# Deaf
# Utopia

# Deaf Utopia

## A Memoir—
## and a Love Letter
## to a Way of Life

## NYLE DiMARCO

### with Robert Siebert

WILLIAM MORROW

*An Imprint of* HarperCollins*Publishers*

This is a work of nonfiction. The events and experiences detailed here are all true and have been faithfully rendered as the author has remembered them, to the best of his ability, or as they were told to him by people who were present. Others have read the manuscript and confirmed his rendering of events.

Some names and identifying details have been changed to protect the privacy of the individuals involved. Conversations were not written to represent word-for-word documentation—especially those that originally took place in ASL. Rather the author has recounted dialogue in a way that evokes the real meaning of what was said, in keeping with the mood and spirit of the event.

Insert photographs courtesy of the author except the following: page 10 by Patrick Wymore/The CW © The CW Network, LLC. All Rights Reserved, page 11 courtesy of Pottle Productions, Inc., pages 12–15 courtesy of Sami Housman, and page 16 by Taylor Miller.

HarperCollins books may be purchased for educational, business, or sales promotional use. For information, please email the Special Markets Department at SPsales@harpercollins.com.

FIRST EDITION

Designed by Nancy Singer

Library of Congress Cataloging-in-Publication Data has been applied for.

ISBN 978-0-06-306235-1

22 23 24 25 26  LSC  10 9 8 7 6 5 4 3 2 1

*To my Deaf family,*
*and the flying hands that gave me wings*

# Contents

# Author's Note

Welcome, reader.

When you crack open these pages, you enter my world: the Deaf world. It's a world within the ordinary world that you know. The two worlds are not separate, but the Deaf world is distinct from the larger one. If you have never met a Deaf person, you likely have seen very little of and know very little about the Deaf world.

For a hearing person who is new to it, the Deaf world can be disorienting. Not impossible to navigate, but the first moments inside can be a bit discombobulating. To ease the transition, here's a quick guide.

First, there is the capital *D* in the word "Deaf." Why?

The word "deaf," spelled all lowercase, is a reference to our medical condition—the fact that our ears don't function the way they're supposed to. The word "Deaf," starting with a capital *D*, signifies so much more than the functional status of the pair of flesh-funnels on the sides of our heads.

As a proud Deaf person, I am a member of a community. Together, we share a common experience, a culture made up of customs unique to our community, and a language—American Sign Language, for the Deaf community in the United States.

The capital *D* is a choice. It's how I see myself, and how I want to be seen. It's my preferred way of naming my identity. Not all people whose ears don't work as intended will choose the same label, and that's fine. Some prefer "deaf," with a lowercase *d*. Some prefer different labels: hard of hearing, late deafened, cochlear implant user, among others. All those are fine, too.

The capital D is *not* a gate. Anyone whose ears are busted in some form or another has the right to use it. It doesn't matter if they sign or not, interact with other Deaf people regularly, have attended Deaf schools, or wear cochlear implants or hearing aids. If you want the capital D, it's yours. If you do claim it: My Deaf ass welcomes you with all my heart.

Second, this book was born out of a partnership between me and my friend and collaborator Robert Siebert. Robert, or Bobby as I know him, is also Deaf, fluent in American Sign Language, and natively familiar with our community and culture.

Our writing process began with my hands. I first told Bobby my stories in American Sign Language—or ASL—in video-recorded interviews, which Bobby then translated into English on the written page. And then together, we worked on the translated source material, chipping away, molding, shaping, and polishing, until it took its final form.

I started the writing process in ASL because it is my natural language, the one I most feel comfortable expressing myself in. ASL is distinct from most other languages, like English. One of the biggest differences between ASL and English is the modality in which each is expressed during conversation. ASL is signed, expressed with the hands, face, and body, and received visually; English is expressed with vocal sounds and received auditorily.

Turning my stories from ASL into written English was a singular challenge. Bobby and I not only had to translate my stories from one language to another; we also had to condense the visual-spatial nature of the source language, ASL, into the linear, two-dimensional symbols of the output language, written English. As always happens during the process of linguistic translation, many elements of the source language got lost in the output language. The beauty, power, *magic*, of ASL is reduced on these written pages.

We attempt to recapture some of that lost magic in different ways in this book. From time to time we describe certain ASL words and phrases in great detail, aiming not only to paint a picture of these signs, but to convey the layers of visual creativity, feeling, and *meaning* behind each of them.

We also write ASL dialogue using an all-caps method called ASL gloss. We borrowed rules and concepts from existing ASL gloss systems and modified them to make our ASL gloss more easily understood by a reader who may have zero knowledge of ASL. Reading ASL gloss may be confusing at first. The first thing you will probably notice is that the grammatical structure of sentences in ASL gloss is different from that of English. This is not because ASL is broken English, but rather because ASL has its own rules, separate from those of English. For instance, in ASL sentences words appear in a different order.

In our ASL gloss, you'll also see hyphenated words. Often, a hyphen is used in ASL gloss to link together multiple English words covered by a single sign. One example is "DON'T-KNOW." While the phrase "don't know" consists of two words in English, in ASL it is expressed using a single sign. Another way a hyphen is used in our ASL gloss is with a repeated term, such as "TRY-TRY." This signifies that the sign is rapidly expressed twice in a row. There are different reasons why a sign is repeated. One is to modify a verb and place emphasis. From the English sentence, "I have been trying to figure out this brain teaser for the last ten minutes," an ASL signer may repeat the sign "TRY" to convey the amount of effort expended. In ASL gloss the same sentence may be written as ME TRY-TRY FIGURE-OUT BRAIN TEASER TEN MINUTES.

The ASL gloss method we use still falls well short of fully capturing the power and beauty of spoken ASL. So many elements of ASL are still missing: the shape your hand takes as it forms a sign; the precise gauge of emotion and intensity emanating from the eyes and brows; the mouth movements that can differentiate a description of a tiny grape-sized ball from that of a big inflatable beach ball; cinematic classifiers, a trademark of the language that can turn a single hand into a Formula One race car with a thrumming motor leaning into hairpin turns on a racetrack. All these beautiful details are tragically absent from the flat and linear scribblings of English on the page.

But the ASL gloss phrases you'll see in this book aren't intended to teach you the language of ASL. If you want to learn ASL, take a class taught by a Deaf teacher. Meet and converse with real Deaf people, the native communicators and torchbearers of our language. Immerse and invest yourself in the journey.

The ASL gloss method has a different purpose: to keep your attention on the fact that the majority of the people in this book are Deaf and communicate using a language that is very different from the spoken ones a hearing person is exposed to in everyday life and in mainstream media. You see, a fascinating thing sometimes happens when all explicit references to Deaf people are taken out of a story. Readers forget that the people are Deaf. We come across as ordinary people doing and experiencing both ordinary and extraordinary things—which is the beautiful truth. We *are* ordinary folks. The ASL gloss dialogue is an occasional tap on the shoulder and whispered hint: remember, these very ordinary folks happen to be Deaf.

On to my third point. I am one Deaf person out of many. The events, thoughts, and feelings portrayed in the book are mine and mine alone. Hundreds of millions of people in the world are Deaf, deaf, hard of hearing, or late deafened or cochlear implant users. Their lived experiences and thoughts and feelings are different from mine. We're not a monolith, and the messages and lessons in this book aren't the last stop for someone looking to learn more about us.

Throughout this book, I intertwine my heritage with my own story, recounting tales and lessons from Deaf history and culture. These are brief glimpses—a small selection from a broad and rich tapestry, stretching back thousands of years. At the end of this book, there's a list of books and other resources on all things Deaf (and deaf and everything in between). It is my hope that as soon as you put this book down, you'll pick up another resource and proceed to the next step in your Deaf education.

Last, a message for my fellow Deaf community members. If you take away only one lesson from this book, I hope it is this: your story has value. Your lived experience as a Deaf person is a vital part of the beautiful diversity of humankind. And you should share your story—as often as you want, and with pride. Doing so may help you better understand and appreciate who you are and can build your identity, giving you the confidence and willingness to embrace it. Personal storytelling is a special kind of love—it is you affirming your existence. It is you telling the world that you matter.

Stories are also the glue that holds communities together. The stories you share will help bond us together and make us a stronger community. Growing up, I was blessed to be surrounded by many Deaf role models around the community and at Deaf schools. They told me their stories, and other stories from Deaf history and culture. Tale by tale, they helped me build an unshakable confidence in who I am and a deep, abiding love, respect, and passion for my culture and heritage. These stories helped make me the proud Deaf man I am today.

And now, I humbly offer my own Deaf story.

YOU-READY? COME-ON, LET'S-GO!

# 1.

# How I Failed My First Test
# the Day After I Was Born

**<0/**
*noun*

a symbol signifying Deaf Power, an expression that embraces and promotes the history, languages, and values of Deaf communities all over the world.

Origin and History: The <0/ symbol is visually derived from the sign for Deaf Power, which is made with an open palm over an ear and the other hand forming a closed fist in the air. As both sign and symbol, <0/ is a bold declaration of profound and defiant pride in our culture and identity as Deaf people.

> *(Definition borrowed from Deaf American artist Christine Sun Kim and Deaf Australian designer Ravi Vasavan.)*

THE DOCTOR ROLLED A MACHINE into the room and parked it at the foot of my mom's bed, next to a pair of bassinets with stainless steel legs and transparent plastic cradles. Inside the bassinets were my brother Nico and me, both of us just a day old. The doctor unspooled wires from the machine and reached down into each bassinet to stick little felt-pad sensors on the sides of our heads, near our ears. He turned back to the machine, pressed a button, and heard a *beep*—the test had started.

Through the clear walls of the bassinets, my mom watched her babies with weary eyes. Nico, my ginger-haired twin, had emerged swiftly and without any issues. Mom and Dad cried and laughed as they saw the first of their twins, a baby with fair skin and hair so light you could barely see the strands in his brows. Mom couldn't celebrate for long, though, because I was still holed up far inside the womb, with no inclination to listen to my mother's pleading for me to come down and out into the world. Mom pushed and pushed, the clock ticked, the doctor and nurses began to worry. Dad clutched my mom's hand and urged her on. Mustering up all her might from a depleted reserve of strength, my mom tried one final time to push me out.

But I would not budge.

The doctor put a stethoscope to my mom's belly and listened close and his eyes suddenly darkened. Everybody out, he ordered, and the nurses ushered Dad away from the bed. Mom asked, *"Why, what was the matter?"*

The doctor started to speak, and Mom's eyes moved to his lips.

The year was 1989. Hospitals weren't required to provide American Sign Language interpreters to Deaf people who requested them. The Americans with Disabilities Act, the landmark legislation that required businesses and service providers in the United States to offer reasonable accommodations for people with disabilities, would not become law for another year.

Without an interpreter, my mom—hours deep into labor—paused her rhythmic breathing and pushing to wipe strands of her deep black hair out of her eyes and get a clearer view of the doctor's mouth to read his lips.

*"The baby's heartbeat,"* she read.

I had overstayed my time in Mom's womb: my oxygen levels were critically low, and my heartbeat had slowed to a faint, weak rhythm. It was an emergency; my life was at stake before I had even tasted fresh air.

Mom watched as the doctor brought a surgical knife to her belly, and then a nurse put a clear mask over her face and everything went black.

Twenty-one minutes after Nico was born, the doctor pulled me out into the world.

Hours later, Mom woke, her mind still mushy and her vision cloudy from the anesthetic. She squinted, seeing three blurry fingers, then opened her eyes wide to bring Dad and my older brother, Neal, into view.

THREE BOYS, Dad signed.

NO GIRL? Mom asked, slightly forlorn.

NO. SECOND TWIN SAME FIRST, BOY.

The nurse brought in her two newborn babies. At first glance, we could not have looked any more different to Mom. Nico had milk-pale skin and straw-colored hair; I had olive skin and deep brown hair. As we lay side by side on Mom's chest, the visual contrast between my twin brother and me was so extreme that Mom had to nudge the nurse.

*"These are mine?"* she mouthed.

*"Yes,"* the nurse reassured her. *"They're yours."* She pointed toward the hospital bracelets on our tiny wrists, and back toward Mom's. The information on the bracelets matched up.

Of course my mom had known that fraternal twins could look different from each other, but she wasn't expecting *this*. In almost every part of our physical appearance, we contrasted sharply. Nico was strawberry; I was chocolate.

With my dark hair and olive skin, I resembled my parents, older brother, and grandparents. It was a no-brainer that I was related to them. Nico, on the other hand, looked like nobody else in my family.

If Nico hadn't been born my twin, there would have been strong suspicion that he was the milkman's baby. But he'd shared the same womb as me, so there was no doubt about his lineage. And when you looked into our brilliant blue eyes you could begin to see our sibling resemblance. It was a trait we inherited from our dad and shared with our older brother.

Mom was exhausted and sweaty and still a little bit dizzy from the anesthetic, but she felt immense pride and joy holding her twins, one in each arm. Then a twinge of anxiety brushed at the edge of her consciousness: the doctor's test. It didn't really matter to her what the results were. She would not forget how close she had come to losing one of her baby boys, so the most important part—the fact that we were alive and healthy—was accounted for.

But one way or the other, my mom wanted us to have the same test result. Differing results could set her boys on paths far apart from each other, and she didn't want that.

The doctor removed the felt pad sensors from my little infant head and walked toward my mom, his hands clasped tightly behind his back. He took a deep breath and started moving his lips.

"[Mumble] bilateral hearing [mumble mumble]."

His hands rose to point at his ears.

"[Mumble mumble] frequency [mumble mumble] failure."

Mom and Dad squinted at the doctor's lips to try to understand what he was saying.

With a lifetime of practice, Mom and Dad had become decent lip-readers. They had to be; back then, they didn't have legally mandated access to ASL interpreters, so lip-reading was an indispensable tool in any Deaf person's communication survival kit. It's still used often by Deaf people today. In fact, when I meet hearing people for the first time, one of the most common questions I often get is "Can you read lips?"

Among the many options available to Deaf people when communicating with hearing people—ASL interpreters, pen and paper, using the Notes app on a phone—many Deaf people will tell you that lip-reading is nowhere near number one on their list. Even with all the practice in the world, lip-reading is notoriously unreliable. By some estimates the average lip-reader captures only around 30 percent of the speaker's words—and the odds are even worse with additional distractions. For instance, chewing gum's a no-no. Missing teeth lead to missing words. And if the speaker has a bushy mustache? They might as well cover their lips; anything but a well-groomed mustache makes lip-reading near impossible.

The man who had delivered Nico and me was a great doctor, but he was a lip-reader's nightmare. His lips moved as if they were stitched up, like Frankenstein's monster. When he spoke, he looked like a ventriloquist speaking for his dummy. Without an ASL interpreter, my parents couldn't understand him.

Grab a pen and paper, my parents motioned.

The doctor flipped over some papers on his clipboard and scratched out: *Your babies have hearing loss.*

Mom pointed at her babies and mouthed, *"Both of them?"*

The doctor hesitated before nodding and wrote: *They both display some level of hearing loss.*

*"What do you mean?"* Mom mouthed, bristling at the ambiguity of the doctor's response. She wanted a straight answer and used her voice to get her point across: "Are they Deaf?"

The doctor took a deep breath and fumbled with his words, trying to find the right thing to say to Mom and Dad.

The *D* word seemed to make him uncomfortable.

*"Well . . . ,"* he started, then stopped and nodded. *"Yes."* He pinched her thumb and forefinger. *"A little bit, one more than the other . . ."*

Mom cut him off with her voice. "Are they both *Deaf*?"

The doctor sputtered and finally gave them the answer: *"Yes."*

Then he wound himself up to recite the speech he had prepared for these situations. The news of a failed hearing test often came as an emotional shock to parents. His first objective was to soften the blow. He would explain how the hearing test worked, introduce the possibility of a false result and how further tests might reveal that there was no hearing loss at all. And then, hedging a little bit, he would share about the technology available to help babies with hearing loss.

Bottom line, the doctor wanted to give parents hope.

The doctor began: *"Please don't worry—"*

He stopped, because Mom had jabbed a pair of thumbs up in his face.

"Good!" she declared. The doctor then noticed Dad thrusting his fists into the air. He laughed and hugged and kissed Mom as if they'd just pulled the winning ticket to the lottery. The *genetic* lottery, that is.

Mom leaned over the bed to look at her two boys, moving carefully because she was still exhausted and dizzy and felt stitches tugging at her tummy. These radically different-looking twin boys were undeniably hers.

Nico and I had joined our older brother as the fourth generation to be born Deaf in our family.

The doctor frowned as he surveyed my mom and dad and brother cheering and signing to each other. His confusion at my family's reaction was and is typical of the medical view on deafness. Doctors often think of deafness as a problem that needs to be corrected instead of a natural difference, one beautiful dot among many on the brilliant spectrum of human diversity, one that was also the crux of a culture, language, and community—a way of life.

Most likely, the moment he confirmed Nico and I were deaf, solutions scrolled through his head: assistive listening devices like hearing aids; organizations and agencies that could provide Nico and I with speech therapy; and even surgical interventions, such as the implantation of sensors that detect sound and send electrical impulses to the brain—also known as cochlear implants.

Likely missing from the list of solutions scrolling through the doctor's head was American Sign Language, the native language of my family—the one my mother and father used to communicate in the hospital room, and the one that Nico and I would learn from birth and come to deeply appreciate and cherish as a cornerstone of our Deaf heritage.

My family barely noticed the doctor packing up and rolling the machine out of the room with a brief, confused nod.

I was less than a day old and had already taken my first test. According to the doctor, my ears did not work the way they were supposed to, and I had failed.

My family saw the test result differently. Dad was elated, because it meant that Nico and I would be able to experience firsthand the culture and language that shaped him as a Deaf person. My brother Neal, only eighteen months old, was too young to understand the test result and its significance—but if he was a little older he would have been giddy at the news, because it meant his little twin brothers would be able to attend the same Deaf schools as him. Mom was just relieved that her boys were safe and healthy and that our test results would not set us on differing paths in life.

My grandparents came to the hospital to visit. After confirming our health—their first and foremost concern—Mom told them that Nico and I were indeed Deaf. A rascally grin came across my grandpa's face as he signed DEAF and then raised a jubilant fist: DEAF POWER.

Whatever the doctor might have thought, the newborn hearing test was never a matter of passing or failing to my family. There was no right or wrong; they didn't consider one result better than the other. If Nico and I had been born hearing, my family would not have been any less thrilled. No matter how our ears fared on the hearing test, we would have been the same chocolate and strawberry bundles of joy to our family.

As for how I felt about the hearing test results? Well, at the time I was most concerned with when my next meal of breast milk was going to be. After all, I had a twin brother to compete with.

But now? I feel that the hearing test revealed only one facet of who I was, still am, and always will be.

I'm Nyle DiMarco. I once dreamed of becoming a math teacher, but life took me on a different path. I won the *America's Next Top Model* and *Dancing with the Stars* reality TV show competitions less than half a year apart. I've advocated for disability rights in a United

Nations conference and given a keynote speech at the Human Rights Campaign National Dinner. I run a foundation and a production company.

I am also Deaf.

It's a fact that's shaped every aspect of my life. The way I experience the world. How I learn new stuff. How I interact and communicate with others, including in English and ASL, the languages I'm fluent in. The community and culture I was born into, and the people I surround myself with and have come to trust.

And, especially, how others perceive me. Anytime I meet someone new, I know the first fact that registers in their heads is that I'm Deaf. Sometimes it puts me behind the eight ball and I have to work a hundred times harder to overcome—and change—the negative stereotypes and stigma surrounding that fact. And other times people think it's nothing short of amazing, and it's all I can do to prove that I'm just an ordinary person who happens to communicate primarily using their hands.

Like any other way of living and being, there is some bad, but there's also a lot of good to being Deaf. There have been times when it's maddening and frustrating and I feel helpless. There have also been times when it's downright glorious and I feel blessed and empowered to be this way. It's weird and remarkable and disturbing and cool, all at the same time.

One thing's for sure: I can't imagine living and being any other way. Being Deaf is part of what uniquely colors the small space of the world that I take up. It is the core of my identity, and I'm damn proud of it.

I've faced countless more tests since that first one, and I think it's only fair that I should be judged by the full breadth of my results. From my point of view, I've passed a heck of a lot of them, with flying colors.

And I've got the stories to prove it.

# 2.

# Queens, New York

**E**very community has a sacred story. For some communities, it is a profound fable with an important lesson, one that impresses the community's most cherished values upon the listener. For others, it is a frightening tale that warns of a significant danger, the avoidance of which is critical for the community's survival.

My community's sacred story is about where we came from and how we started. It begins at the beginning.

The year was 1813 and the town was Hartford, Connecticut. The Reverend Thomas Hopkins Gallaudet saw a girl sitting under a tree, apart from her siblings playing in the yard. Gallaudet sat down next to her. He spoke to her, but the girl, Alice Cogswell, did not respond to his voice. He thought for a moment, then he picked up a stick and started scratching at the dirt: H-A-T.

Gallaudet took his cap off, then pointed at the letters in the dirt and back to his cap. The girl's eyes lit up with understanding.

The girl's father, a wealthy man, was thrilled. He had been confident that his daughter was capable of learning, but now he had confirmation. There was no school for the Deaf in America, but he had heard of schools across the ocean that had been successful in *teaching the Deaf. He sent Gallaudet on a trip overseas, with the goal of attaining enough knowledge to start a school for the Deaf in America.*

*Eventually, Gallaudet alighted on the Institut Royal des Sourds-Muets in Paris. He was guided by the school's headmaster, Abbé Sicard, and two Deaf teachers. Everyone at the school communicated by hand, through French Sign Language. He was awed by the intelligence and robust communication of the school's Deaf students. Gallaudet approached one of the Deaf teachers, Laurent Clerc, and asked him to go to the United States to help Gallaudet start the first school for the Deaf there.*

*Clerc agreed. On the long sea voyage, they learned from each other: Gallaudet taught Clerc English; Clerc taught Gallaudet French Sign Language.*

*In 1817 in Hartford, the American School for the Deaf, the first school for Deaf children in the United States, opened its doors. There, the French Sign Language of native speaker Laurent Clerc, the signs of the large Deaf community 175 miles to the east in Martha's Vineyard, and various local sign systems and dialects used by Deaf people, including Native Americans, all blended together.*

*Soon, an entirely new language was formed—a language different from French Sign Language or any other local signed dialect, a language I would one day proudly claim as part of the Deaf heritage I inherited: American Sign Language.*

I WASN'T TAUGHT AMERICAN SIGN Language; I was submerged in it.

That's how people acquire their native language: they don't learn it consciously; they naturally absorb it from the available language input in their surroundings. The key is a vibrant and accessible language-rich environment. That's the vinegar that turns cucumbers into pickles. If you drop a baby into an accessible language-rich jar and give it time, that baby's going to turn into a native communicator in that language.

For a Deaf baby like me, there were few jars more American Sign Language–rich than the A-frame Tudor-style house where I grew up, located in the Bellerose neighborhood in Queens, New York. Under that roof lived my parents, brothers, and maternal grandparents and uncles—all of whom were Deaf. My grandpa had lived in the house since he was fourteen, and it was passed down to my grandparents from my great-grandparents. My grandparents raised my mom, Donna, and her two brothers, Robert and Charles, there. When Neal, Nico, and I came along, we became the fourth generation of the DiMarco family to live in the house.

As is the case for many Deaf and hard of hearing people in the United States, Canada, and numerous other countries around the world, American Sign Language, or ASL, is the native language of my family. It's a visual language, expressed through handshapes; facial expressions; movements of our hands, arms, and shoulders; and the use of the space around our bodies. It's also received visually, which means you listen to ASL through your eyes.

ASL has letters, too. The ASL alphabet mirrors that of English, with each letter represented by a handshape or a sign. Those hand-shapes form a key foundation of the language; many signs are made using a single letter handshape that is presented in different positions and movements. For instance, the $x$ handshape—a hook formed with the index finger—is used to form the signs for "addiction," "mining," "key," "time," "hockey," "electricity," and so forth.

The ASL and English alphabets may be closely related, but ASL has its own rules, grammar, and syntax, separate from English. For example, in English you might say "I'm going to the store." In ASL you'd sign STORE ME GO.

Like English and any other vocal language, ASL has dialects, or variants, based on geographical region, age, and ethnic group. In other words, there are accents in ASL. ASL dialects differ from each other in many ways: speed of delivery, placement of hands when making signs, facial expressions. Some words are signed completely differently based on dialect. For instance, the word "birthday" has at least a half dozen signs in ASL, differing by dialect. Sometimes, we can even guess where someone is from based on how they sign ASL.

One prominent ASL dialect is Black ASL, or BASL. Racial segregation in schools for the Deaf gave birth to BASL. Based on research championed by Dr. Carolyn McCaskill, a Black Deaf professor of ASL and Deaf Studies at Gallaudet University, signers using BASL have been found to use larger space around the body to form some signs and use two-handed variants of signs more often.

ASL and other sign languages around the world are the beating heart of Deaf culture. They are the thread that connects Deaf people to one another and holds the Deaf community together. As a visual language without sound, sign languages are naturally accessible to Deaf people.

From birth, I feasted on an all-you-can-eat buffet of ASL. Every conversation in the DiMarco household was readily accessible to me in ASL. When my mom and grandma leaned over me in the cradle for some baby talk, they showered ASL words onto me. Whenever I crawled my way into the middle of a conversation between my dad and uncles, their words, in ASL, were there for my eyes to drink in.

WHEN I TALK ABOUT MY pride in my Deaf identity and how much I cherish ASL as my language, so much of that comes from my mom. She was, and still is, a proud Deaf woman. She preached to us constantly about the value of ASL: How rich and beautiful it is. How it helps us develop and shape our minds, sharpen our critical thinking skills, and become strong and independent people. How, as a means of communication and education, it enables us to access the world.

My mom took it upon herself to introduce my brothers and me to the full beauty and power of ASL. Through her storytelling, my mom guided us further through the wonders of ASL. Every night, with the dedication of a devout Catholic praying the rosary, she signed stories out loud to us boys. I delighted in her animated signing, and how she used her eyes and mouth to add color and imagination to the books she read to us.

Our favorite book was *Are You My Mother?* by P. D. Eastman. Mom twisted her face as she transformed into characters: signing meek and small as the little bird seeking out his mother; growing big, wide eyes as the kitten; springing a rubbery neck as the clucking hen; putting on dopey eyes and languid signing hands for the dog; and flaring nostrils, frowning eyes, and big, wide, stomping hands as the cow. Following a treasured ASL storytelling rule, she shifted her shoulders from one side to the other as she switched from the little bird to the different animal characters it talked to throughout the story.

A skilled ASL storyteller can create a cinematic effect. Watching my mom signing stories was like seeing a movie for me and my brothers. The story times weren't all just for fun, however. Mom made sure we were paying attention.

WHAT-IS THIS? she would ask, pointing to the cow.

COW.

GOOD. COWS EAT WHAT?

HAY!

GREAT! Mom reached out to tousle my hair. We were drawn into Mom's storytelling and whenever she threw us a pop quiz question, it jolted us wide awake. When we got a question right and were rewarded with Mom's smile, it was the best feeling in the world.

She gradually increased the degree of difficulty of her questions, pointing at words in the books and asking us what they meant. We looked at a word and then the pictures, searching for clues in the drawings. We threw out guesses—BOY! GIRL! HOUSE!—and Mom kept shaking her head until we got it.

RIGHT! Mom signed, and again I was rewarded with the best feeling in the world. Next, she asked us how to spell the word. Using ASL handshapes of the alphabet, we spelled the word out letter by letter. Sometimes she covered the word in the book with her hand, which made it harder, but she gave us several tries until we got it.

Mom knew that our primary language, ASL, was our path toward building fluency in our second language, English. During these story times, she used our fluency in ASL to help us recognize and understand English letters and words in print. Slowly, book after book and quiz question after quiz question, she laid the building blocks for our lifelong success in the world out there that is dominated by English.

To nurture our burgeoning language fluency, Mom also sought out videos that featured ASL, which was a lot harder than it might seem. Remember, this was the early-to-mid 1990s, back when the internet was little more than an idea. Nowadays, a YouTube search returns *thousands* of ASL videos with a single click. (Granted, a lot of them are terrible music videos performed by beginner hearing ASL students, but there are a lot of accurate and genuinely helpful ASL videos available—look for those made by bona fide Deaf people.) But back then? You had to *work* to find them and get them to the TV in your living room for your kids. I'm talking, of course, about old-school VHS tapes. My mom would keep her eyes peeled for tips about new ASL videos from friends, family, and teachers at our school. Whenever she learned about ASL videos, she'd order them to be delivered to our home, sometimes whole sets.

My favorite ASL video set was an educational video series that showed a fictional Deaf family, the Bravos, that communicated in ASL. The family went through assorted everyday scenarios, like going to the dentist, all the while teaching different relevant ASL vocabulary, including words for having your teeth checked for cavities and so forth. The show captivated me in ways that non-ASL shows could never achieve. The actors onscreen were Deaf *like me,* and they talked in *my* language. I'd watch the video set from start to finish over and over again, clutching my favorite blanket and sucking my middle and ring fingers (which made an I love you handshape, which my mom thought was absolutely adorable) as my eyes were glued to the screen.

Besides the Bravo family, there was also *Sesame Street* on PBS. Deaf actress Linda Bove appeared regularly, teaching ASL signs alongside Big Bird. My brothers and I loved *Sesame Street*. My older brother Neal even had a Big Bird stuffed animal he carried around with him.

LIKE MOST TWINS, NICO AND I did everything together and shared everything with each other while growing up. But, like our hair color and skin complexions, we had opposite personalities.

When Nico and I were toddlers, Mom and Dad put us in baby walkers and let us dodder around the family room. The room was separated from the hallway by a little step that would stop the walker in place and prevent us from leaving the room. It took me numerous tries—and painful falls—but eventually I figured out how to pick up my walker myself and carry it with me over the step, all by myself. Nico adopted a different method: he stopped his walker at the step and cried his little heart out until someone came along and picked him up.

I had an independent, mischievous streak. I tested limits and had an endless curiosity I sought to satisfy by trying new stuff. My mom would refer to me, affectionately, as her little devil. Nico was my celestial antithesis, a perfect angel with his halo of ginger curls. He was thoughtful, caring, and sensitive, and approached new challenges with caution, tending to think twice before acting. If he did a bad deed, it was because Neal and I convinced him to do it with us. Even then, it rarely took long before his conscience caught up to him.

For example, when Nico and I were about five, my brothers' and my favorite part of our house in Queens was probably the aboveground pool in the backyard. We passed many sunny summer days splashing around, racing each other swimming freestyle from one end to the other, jumping in from the wooden deck, and seeing who could hold their breath underwater the longest. While submerged in the pool, we made the delightful discovery that we could talk to each other underwater by using ASL, something that hearing folks couldn't do.

One of our favorite things to do in the pool was to throw objects that sank to the bottom and dive in to retrieve them. The best and most readily available sinking objects, we found, were the rocks that surrounded the pool's perimeter. We tossed them in, a handful at a time, and dove in, pumping our little arms and legs until we grabbed one or two rocks and carried them to the surface. We often threw in too many rocks, and nearly always left some in the pool when we were finished.

This drove my mom and grandparents crazy. They kept finding rocks in the pool, which they had to clean up every time. They weren't sure who was doing it.

THROW ROCKS IN POOL, YOU-THREE? Mom asked.

NO, we said, NOT US. We were afraid she'd punish us, maybe take away our pool privileges, so we lied.

Figuring our denial would keep us safely out of suspicion, the very next day we went back to tossing rocks into the pool and leaving them behind when we'd finished. Mom and my grandparents couldn't figure out who was causing this ongoing problem. Maybe it was some kids from the neighborhood? they thought. But it happened so often that there really were only three possible culprits. Mom didn't waste her energy trying to get the real story from Neal and me. She pulled Nico aside to talk with him privately.

TELL-ME TRUTH. ROCK POINT-AT-POOL, WHO THROW?

Without Neal and me by his side, Nico never had a chance. He confessed to the entire thing before my mom finished her question, ratting me and Neal out.

BUSTED, Mom told me and Neal.

NICO! Neal and I grumbled. But we forgave Nico afterward, like we always did. We knew he couldn't help himself. That was just his nature, and we loved him for it.

EARLY IN MY LIFE, I began a bad habit: getting lost. Practically as soon as I learned to walk, I wandered every which way, as far as I could—consequences be damned. I always went alone, of course—Nico never joined me in my reckless wandering.

When I was four, I disappeared from the house in the middle of the day. This wasn't an easy feat—remember, I grew up living in the same house with my two brothers, my mom and dad, my grandparents, and my two uncles. Somehow, among all these people, four-year-old me slipped out of the house without anybody noticing.

My mom was the first to realize I was missing. She checked the swing set and pool in our backyard, walked up and down to check all four floors of the house twice, and looked out the front door at our yard and the street. I was nowhere to be found. Panic setting in, she grabbed my dad and they started knocking on our neighbors' doors. They used different communication tools, combining them into a frantic mishmash of signing, gesturing, and mouthing words.

*HAND-WAVE "Hi!" POINT-AT-NEIGHBOR "Have you" POINT-EYE "seen" POINT-AT-CHEST "my" FLAT-PALM-BY-WAIST PAT-PAT "boy" SHRUG "?"*

The method may have been unorthodox, but my parents got the message across. None of the neighbors who answered their doors had seen me, though. Uncle Charles, my mom's brother, drove my dad around the neighborhood while my mom kept looking on foot, walking past each house on our block, checking the front yards and backyards.

Finally, my mom spotted me, in the backyard of a house across the street. I was sitting on a swing with my neighbor friend, laughing and playing and carefree.

She grabbed onto my hand tight and brought me straight home.

NEVER, NEVER LEAVE HOUSE WITHOUT TELL MOM DAD FIRST, she scolded me. She pointed to my dad, my brothers, my uncle, my grandparents.

ALL-OF-US SCARED. WHERE NYLE? WE LOOK-LOOK LONG TIME.

For all the trouble I'd caused my mom and my family, you'd think I'd feel guilty as heck. But I didn't. When my mom scolded me, I showed remorse, because I knew it was expected of me and that doing so would help reduce any punishment that might come my way. But inside I wasn't sorry. The whole time I was away and alone, I didn't feel any fear. I was doing exactly what I was supposed to be doing, wandering and exploring.

I got lost again when I was a little older, around seven years old. My brothers, Mom, and I were at a waterpark. While I was walking around, a game booth caught my eye and I wandered off on my own, without thinking. When I turned around I saw that I was alone and that my mom and brothers were nowhere to be found.

I didn't freak out or bawl my eyes out or think at any moment that the world was ending. *Oh, I'm lost,* I thought. *Time to fix it.* Calmly, I spotted a security officer, walked up to him, gestured for a pen and paper, and wrote that I was lost.

The security officer nodded, spoke into his walkie-talkie, then took me to the security office, where I sat and gazed at the officers bustling about, doing their work. Eventually Mom and my brothers burst into the office, Mom's arms reaching out and squeezing me tight.

She told me that she looked all over the waterpark for me, that the entire park had to be closed off to find me, that she was upset, my two brothers were upset.

SORRY, I said. But again, I didn't cry, and wasn't scared or truly apologetic.

I wasn't trying to make my mom's black hair go prematurely gray with my wandering, at least not on purpose. Causing trouble was never the point. I was just drawn to the world and was content to let my curiosity guide my feet in whichever direction appeared most interesting.

It makes me feel bad to look back and realize how much stress I must have put on my mom in those early years. She rarely let on, though, because she's a superhero. There's no doubt about it, I wouldn't be where I am if not for her. Not only did she do so many things for me and my brothers, she did it while functioning like a single mom most of the time, while my dad continually moved in and out of our lives, battling his own demons and alcohol and drug addiction.

Part of Mom's resilience and strength as a woman and mother was drawn from her hero, Princess Diana. Mom adored Di and the example she set for the rest of the world. She loved how compassionate Di was and how much empathy she showed for others, especially groups of people that the world had shunned. She was a *good* person, radiating kindness and grace. Proudly, Mom signed out to Neal, Nico, and me the story of how Di had taken off her glove to shake the hand of a man who had AIDS, to shatter the misconception that HIV/AIDS could be spread through physical touching. With such a small, simple act of kindness, Di sent a message to the rest of the world that it was okay to touch those with HIV/AIDS, to hug and hold them, to continue to give them the love they deserved as they endured.

Princess Diana's advocacy touched the Deaf community, too. In the 1980s, she became a patron of the British Deaf Association, a U.K. organization that advocated for access and equality for Deaf Brits and was led by Deaf Brits, and she learned British Sign Language, or BSL. When my mom saw footage of Princess Diana signing BSL with Deaf people on *Deaf Mosaic,* the Emmy Award–winning television magazine show on Deaf news, her heart swelled. Princess Diana was an exemplary role model, and her actions delivered important lessons on compassion, empathy, and caring that Mom wanted to pass along to us boys.

Even as my mom took on all those hats as our superhero de facto single parent, telling us stories, instilling values of love and respect, laying the foundation of our language acquisition, and taking us out to have fun to remind us to have joy in life, she still found the time and energy to take on the role of the strict parent. Indeed, she wasn't all fun and games. If we crossed a line, she never hesitated to discipline us. She knew she couldn't be reluctant when it came to disciplining her boys—if she didn't, then who would?

My mom's discipline scared the bejesus outta me, in a good way. Her punishments stuck with me, making sure I learned my lesson. And they could be quite embarrassing.

One time when I was five, my mom took me and my brothers grocery shopping. At the checkout register, I spotted a candy bar I wanted, and I asked my mom if I could have it. She had loaded our grocery items onto the conveyor belt and was getting ready to pay.

NO, she said. FINISH GET EVERYTHING WE NEED. CANDY BAR PUT-BACK.

My mom paid, packed up her grocery bags, loaded her boys into her car, and drove all the way back to our house. As she unpacked the grocery bags and put the food into the fridge, she spotted me holding something to my mouth.

WHAT-IS THAT? she asked.

UHH. Busted.

She grabbed the half-eaten candy bar and dragged me to the car. Starting the ignition, she told me that she was taking me back to the grocery store.

STORE MANAGER, YOU TELL-HIM YOU STOLE CANDY BAR, she said.

Tears immediately started streaming down my cheeks. I was *terrified*. Stealing was wrong, and I would be headed straight to jail. Cops were going to slap handcuffs on my wrists and haul me to the slammer in the back of their car. I was a bad person, about to be branded a criminal for the rest of my life. There was no turning back.

NONONO ME SORRY! DON'T-WANT GO! PLEASE! I begged and pleaded, only stopping to use my hands to wipe the snot and tears that dripped and drooped down my face.

My mom was resolute. YOU MUST TALK-TO MANAGER.

She parked and pulled me by the hand all the way to the grocery store manager's office.

She held out the candy bar and signed: NYLE, TELL-HIM.

I felt like crapping my pants. My hands shook as I stammered out what I'd done: CANDY BAR ME STEAL. ME SORRY.

My mom repeated what I said, using her voice and mouthing to make sure the manager understood. The manager's face turned stern. He *tut-tut* waved his finger and told me, with my mom's help interpreting, that what I'd done was wrong and if it happened again there might be worse consequences.

I took his scolding with a large lump in my throat, waiting for the hammer to drop. It was coming, I knew, it was only a matter of time. I braced myself.

Then he pointed toward the door. He was letting me go. That was it. No cops or handcuffs, no jail, no criminal record.

Satisfied, my mom took my hand and we drove back home. I was furious and nearly burned a hole in the back of her head with my angry stare. I promised myself I would never forgive her.

I was wrong.

# 3.

# Fire in the Belly

In the year 1880, a bunch of older white men with prim side-parted coiffures and handlebar mustaches descended upon Milan, Italy. They had come from all over Europe and the United States for the International Congress on Education of the Deaf.

It is now known simply as the Milan Conference—one of the greatest tragedies in the history of the Deaf community.

James Denison, from the United States, was the sole Deaf delegate in attendance. The purpose of the conference was to decide the best, most effective approaches to educate the Deaf, and only 1 of the 164 delegates in the room making those decisions was Deaf.

Also in attendance was Edward Miner Gallaudet, the youngest child of Thomas Hopkins Gallaudet, who in 1864 had founded the world's first and only college of the Deaf, Gallaudet College (today called Gallaudet University).

Since the American School for the Deaf had opened in Hartford in 1817 under the leadership of Laurent Clerc and Thomas Gallaudet, dozens of schools for the Deaf had been established all over the country. In these schools, American Sign Language was used to teach Deaf students and unlock their potential.

*It was the golden age of Deaf education in the United States. It didn't last forever. Sign language had too many enemies.*

*One was Alexander Graham Bell. Bell was a treacherous man who espoused many ideas that deeply harmed my community. He did not even do the thing he was best known for: inventing the telephone. The idea and design for the telephone was first created by a poor Italian American named Antonio Meucci, with whom Bell shared a lab. Meucci could not afford the patent; Bell could.*

*Anytime I see Bell's name, I feel pain and anger. Bell would have been opposed to the very idea of my existence as a multi-generational ASL-fluent Deaf man. He devoted his life to the study of speech and teaching Deaf children how to speak. He propagated the eugenicist view that Deaf people should not marry each other (so they couldn't make more cute Deaf babies like me) and advocated for oral education of the Deaf—or teaching the Deaf through auditory languages. He was opposed to teaching Deaf children sign language; he and Edward Miner Gallaudet frequently clashed over this topic.*

*The Milan Conference gave Bell the upper hand. Despite Edward Miner Gallaudet's passionate pleas for sign language education during the conference, the delegates voted overwhelmingly in favor of oral education as the preferred method of instruction for the Deaf. The delegates also voted to declare sign language harmful to learning how to speak, lip-read, and understand ideas, establishing so-called pure oral education as the preferred method and effectively banning sign language from the education of the Deaf.*

*Thus, in part because of the Milan Conference, began the decline of the golden age of Deaf education. For decades, the oral education method proliferated in Deaf schools in western Europe and the United States. At those schools and elsewhere, hearing administrators decided that Deaf people who communicated in ASL were incapable and stripped them of their jobs.*

*Some Deaf community members, however, continued to use ASL with pride. At home, Deaf parents taught it to their children. Black*

*Deaf people, whose segregated schools in the South continued to use ASL, were instrumental in carrying our language through this dark age. Despite our community's best efforts, as the years passed, ASL became less and less accessible to the majority of Deaf people, who were born into hearing families.*

*Shockwaves from the Milan Conference were still rippling through Deaf education more than a century later, when I enrolled in the Lexington School for the Deaf in Queens.*

YOUR HEARING AIDS WHERE? MISS Dawes, my teacher, asked.

ME FORGOT, LEFT-AT HOME, I signed back. I tried my hardest not to smile, because Miss Dawes would get mad if she knew I didn't bring my hearing aids to school on purpose.

Every morning in class, we repeated a daily ritual to make sure we had our hearing aids and that they were working properly. After putting our backpacks away in our cubby holes, we placed our hearing aid devices on a table in front of Miss Dawes. She took the little battery cells out of our aids and inserted them into a black device with a needle that swung from 0 to 100. If a battery cell made the needle swing to 100, that meant it was full of juice and Miss Dawes would congratulate us with a big smile and a cheer. There was only one battery tester, so we lined up and took turns testing the batteries on our aids one by one.

I dreaded this ritual. It was boring and a waste of time. But more importantly, I despised my hearing aids. Putting them on was like letting a dam open to a flood of noise. My classmates yelled, hands banged on tables, paper crinkled. The ear molds burrowed uncomfortably into my ears, and sometimes if there was too much loud noise, or if something pressed close against my molds, a piercing *EEEEEEEE!!* burst out in my aids. That high-pitched sound made me want to rip off my ear molds, then dig into my ear canal and itch and rub until the noise was gone and there was just numbness. At home, I hardly ever wore my hearing aids. Everybody in my family talked in ASL, and we could all understand each other just fine without the aids.

At school, Miss Dawes signed, too. But she also used her voice to speak English while signing at the same time, a form of communication called simultaneous communication, or sim-com. For sim-com to be effective, both voiced and signed modes of communication need to be delivered equally—both in substance and clarity. That's how it works, in theory. But in practice, the speaker will usually lean toward one of the two, typically the speaker's dominant mode of communication. For Miss Dawes, a hearing person, that was spoken English. She leaned heavily on it, and often only signed every second or third word she spoke. She also exaggerated her mouth movements, encouraging us to work on reading her lips and understanding her voice. I kept trying to figure out which part of her communication to focus on. When I tried to concentrate on her spoken English, I had to cut through the static from my hearing aids and the atmospheric noise in the classroom to focus on Miss Dawes's voice. At the same time I kept my eyes glued on her lips, trying to match up some of the sounds and lip and tongue movements and make words from them. Trying to decipher Miss Dawes felt like one of those word games we played sometimes in class, where we took strings of mixed-up letters and tried to unscramble them into real words. The process exhausted my brain.

Learning through my eyes was much easier. When I talked with anyone in ASL, I understood the words as soon as the signer's hands made them. Miss Dawes wasn't very good at signing, and her hands kept skipping words. But even then, I could still understand her a lot better when I focused on her signing instead of trying to listen to her spoken English. I couldn't understand why I needed to wear the hearing aids at school and go to all the trouble trying to understand the sounds when I understood the words so easily by seeing them in sign language.

What I didn't know then was that I didn't have much of a choice. All the Deaf schools in New York City taught their students this way, mandating hearing aids and using sim-com in classrooms. Another option was mainstream school, but that would have meant Nico and I would have been the only Deaf kids in our classes, funneling all of our

communication with the teacher and our peers through a sign language interpreter. We wouldn't even have the scraps of signing we got
from Miss Dawes's sim-com—no one else in our mainstream classes,
other than the interpreter, would be able to sign with us.

I might have been stuck at this school, but I wasn't going to take
its hearing aid mandate lying down. One morning before school, I had
an idea: if I forgot my hearing aids at home, maybe Miss Dawes would
give me a break for the day. Even better, she might realize that without
my hearing aids, I would be able to understand only her hands. Just
perhaps, she would try harder to sign clearly.

After I told her I'd forgotten my hearing aids at home, Miss Dawes
took a deep sigh and shook her head.

"You KNOW you need to BRING your HEARING AIDS to school
EVERY DAY," she sim-commed, signing fewer than half the words
she spoke.

"YOU need to become MORE RESPONSIBLE," she said.

I nodded solemnly, accepting this gentle chastisement with all the
graceful regret I could muster. I wanted Miss Dawes to skip to the
part where she let me go through the rest of the school day without my
hearing aids. Out of the corner of my eye I could see Nico shaking his
head at me. As the cliché goes, we all have an angel on one shoulder
and a devil on the other; I swear Nico has an angel on *each* shoulder.
He showed up to school every day with his hearing aids in hand and
the batteries fully charged.

"I KNOW you're WORRIED about MISSING INFORMATION
today without your HEARING AIDS."

Another solemn nod from me.

"BUT you DON'T have to WORRY!"

*Wait, what?*

Miss Dawes grabbed hold of my hand and walked me down the
hall to the area where the speech teachers' classrooms were, and the
office that we knew as the audiologist's. I knew the audiologist as
the special doctor that focused on our ears. I'd gone to the audiolo-

gist's office before, where she put me in an enclosed sound booth and turned on different noises to test my hearing.

There was a long line outside the office. Some of the other students in line didn't have hearing aids in their ears. Some of them held broken ear molds. Miss Dawes dropped me off at the end of the line and told me to come back to the classroom when I was finished.

*What was I waiting in line for?* I wanted to ask Miss Dawes, but she'd already gone.

One by one, the kids ahead of me filed into the office and then came out with new hearing aids and earmolds fit snugly into their ears. My spirits sank lower and lower with each student who filed in and out.

The line dwindled until it was my turn.

Rows and rows of drawers lined the walls of the audiologist's office. The audiologist smiled and sim-commed, "FORGOT your HEARING AIDS, huh? Let me see, NYLE . . . Nyle . . . oh! Here we are."

She picked out two ear molds from a drawer labeled with my name. Then she opened another drawer and pulled out new hearing aid devices, exactly like the ones I'd left under my bed that morning. She connected the ear molds to the aids, then inserted them into my ears. The rubbery plastic of the molds felt cold to the touch. The audiologist reached behind my ears to switch the aids on, sending a wave of static through my ear canals.

"Okay!" the audiologist said, her voice amplified. "You're ALL SET!"

She grabbed me by the shoulders, spun me around, and nudged me out the door.

Miss Dawes greeted me as I slunk back into the classroom. She inspected my ear molds and said, "CAN you HEAR me NOW?"

I gritted my teeth and fake smiled. Miss Dawes cheered and gave me a big thumbs up.

"NOW YOU'RE READY TO START LEARNING!"

Those last words from Miss Dawes made me feel uneasy. Earlier

that morning, I decided to leave my hearing aids at home because
they irritated me and I didn't like wearing them. It never crossed my
mind that I left them home so I could get out of learning that day.
The opposite, actually, was true: without the distraction of the hearing aids and being forced to pay attention to two things at the same
time—Miss Dawes's voice and her signing—I would have been more
ready to learn than ever.

I didn't need the hearing aids to learn, and it confused me that
Miss Dawes thought I did.

I fumed silently in my seat. Miss Dawes and the audiologist might
have outsmarted me this time, I thought, but I wasn't going to give up
anytime soon.

THE LEXINGTON SCHOOL FOR THE Deaf has been around since the
Civil War. My brothers and I were the third generation of our family to
go to school there; my grandma was the first, starting way back in the
1940s. The Milan Conference had taken place more than sixty years
before, but its long shadow still darkened the halls of Deaf schools;
the pure oral education approach the conference had endorsed was
ironclad law at Lexington. Its Deaf students, including my grandma,
were expected to use their voices at all times. Using the hands to communicate was strictly banned and looked down upon with disgust and
disdain by teachers and administrators—all of whom were hearing.

My grandma was born Deaf to hearing parents. Her father was a
distinguished family doctor, carrying on a proud family tradition as
the fifth generation to practice medicine. Her mom taught courses on
shorthand at a local business college. Though she lived just a fifteen-
minute drive away from the school, her parents had her sleep in the
dorm on weekdays, and she came home only on the weekends. Her
parents hoped the more time she spent immersed in the Deaf school
surrounded by teachers and other staff who reinforced speaking, the
stronger her speaking and listening skills would become; perhaps she
might even progress enough to pass as hearing.

It was a misguided hope. The goal should never be for Deaf

people to pass as hearing, but to achieve their full potential using methods and languages that work for them. Speech didn't work for my grandma; she never learned how to speak well. To this day, she has no ability to articulate words clearly using her mouth.

The school, as is typical of the oral education school of thought, confused speaking ability with intelligence and potential to learn. They saw my grandma struggle with speech and put her on a vocational learning track. In high school she took life skills courses and learned how to cook and sew; she didn't take more academic classes, such as history or English literature, that would have rounded out her education, improved her world knowledge, and honed her ability to think critically.

It turned out to be a blessing in disguise that my grandma's parents had her sleep in the dorm, because it was the one place in school where Lexington students could use sign language. The school's strict ban on signing faltered at the thresholds of the dorm buildings, and beyond them, the Deaf students thrived. Their hands flew, and their eyes eagerly drank in the information these hands presented. In the sanctuary of the dorms, my grandma learned sign language from her Deaf peers who had grown up in Deaf families. It was her saving grace.

Grandma's parents looked down on sign language. They did not sign and adamantly spoke when trying to communicate with her. When she was thirteen years old, her grandparents moved in to live with her family. Her parents told her she shouldn't dare use her hands to communicate, not even to make a gesture. Grandma's parents thought signing was beneath humans—that it was for monkeys.

But when her parents were out of the house and she found herself alone with her grandpa, he did something that floored her. He approached her, put up his hand, and started fingerspelling. Surprised, she asked her grandpa how he had learned. Continuing to fingerspell, he told her that his brother, my grandma's great-uncle, was Deaf like her. As he ended the conversation, he put a finger to his lips and mouthed to my grandma, *"Don't tell your mom and dad."* He knew her parents wouldn't be pleased if they knew he'd communicated with her in sign language.

Grandma was surprised by this new information from her grandpa. She had only met her great-uncle once, when she was five, and didn't remember him. Her parents had never told her that there was another Deaf person in her family. She later learned that her Deaf great-uncle was a printer—a common occupation for Deaf people because they were impervious to the awfully loud racket that printing machines made. The printing trade was often taught at Deaf schools, and printing jobs provided many Deaf people with a comfortable income to support their families. But my grandma's father, the fifth-generation doctor, looked down on the printing trade, and prayed that his daughter would learn to speak capably and achieve a career that was, in his eyes, more sophisticated.

Grandma put her head down through her vocational classes at Lexington, snatching what little she understood from the teachers who taught orally. Her final courses at Lexington trained her how to be a keypunch operator for IBM computers. But every day she looked forward to when the final school bell rang and she could run to the dorm and start signing with her friends. After she graduated, she met my grandpa, who had attended another Deaf school in a different part of the city. He too had endured oral education and had learned ASL the same way she did—through friends, out of sight of the school's administrators and teachers. They started a family, my mother being the first of their three Deaf children, and Grandma became a devoted mother and homemaker.

One thing that stayed with Grandma from her time at Lexington was the punishments the teachers gave to students who violated the no-signing rule, herself included; she was a common rulebreaker. She and her other friends couldn't help it—signing was natural to them. They felt compelled to use their hands and faces to communicate, and they relished the full access to information they had when they signed. But each punishment was humiliating. Sometimes it was multiple sharp raps of a wooden ruler across the legs and the knuckles, or a literal dunce hat, which the offending person had to wear while sitting in the corner. Other times, Grandma told me, the teacher handed her a long piece of chalk, put her in front of the blackboard, and instructed her to scratch out, hundreds of times:

*I will not sign in class.*

*I will not sign in class.*

*I will not sign in class. . . .*

And twenty years later, the very same words were being written on the very same blackboard, only the hand holding the piece of chalk was my mom's. Little had changed at the school in the generation that passed since Grandma finished her schooling. The oral education philosophy still ruled, and signing was still banned, looked down upon, and met with severe, degrading discipline. But there was one significant difference: the advancement of technology had brought forth hearing aids, which Mom started wearing at the age of three, as mandated by the school.

At Lexington, Mom learned how to use her voice to speak better than Grandma had, but her skill was still marginal. Often, she could only articulate single words, and sometimes, if the words were easy enough, maybe a full sentence. Though it was nowhere near the competency required for effective everyday communication outside the school, Mom still spoke better than most of her classmates and was considered a model student. The school shrewdly reinforced speaking among its students by handing out awards for the best students, and once gave Mom the Speech Student of the Week award. It came with a pin featuring those exact words, which she wore on her shirt with pride. She was only seven then, and the award boosted her self-esteem.

Yet anytime she found herself with her friends out of sight of the teachers, she would sign. As for my grandma before her, signing came to her naturally. Mom was more fortunate than my grandma because she had Deaf parents and lived in a signing household. Many of her peers came from Deaf families, too, and friend gatherings outside of school helped her build her signing fluency far more rapidly than her speaking ability. And so, even with the speech award pin on her chest, when Mom went to the restroom and bumped into a friend, she immediately started chatting with her in sign language. They were in one of the school's few safe spaces, beyond the vigilant gaze of teachers, administrators, and other strict signing ban enforcers. Without thinking, they continued to chat in ASL as they opened the restroom door and walked out into the hallway. Mom, whose head was turned as she walked to keep her eyes on her friend's signing, was not watching where she walked. Wham! She walked smack dab into a massive belly. She craned her neck up and up until she could see the person's face and gasped. It was the school superintendent, and he was not pleased.

*"Why are you signing?"* he spoke. Mom didn't know what to say.

The superintendent's eyes darted to Mom's shirt. He looked at the pin, and then back at my mom's face.

*"Give that to me, please."*

Mom's self-esteem dropped to the floor. Today, she knows that the award meant nothing, and that she shouldn't have felt bad for having it taken away. But at age seven the school had so conditioned her—*brainwashed* her—to take pride in her speaking ability that the order to return the pin deeply humiliated her.

Delivered in oral education for Deaf students that clearly struggled with it, classes progressed as slow as molasses. Mom and her classmates didn't learn and thrive; they survived. They made do with the few words they caught from the teacher's slow-moving lips, scribblings on the blackboard, and assigned readings.

The teachers led activities that had zero educational benefit. In one game they played, the teacher pressed a piece of chalk on the blackboard; upon her signal the students would start humming and she would slowly move the chalk across the board, forming a line while the students went:

*"MMMMMMMMMMMMMMMMMMMMMMMMM!"*

The room rumbled with the class's mournful chorus, growing quieter when students tapped out, one by one; the teacher moved the chalk until the very last student's vocal cords gave out. The game was supposed to exercise the students' voice boxes.

The school gradually relaxed its signing ban as Mom grew older. Part of the reason was that new research, proving that ASL was a language, was gradually advancing through the Deaf education community, slowly changing some Deaf educators' perspective on the merits of ASL. Another reason was that the students simply could not be stopped from signing at all times. Violations of the school's signing ban were too frequent, the transgressors too rampant in the student body. Concessions had to be made, the school finally decided. The rule wasn't as strictly enforced during lunchtime, and the cafeteria joined the dorms as a signing haven on the Lexington campus. By the time Mom started high school, the signing ban was even relaxed in the classrooms. Tired of the slow pace of oral education, many teachers would close the door and start signing their lessons. The school even hired a Deaf teacher, Mom's first and only one in her time at Lexington, and looked the other way as the teacher conducted classes in sign language.

One change the school made in the time between Grandma's and Mom's enrollments turned out to be critical for Mom. Unlike my grandma, who was relegated to life skills courses because the school equated her inability to speak with a lack of intelligence and potential to learn, in later years the school had changed its philosophy significantly enough that Mom and many other Deaf students were allowed to stay on the academic track and take more intellectually challenging courses. After graduating from Lexington, she continued her education at the National Technical Institute for the Deaf in Rochester, New York. She was the first in the DiMarco family to attend college.

Her path led back to Lexington when her three boys were enrolled there. Miss Dawes and all the teachers, administrators, and staff at the school treated Mom with respect and deference to her face. In addition to being a part of the DiMarco family and an alum of the school, Mom also was the president of the parent-teacher association. And, perhaps most fear-inducing of all, she was an *educated*

Deaf parent who was a proud, articulate, and outspoken advocate of Deaf education, especially when it concerned ASL.

Oral education was *still* the norm at Lexington when my brothers and I were students there. Understand that this wasn't the distant past; this was the mid-1990s. Just two and a half decades have passed between then and the day I'm writing this sentence.

Fortunately, Mom was armed with knowledge of the educational system and strong advocacy skills. She knew that laws like the Individuals with Disabilities Education Act armed parents like her with powerful rights pertaining to the education her disabled children received. She requested that Lexington provide my brothers and me with sign language support services. The school resisted Mom's request, but she persevered, and won.

That was how my teacher, Miss Dawes, came to start signing with me and Nico in class. But friction remained between Miss Dawes and Mom, with language fluency at the heart of the issue. Having never been required to sign in class before Mom's request, Miss Dawes simply was not fluent enough to converse with Mom, or any of her Deaf students, in ASL. She not only sim-commed, she used Signed Exact English (SEE) instead of ASL. SEE follows the grammatical structure of English, which is way different from that of ASL (remember the STORE ME GO example of ASL grammar from earlier?) and adds invented signs to show phonological aspects of English words and how they're ordered in English sentences. Oralists prefer SEE over ASL, under the unproven assumption that SEE's closer resemblance to the English language will be more effective in helping Deaf children learn how to speak English.

Mom labored to understand Miss Dawes's sim-commed SEE. It pained her to think about how much tougher it was for Nico and me to understand Miss Dawes in class. She went to the principal and asked for an opportunity to get involved in her boys' classes; she could be a Deaf adult language model and help her sons and our peers develop our ASL competency. The principal reluctantly consented to Mom's request because it would reinforce the sign language support services that she had requested for her boys. But she was only to participate in classes with her sons in them; none of the kids in other classes had approved sign language support services.

Nico and I and our classmates hopped and clapped every time we saw that Mom would be spending the day with us. We especially loved reading time, when we would clamor for my mom to read out loud instead of Miss Dawes. It wasn't only us; the entire class joined in the request. Just like at home, her colorful and cinematic ASL story times delighted and fascinated us. When the book ended, we would groan, bunch all the fingers of both of our hands at the tips and tap them together: MORE.

We wanted more of Mom's signing and dreaded the moment the control of the classroom shifted back to Miss Dawes's stilted sim-com and SEE.

Word of Mom's ASL storytelling rippled through the school, and soon students from other classes crashed our reading times, eager for my mom's accessible, entertaining ASL tales. The principal found out and immediately put a stop to it. My mom's ASL support was for her sons' classes only, he said, chastising the other teachers.

Whenever Mom volunteered at school, all my classmates crowded around her. None of my classmates had Deaf parents, and very few of their parents signed. They craved natural ASL communication, and Mom was the rare Deaf, ASL-fluent adult who came into their lives. They tapped her shoulder and asked her questions with their little hands, their eyes glued to Mom's hands and face, absorbing all the ASL input she gave them. It broke her heart when she had to leave school every day, knowing that these kids wouldn't get accessible communication the rest of the school day or at home, when they would return to parents who didn't know enough ASL to communicate with their child—or disdained signing and refused to use it at home, as my grandma's parents did.

The parents weren't always at fault. The issue was systemic:

parents of Deaf children rarely received sufficient information from doctors, social workers, or educators about ASL to understand how beneficial it could be for their Deaf child.

Mom knew how the system worked against ASL and tried to push back. She advocated for more ASL input in the school so her boys and their classmates would receive the natural language input they desperately needed. She tried to talk with the principal about the language environment in her boys' classrooms. Deaf kids needed a rich, accessible language environment led by teachers fluent in ASL, she told the principal. We started to struggle and fall behind when we were forced to hear words through our hearing aids. We strained to read the overenunciated words on teachers' lips and scrambled to catch leftover crumbs of sentences from teachers' hands. This was not the right way to teach Deaf kids, Mom argued.

The principal wasn't unsympathetic, but he explained that there was nothing that he could do about it. The school had used the oral education so long that it had calcified in the mindsets of administrators, teachers, and parents. Speaking and listening, sim-com, and SEE were here to stay. There was strong resistance to ASL from many stakeholders. Making a change would be extremely difficult, if not impossible.

In the early 1990s, the New York City Department of Education had formally recognized American Sign Language as a foreign language that could be taught at schools throughout the state. ASL lessons boomed among hearing kids, who thought it was cool to learn a new language using an entirely different modality that involved their hands, faces, and bodies. Mom pointed this out to the principal.

"Hearing students learn ASL throughout the state and the city. Why can't we do the same here?"

No can do, the principal said. Bureaucracy would make such a significant change too difficult. Too many hearing parents of students at the school wanted their kids to speak. My mom clenched her teeth in frustration; learning ASL enhanced language development for Deaf children and didn't hinder a Deaf child from learning to speak.

"The Department of Education is inviting hearing kids to learn ASL," Mom said. "But Deaf people, the very people that the language was created to empower, can't even use it in their school?"

The principal didn't respond.

The deep and painful irony of the idea that hearing kids learned ASL freely while their Deaf counterparts scraped along in Deaf schools that disdained the language angered my mom. But she didn't give up. She couldn't—for the sake of her boys and their classmates.

ONE MORNING MY MOM DROVE us boys to school, ushered us into our classroom, pulled out our hearing aids from our backpack, and helped us put them on. Out of the corner of her eye she spied another parent asking Miss Dawes why my mom didn't make her boys wear hearing aids at home, since the teachers at the school trained parents to put hearing aids on their kids as soon as they woke up. The hearing aids were to be kept on all day long, at home and at school, through the night up until it was time to go to bed.

My mom read Miss Dawes's lips as she responded: "*Well, she doesn't have time. She has three children.*"

There's a sign in ASL that places a fire in your belly. Combined with a frown and gritted teeth, it indicates a smoldering and seething anger burning hot inside you. At that moment, a blazing inferno was in my mom's belly.

Later, after her initial anger had subsided, Mom met with Miss Dawes to tell her how she felt.

"I may be a busy mom," Mom signed, "but that isn't why I don't make my boys wear hearing aids. We communicate in ASL just fine at home. If my boys want to wear hearing aids at home, I'm okay with that. If they don't want to, I'm fine with that. I won't make them."

Knowingly or not, Miss Dawes had lied to that parent, Mom told her. More than that, it was Miss Dawes's responsibility to ensure that parents were educated on the uses and benefits of hearing aids, as well as other communication methods and languages, like ASL.

Embarrassed at being caught, Miss Dawes apologized.

Mom wasn't finished. At home, she printed out copies of fact sheets related to ASL and the benefits of hearing aids. The handouts described what ASL was and its various grammatical rules; explained how hearing aids worked and who would benefit from them; and discussed deafness, including the different levels and types of hearing loss. She passed them out to the other parents at school. The parents could read them, keep them, or throw them out; it was their choice. She only wanted to ensure they had access to this information.

Miss Dawes remained silent as my mom handed out the fact sheets in her classroom. It was one of the only times I saw her speechless.

Mom found other ways to help educate parents at the school. As the president of the PTA, she made ASL awareness a focal point and educated the other parents on the merits of ASL, that it was a language, and that it didn't harm Deaf kids' development in other areas, like learning to speak. Slowly, she helped some parents change their mentality to the mindset that being Deaf is fine, and to embrace ASL.

For many of these parents, their Deaf child was probably the first Deaf person that those parents had ever met in their lives. Mom thought that they might appreciate learning how Deaf adults and families lived. She hosted a party at our house and invited the other parents to come over. She showed them how, when the doorbell or phone rang, the lights on the house flashed on and off. She showed them how we would make phone calls, typing out a call made on our teletypewriter (TTY). For some parents, that party was their first time seeing a dinner conversation entirely in ASL.

Mom began to gain the trust of the other parents. Over time, many of them started calling on her for advice. They asked questions about Deaf culture and ASL. Some borrowed VHS tapes from her collection of ASL videos. Others wanted to make their home more Deaf-friendly and asked how they could set up doorbell and phone light-flashing systems and install TTYs.

Mom's advocacy was worthwhile and fulfilling, but it had its emotional peaks and valleys. She slipped, painfully, into one of the valleys at a support group for parents held by a counselor at the school. While Nico, Neal, and I played with the other Deaf kids at one corner of the classroom, the parents huddled together in a circle to talk with other parents and sip stale coffee from Styrofoam cups. Most of the parents were struggling to cope with the fact they were raising a Deaf child and came to the group for support and guidance. Being Deaf herself, Mom had an entirely different perspective from these hearing parents. She attended to meet and get to know the other parents and support them by sharing her point of view as a Deaf adult who was the parent of Deaf children.

During one gathering, a mother stood up to say that having a Deaf kid was the hardest thing she had ever experienced in her life. She had a vision of her child, perfect and vibrant and intelligent, with limitless potential; this vision was dashed when she'd found out that her daughter was Deaf. She cried every night, wondering what she did wrong. She said she prayed to God regularly that her daughter would fully regain her hearing.

The school counselor said, "That would be a miracle."

Mom couldn't believe what she had just seen. The fire in her belly, the smoldering anger, burned inside her again. She understood the pain and frustration the mother was going through, but it was inappropriate and counterproductive for the counselor to encourage the mother to wish for her child to regain hearing. False and misplaced hope would keep the mother focusing her energy on the impossible. That energy could be redirected and used far more effectively if the mother learned ASL along with her Deaf child and focused on her language development and rounding out her education. Her daughter was not a lost cause; she was a bundle of *potential*, which was being squandered every moment the mother despaired for something that would never happen.

The counselor continued to console the grieving mother. My mom, the sole Deaf parent in the circle, sat in silence for the rest of the session.

After the counseling session finished, my mom rushed us to the car. Looking into the rearview mirror, I could see tears streaming down my mom's cheeks as she drove. That night at home, Mom gathered everyone around the dinner table—my grandparents, my dad, my uncles—and told us what happened.

Mom wondered: Were Deaf people's lives worth living in the eyes of the mother and the school counselor? Mom had left the support group feeling like a nobody, that all Deaf people were nobodies. The world continued to view us as broken beings, that we needed to be fixed and regain our hearing in order to be able to succeed.

Mom refused to accept this as fact. She set a meeting with the school counselor and told her how she felt. It was wrong of the counselor to support and reassure the mother after she made her comment. Instead the counselor should have given her tools and guidance on how she could raise her child to be successful in this world. The counselor also could have, after acknowledging the mother's feelings, opened the discussion to the room—offering my mom an opportunity to be included in the discussion.

Above all, Mom told the counselor, it was irresponsible for the school counselor to say that Deaf kids regaining their hearing was a miracle.

"Am I not a miracle to you?" Mom asked the counselor. "How about my Deaf boys? I don't want my boys to ever think they're not good enough. They *are* miracles. I *refuse* to let anyone tell them otherwise."

To her credit, the counselor understood and immediately apologized. Mom asked the counselor to address the situation in front of the parents during the next session, and the counselor agreed. When the counselor did so, the mother who'd wished for a miracle turned to face my mom.

Mom smiled at her and said, "I'm doing fine. I'm not less than a miracle. I am an independent and capable woman. I drove down here myself. I can communicate using sign language. My three beautiful Deaf children communicate in ASL, too."

The woman nodded slowly. I like to think that she was finally seeing my mom for who she was, a fully actualized Deaf adult human. A miracle, just like her own beautiful Deaf child.

Mom had spoken her truth. And in doing so, she felt empowered. She had reclaimed the dignity and pride that had been stolen from her.

WHILE MOM WAGED HER BATTLES with the school, I persisted in my own tactical skirmishes with Miss Dawes and the school audiologist. Whenever I had the chance, I left my hearing aids at home. After receiving a note from Miss Dawes expressing concern about my attending school without my hearing aids at an alarming frequency, Mom made half-hearted attempts at checking I had them in my backpack in the mornings before going to school. I devised my strategy by waiting to hide the aids until after my mom checked my backpack. I kept finding creative new places to hide them, tucking them under my pillow or mattress, covering them up beneath my boxers and socks in my drawer, stuffing them into an old shoe, slipping them between the seat cushions in the car.

The dull hearing-aid battery-test routine at school every morning turned into a new, exciting dance between Miss Dawes and me. Every time I came to the front of the line, I began frantically digging around in my backpack, stopping after an appropriate length of time had passed to look up with feigned dismay at Miss Dawes.

Again and again I claimed to have forgotten my hearing aids. Each time, I pushed Miss Dawes closer to the edge of her patience. With dwindling composure, she pointed me down the hall, where the audiologist, growing equally impatient, gave me my backup hearing aids and ear molds.

Miss Dawes and the audiologist grew suspicious that I was forgetting the hearing aids on purpose. Finally, one morning my feigned forgetfulness pushed Miss Dawes all the way to the brink.

"If YOU FORGET your HEARING AID one more time, WE will have CONSEQUENCES," she sim-commed.

The next morning I came in without my hearing aids again.

"That's it," Miss Dawes sim-commed. "DETENTION for YOU during lunch and recess."

That day, instead of eating with my classmates at the cafeteria, I sat across from Miss Dawes in the classroom. I munched in silence and watched out the window as my classmates played outside during recess.

At home that afternoon, Mom asked us boys how our day went.

Nico, the goody-two-shoes blabber-hands, was more than happy to tell Mom.

NYLE LUNCH DETENTION.

Mom turned to me. WHAT HAPPENED? I told her.

HEARING AID YOU NOT BRING, THAT ONLY REASON? OTHER REASONS, NONE?

I shook my head. I didn't act up or cause any trouble. My missing hearing aids were the only reason for the punishment.

The fire in her belly lit up once more. She walked into the principal's office the next morning.

"Yesterday, Miss Dawes gave my son detention for forgetting his hearing aids," Mom told the principal. "I understand why; it's school policy and hearing aids are considered an important communication tool in the classrooms here. Do you know what else is important for communicating with Deaf students who sign? Fluency in ASL. Unfortunately, my six-year-old son is more fluent in ASL than his teacher."

Mom paused to look the principal in the eyes. "Will you be punishing Miss Dawes as well, for her lack of fluency in ASL?"

The principal sat there blinking. Mom didn't wait for him to respond. She walked out.

Mom could not fathom how a teacher who had worked at a school for the Deaf for years could be allowed to get away with not acquiring at least a conversational level of ASL fluency. She couldn't see why the school would not blink at punishing a six-year-old for not bringing hearing aids to school, but let the teacher get away with continuing to make the classroom inaccessible for her sons and dozens of other Deaf students.

To Mom and me, hearing aids were optional. We'd wear them if we felt they helped with communication. American Sign Language, on the other hand, was essential. Our communication began and ended with ASL. Unfortunately, the school's views were flipped the other way around. Hearing aids were required; ASL was an afterthought.

Mom wrote a letter addressed to the school's superintendent.

> *My sons have experienced teachers with limited to poor communication skills, low expectations for their students, and no sensitivity or concept of Deaf culture or ASL. . . . As a Deaf parent of Deaf children, I have had to suffer exclusion from conversations (even when they directly pertained to me) and prejudicial statements regarding the Deaf by those who call themselves professionals in the field of Deafness.*
>
> *Without acceptance of ASL, the school cannot possibly be focusing on the Deaf child's full development of language. Reading, writing, and learning about other subjects is too difficult without the full development of language.*
>
> *I leave this school because I cannot afford to waste anymore of my children's academic life.*

My mom signed her letter as a parent, former parent-teacher association president, and an alumna of the school. The moment my mom sealed her letter, the decades-long tradition of DiMarcos at the school came to a halt.

Leaving Lexington wasn't the only change Mom was making. New York City had been home to my mom and us boys for our whole lives, but it was time for somewhere new. Where would we go next?

Go to Austin, Texas, said a friend of my mom. There was a large and growing Deaf community, and a great school for the Deaf located just down the road from the Texas state capitol building on South Congress Avenue. There were good teachers who were fluent in ASL and classes filled with smart students who would challenge my brothers and me.

Austin was also a beautiful city, with winters much milder than New York's, and scores of watering holes to keep us cool during the scorching summer months.

Of course, my grandparents decided to come along with us. My uncles had already moved out of our house in Queens by then, so my grandparents put it up for sale. We packed up our bags, said goodbye to my grandparents' house, and set out across the country in search of a fresh start and better Deaf education.

THANKFULLY, THE LEXINGTON OF TODAY is not the same Lexington of my childhood. For one, it now has Deaf leadership. In the mid-2000s, the school hired the first Deaf superintendent in its history. Since then it has hired two more Deaf superintendents, including the one leading the school at this time of writing.

ASL, once upon a time banned at the school, and later limited to children whose parents requested it in their Individualized Education Plans, is now the primary mode and language of communication in most classrooms at the school.

Slowly, the Lexington School is emerging from underneath the shadow cast by the Milan Conference, working its way toward a more inclusive and accessible environment for its Deaf children.

# 4.

# Roadside Arts and Crafts

Though ASL was their primary language, my grandparents put their own spin on it, creating unique signs that I have never seen used by any other ASL signers. These signs came from the home signs my grandpa used with his hearing parents growing up. My grandpa's native language is ASL, but his hearing parents, my great-grandparents, never learned it. Instead, they communicated with my grandpa by blending spoken English and their own made-up home signs, many of them adopted from common Italian gestures.

An example: the ASL sign for "beautiful" is made with an open palm and a circular motion in front of your face, with the palm closing as your hand completes the circle. In my grandpa's home sign for "beautiful," he closes his thumb and index finger in an o, leaving the remaining three fingers extended, moving this handshape across his chest. They're completely different signs, and my grandpa's version is unrecognizable to people fluent in ASL. My grandpa has different signs for other words, too, like "help," "delicious," "dislike," "bread," "dead," and many others.

My grandpa kept using these home signs after moving out of his parents' house and passed them on to my grandma; years later, after my brothers and I were born, and even now, my grandparents have *continued communicating with their home signs. I was proud of my grandparents' old-school way of signing. The signs they used looked retro, and it felt like our family had its own unique, secret version of ASL. And I especially enjoyed seeing the confusion on my Deaf friends' faces when they joined the DiMarco dinner table.*

*My grandpa would flirt with my grandma, signing that she was beautiful. It made her blush and she'd pat his hands away to make him stop. Suddenly my friend would elbow my ribs and whisper to me. In ASL, whispering is quite different from whispering when using your voice. Instead of worrying about being heard, you worry about being seen. My friend kept his hands out of sight under the table as he whispered with a bewildered frown: YOUR GRANDPA SAY WHAT?*

THE MOVING TRUCK REMINDED ME of a giant eighteen-wheel semitruck, the kind my brothers and I would pump our arms at while chugging along the interstate. We would cheer, not at the blow of the truck's horn, but at the sight of smoke clouds that happened to belch, with purely coincidental timing, from its vertical exhaust pipes.

Few things in life gave seven-year-old me more pleasure.

Dad drove the moving truck and my older brother, Neal, rode shotgun, while Nico and I traveled with my mom in our Dodge van. It was a three-day cross-country trip, with stops at hotels each night. On the road, Mom followed close behind the moving truck, keeping it within direct eyeshot. We didn't want to get separated, because we had no way to stay in touch if we did; the year was 1996 and the smartphone was little more than an idea. If either vehicle moved out of sight distance, we wouldn't know if one of us had taken an exit to fill up on gas, or stopped because of a flat tire or engine trouble, or worse, if a cop had flashed its lights and pulled either of us over. Indeed, when we wanted to stop for gas or to eat, we had a way to communicate with each other. Mom would move to the left lane and gun the van's engine until we pulled alongside the moving truck, and through the passenger-side window of the van and the driver's-side window of the truck, Mom and Dad hastily signed out trip logistics.

Mom: NEED GAS! NEXT EXIT.

Dad, swiveling his head from the road to his window: OKAY! MAYBE EAT? ME HUNGRY.

Mom: FINE!

Ah, the days before smartphones and texting systems. Our (literally) high-speed interstate communication system worked, pure and simple . . . until it didn't.

A few hours from Austin, the moving truck disappeared from view. Had the truck pulled over or slipped behind us without us noticing? We had no idea. Mom pulled over at the next exit and circled back down the interstate the way we had already come, thinking maybe the truck had a flat and my dad was pulled over somewhere. We couldn't find him the first go-around, and we went around a couple more times, going further and further back each time. But Dad, Neal, and the truck were nowhere to be found. We didn't know if something had happened to them, and even if everything was fine, we weren't sure if they knew where to meet us in Austin. Mom couldn't remember if she'd given my dad the address of the place where we were going.

Suddenly, Mom pulled the van over to the shoulder, opened the back door, and started unloading our moving boxes. Nico and I had no idea what she was doing. Nico tapped her on the shoulder.

YOU DO-DO WHAT?

She ignored Nico, continuing to toss boxes and other stuff out onto the grass. We stood by and waited until she found the box she was looking for. She ripped it open and started pulling out its contents: posterboards, paint brushes and cans, markers, Elmer's glue. I recognized it—our arts and crafts box. I looked at Nico, who returned my quizzical look. We had a roadside emergency and Mom wanted to start a DIY project? She grabbed a black marker, placed the posterboard on the asphalt, and knelt over it.

Nico and I peered over her shoulder to see what she was drawing.

Slowly, the black lines she drew turned into block letters, which read: PLEASE CALL POLICE.

My mom got up and started handing out posters and markers and told us to make copies of her poster. I was mortified. Did Mom expect us to stand by the road holding signs we'd hastily scrawled ourselves? I turned to Nico.

MOM SERIOUS?

ME WON'T DO THAT.

NO WAY.

We turned to Mom to start our protest, but the look in her eyes stopped us. She didn't say a word, but her face threatened: "I dare you to challenge me right now. I *dare* you."

Moments later, as vehicles zoomed by, we stood by the road lifting our signs above our heads and waving them back and forth to get someone's attention. I felt like one of those sign spinners standing on a street corner. These spinners made their job look halfway fun; this was *not*. The Texas sun beat down on our backs. Speeding semitrucks and SUVs kicked up suffocating clouds of dust and exhaust that enveloped us and triggered occasional fits of intense coughing, adding injury to the insult of my intense embarrassment and shame. Nico and I looked at one another.

WE STAND HOLD-UP SIGN, HOW LONG?

ME TIRED.

THIS-IS STUPID. WON'T WORK.

SHH! MOM WILL SEE US TALKING.

Just then, Mom tapped me on the shoulder.

STOP TALKING. SIGN HOLD-UP-HIGH, DRIVERS SEE CAN. BE-PATIENT, POLICE CAR APPROACH-US SOON WILL, ANY TIME.

We waited and waited. Sweat beaded on our bodies and our shirts clung to our torsos, wet and clammy. Dust coated our faces, and I felt the unnerving grating of fine sand each time my teeth clicked together.

Eventually, finally, mercifully, a police car approached and pulled over. Gesturing and writing with a pen and notepad, Mom explained the situation. The police officer nodded and leaned chin to chest to speak into the radio in his shirt pocket. After a moment he notified us that nobody on his squad had seen a moving truck pulled over any-where near this stretch of the interstate. He sympathized with our trouble and encouraged us to get out of harm's way and safely back on the road. Mom agreed, figuring that if police didn't see something as big and visible as Dad's moving truck, then he must not have pulled over and was probably still on the road to Austin. We set off for Austin, where we fortunately found Dad waiting for us at the place we'd planned to stay.

My embarrassment aside, it's amazing to me how resourceful and creative my mom was in that situation. She had to be because there were few communication options back in those days. Smartphones and other technology have made life so much easier for Deaf people.

I WASN'T ALIVE IN THE middle of the twentieth century, but I have some idea of how tough it was for Deaf people in that era because of my grandpa. The DiMarco family's Sunday pasta dinner tradition existed because of him; it was a birthright from his Italian heritage that he passed on to his children and grandchildren. And when we gathered, we gravitated toward him. He'd asked how we are, laughed along with us when we'd tell him a funny story, and told jokes with a conspiratorial wink that made you think the punchline is just for you and him. Later in the evening, after our breadbasket and bowls of pasta emptied and the sun had set, Grandpa would tell us stories from his past.

He told us about how he made a living as an assembler-riveter, helping build planes for the army. Many Deaf people worked with him at the same plant. They were so good at their jobs that Grandpa and his fellow Deaf plane builders often won safety awards. Once a heavy smoker, every work break he would go outside with his Deaf cowork-ers and—cigarette in one hand and signing with the other—catch up on the latest news with his buddies.

NOT LIKE TODAY, he told me and my brothers. BETTER TECHNOLOGY, EASY FIND-OUT NEWS. YOU LUCKY.

One story Grandpa loved sharing was about how much work it

took to arrange a visit with friends when he and my grandma were much younger.

BEFORE-BEFORE PAST, YOU MAKE-PLAN, YOU STAY-WITH PLAN, he signed. There was no last-minute bailing, as people do via text message these days. Back then, if a plan was set for Friday evening at a friend's home, when Friday evening came, my grandpa and grandma went, period.

The way my grandpa tells the story, a trip to their friend's house was an epic journey. My grandparents would trudge five entire city blocks to the subway station, where they boarded a train. After a ride that lasted an eternity (twenty minutes), my grandparents would get off at their stop and walk yet more blocks to the front door of their friend's place. The whole trip took well over an hour, which would have been fine—unless they rang the doorbell and received no answer. They would ring again, bang on the door, and wait another fifteen minutes, peering into the windows to be certain there was no one home. If there was still no answer, Grandpa would take out a notepad and scribble a message to slip under the door.

*The DiMarcos were here. We missed you.*

And then my grandparents would walk all the way back to the subway station, board a return train, get off at their stop, and walk all the way back home. They would have to wait until they bumped into that friend again to make another plan. If it was a friend from work, then my grandpa would find out what was up the next workday. Sometimes they would have to wait until the next gathering at the local Deaf club, where the friend was also bound to turn up. And if a visit was rescheduled, when the time came, my grandparents would go through the whole walk-subway-walk journey again.

In the 1960s, a brand-new invention would change the game for my grandparents and their Deaf generation. It was called the tele-typewriter, or the TTY.

TTYs were big, clunky machines with keys that connected with other TTYs through a phone line. On a small horizontal screen you typed out and received messages. TTYs had their own lingo—

abbreviations to take turns and finish the call. GA meant "go ahead," which indicated to the other person that you were finished typing and they could begin; SK was "stop keying," which you used to let the other person know that you were ending the call.

TTYs made it a heck of a lot easier for Deaf people to communicate with each other. They allowed us the easy freedom to make plans and also enabled us with the power, as gracefully as I can put it, to flake out—as in, to shamelessly cancel on plans at the last minute.

```
HI ALFRED HERE WHO IS THIS GA     HI THIS IS LORENZO
DIMARCO HOW ARE YOU GA     I AM FINE, THANK YOU. WANDA
AND I ARE EXCITED TO HAVE YOU AND JANICE FOR DINNER
TONIGHT GA     THAT IS WHAT I AM CALLING ABOUT. WE
ARE NOT FEELING GOOD. IT MUST BE THE FLU THAT IS GOING
AROUND. UNFORTUNATELY IT WOULD BE BEST IF WE STAYED HOME
TONIGHT GA     OH WE HOPE YOU FEEL BETTER SOON. THANK
YOU FOR LETTING US KNOW. LET'S MAKE DINNER PLANS FOR SOME
OTHER TIME GA     THANK YOU WE WILL CALL SOON GA     GOOD
BYE GA TO SK
```

Basically, TTYs were the original text messaging system. Deaf people were texting long before everyone else caught up. It took the rest of the world decades to discover the joy and convenience of conversing through text. Nowadays, TTYs aren't as prevalent in the Deaf community. To communicate with each other in real time, most Deaf people use video calling technology or (modern) text messaging.

While Deaf people were ahead of the game with text messaging, throughout the latter half of the twentieth century we were still far behind in many other areas of communications and media—especially when it came to accessing the news. With newspapers, Deaf and hearing people were equal; we could read papers just as well, there were no barriers there. But newspapers were delivered only once a day, and technology forged ahead, creating newer, better ways to get news to people faster.

With the invention and spread of TV, news programs gave hearing people a new way to access information. However, for many years, TV was inaccessible to Deaf people because television programs didn't have captions. While hearing people learned about breaking stories during the 6 P.M. news shows, Deaf people had to wait until the newspaper came out the next morning. Eventually technology was created to enable captions on TV, and yet later still captions became federally mandated for TV programs, and Deaf people finally gained access to the news on TV.

That left the radio: a rapid, up-to-date source of information that Deaf people didn't—and still don't—have access to. So, hearing people with access to a radio almost always learned about big news before the Deaf community did.

But if a piece of news is huge, shocking, and earth-shattering? It doesn't take long before it finds its way to Deaf people.

It was August 1997, and we had just moved to Austin. We were starting to get to know the new city we lived in. Of course, Mom was quick to make friends. One of them was a sweet cashier at the grocery store where we shopped. The cashier would always make small talk with Mom as she rang up our groceries, asking how she was doing and commenting about how cute we boys were. The cashier would speak slowly and clearly, enunciating every word to make sure Mom understood. She knew how to fingerspell, too, and would bring up a hand any time Mom couldn't catch a word off her lips. Mom enjoyed these little chats and became fond of the cashier, with her warm personality and uncommon enthusiasm and patience in communicating with Deaf people. Every time we went to the grocery store, Mom would try to search out the cashier so she could chat with her while checking out.

One time, as the cashier checked us out, she asked my mom, enunciating:

*"Did you hear what happened?"*

Silly question. Of course we hadn't. My mom asked her what had happened.

*"Oh my. It's so sad. Princess Diana died."*

Mom stared back at the cashier in disbelief. The cashier nodded and told her that she had heard it on the radio. They said there had been a car accident.

Tears ran down Mom's face, right there in the checkout line, as she shared her grief with a friendly grocery store cashier who happened to know a little sign.

I knew what the word "died" meant, but until that moment didn't truly understand the impact of it. Watching tears roll down my mom's face, I knew suddenly that it meant Princess Di was gone, and she wasn't coming back. I understood, for the first time, how death was supposed to make you feel. Knowing how much my mom adored Princess Di, I felt the deep pain and sorrow that she was feeling.

That moment, my first true encounter with death, spurred by a cashier who had heard the news on the radio, still sticks with me to this day.

For a long time, Deaf people were left out from accessing up-to-the-minute breaking news that radio offered hearing people. Then pagers came along, which gave way to smartphones, which eventually added social media applications, like Twitter. With the speed at which Twitter delivers information to your fingertips, it's the rough equivalent of what the radio gave hearing people for so long. That's probably why I love Twitter so much. It helps level the playing field of information communication and sharing for Deaf people. Now I can't imagine life without my smartphone always in hand and Twitter at my fingertips. With my smartphone, I have access to so much.

However much my grandpa enjoys telling stories of how it was back in his day, I know he wouldn't go back and relive it. He loves his smartphone too much. In fact, he's downright spoiled by it. Now, I fully concede that he has earned the right to be spoiled after living so long unable to make and change plans (and communicate with the world in general) easily.

As an example of how Grandpa maximizes the use of his smartphone, I might get about five Instagram DMs from him in a day—all links to delicious Italian dishes that caught his eye.

"Knock it off, Grandpa," I'd tease back on IG DM. "Your doc's been telling you for twenty years to stop eating pasta. It's bad for your health."

"Well," Grandpa would respond, "I'm eighty-seven and still strong as an ox. What do doctors know?"

Grandpa can take the conveniences of modern technology to some wild extremes, though. I get FaceTime calls from him often, just to check in. He doesn't always have something to say; he only wants to know how I'm doing. But once, when I was visiting home, my phone buzzed with a FaceTime call from him.

HEY. CAN-YOU GRAB BOTTLE WINE FOR-ME? he signed over our video connection.

WHAT? UM. SURE? There was something weird about this call, something about the backdrop behind my grandpa. But it took me a full beat before I realized it.

WAIT. YOU HOME? YOU CALL-ME DOWN-THERE BASE-MENT THIS HOUSE?

NEVER MIND. MERLOT, WE HAVE? MY FAVORITE. OR CABERNET SAUVIGNON? ME LIKE, TOO.

# 5.

# Wanderings

**M**any Deaf schools tell their students stories about Deaf history and culture to build up a sense of identity and pride. The tale of Laurent Clerc, Thomas Hopkins Gallaudet, and the founding of Deaf education in the United States is one such story. As a young boy at the Texas School for the Deaf, I learned another.

In 1988, Gallaudet University had been around for 124 years. In all of that time the hallowed institution of higher education had never had a Deaf president. It was long overdue, Gallaudet students, faculty, alumni, and the greater Deaf community agreed. The previous president had retired, and the university's board of trustees had narrowed their search to three candidates. Two were Deaf men and the third was a hearing woman.

The board announced their selection: the hearing woman.

The students and faculty walked out of the audience midannouncement. The next day, the campus shut down as the students and faculty staged a protest. Again and again the protesters chanted their simple but profound demand: DEAF PRESIDENT NOW!

The protest lasted one week. It captured the nation's attention and the support of many key allies, including the Reverend Jesse Jackson, who in an open letter addressed to Gallaudet students wrote: "The *problem is not that the deaf do not hear. The problem is that the hearing world does not listen."*

*The protest reached its peak when it was featured on ABC's* Nightline. *Elisabeth Zinser, the hearing woman who had been selected as Gallaudet's president, was interviewed along with Gregory Hlibok, a key student protest leader, and Marlee Matlin, the Deaf actor who was just two years removed from winning the Academy Award for Best Actress for* Children of a Lesser God. *Hlibok and Matlin were eloquent in their passionate appeal for the selection, finally, of a Deaf president to lead the world's only liberal arts college for the Deaf.*

*On the fifth day, Zinser resigned. On the eighth, the hearing chair of the board resigned, and the university's first Deaf president in its history was named. The Deaf community rejoiced.*

*I felt awe when I first learned this story. We claimed what was rightfully ours and had changed the course of history. We did that. Deaf people. Us.*

WHEN I WAS NINE, OUR family went out for a bike ride at a large city park about three miles from our house. We parked our van in the parking lot, unloaded the bikes, and rode out on the park trail together.

I rode just ahead of my mom, dad, brothers, and Uncle Robert, who was visiting at the time. I liked going fast, pretending I was winning a race that only I was aware of. The popular trail was crowded with bikers, joggers, and inline skaters that day. It was annoying getting stuck behind groups of plodding joggers.

*Slowpokes,* I thought. I wanted to go faster; I didn't have the patience to wait behind anybody. I studied the trail: it twisted and curved around thick woods and prickly pears. Where it curved I spotted gaps just off the trail.

I thought to myself: If I ride off the concrete trail and straight through the woods, I'll meet the trail again at the other end of the curve. I could avoid the slowpokes on the trail and go faster.

I looked at my slick BMX bike.

*Yeah, this baby can handle some off-road riding.*

I turned the handlebars and veered off concrete and onto dirt.

Looking between the trees, I could see that I was riding parallel to bikers on the paved trail, and I rode farther and farther and the woods grew thicker and thicker, until I couldn't see the other bikers at all. I went deeper into the woods, expecting the trail to pop up at any moment. It didn't. Suddenly, with a sinking feeling, I remembered that the trail was a loop. I must have veered off the trail just as it curved into the loop, and I was very far away from it now. I reversed my bike and stared at the woods in front of me.

Where had I come from? Where was the trail?

Uncertain, I picked a direction and pedaled forward. I kept my eye on my right, where the trail should be. But I saw no glimpses of bikers or slivers of concrete; the trail wasn't there.

Had I gone in the wrong direction coming back?

I stopped, took a deep breath, and thought for a moment.

It was growing dark. Would I get stuck at the park overnight? Was I going to spend the night alone, huddled on the forest floor?

*Stop! Don't panic.*

I blocked out the scary thoughts.

*Focus. Okay. Think about the main road, where we drove on the way here. That's where I need to get to.*

I tried to remember the spot where I turned off the trail. I oriented myself in one direction away from where I thought that spot was.

*This way, if I bike long enough, I'll get to the main road.*

I'm not sure how I knew, but I knew.

My feet pushed the pedals. My BMX bike slipped out of thick woods and glided across grass fields, skidded on dirt patches, and maneuvered around treacherous bunches of prickly pears. After what seemed like forever, I finally reached the main road.

*Yes! Now what?*

I looked left, then right. I realized I couldn't tell where the parking lot was from there.

All this time I'd been baking in the 100-degree-plus-heat under the scorching summer Austin sun. Big fat rivulets of sweat ran down my face and back, soaking my shirt. I looked left and thought that home might be that way. Exhausted and dehydrated, I told myself: *Just go home.* My family might spend some time looking for me around the park, but eventually they would figure out I wasn't there and go home. And then there I'd be, on the front steps. It was a plan. I looked left and right again and felt confident that my home was down the road to my left.

The first intersection I arrived at looked familiar, thanks to my dad. While driving home, Dad would often test our sense of direction. At a stop sign, he'd tap my shoulder, point left, straight, and right and ask: WHICH?

Over time, I got better and better at these pop quizzes and knew the way home from practically anywhere a couple miles out from our house. Riding on my bike, I knew the turns at this intersection, and the next, and the next, all the way home.

There was nobody home when I got there. I sat on the front step and waited. And waited. And waited.

The sun set. The sky turned dark; the streetlamps flickered on.

At last, a pair of headlights shined on the driveway. I looked up. My family was out of the van, running. Nico's face was red and his eyes were swollen from crying. Mom's hands stretched toward me, her face awash with terror, exhaustion, and relief. As she ran, she shouted: HOW?! WHY?!

A moment later, I was buried in my family's arms.

THE BMX BIKES THAT MY brothers and I rode were a gift from Dad. When we saw the brand-new bikes under the tree on Christmas morning, all our jaws dropped—including my mom's. The day before, Christmas Eve, Dad had gone out and bought the bikes for us boys without telling Mom. She found out about the gift at the same time as me and my brothers.

Privately, Mom asked Dad how they could afford to pay for the bikes. Dad just shrugged and said he wanted to do something nice for his boys.

The bikes weren't Dad's first time impulsively spending our family's money and wouldn't be his last. His splurging was a habit that seemed innocent on the surface, especially to me and my brothers. We were too young to understand that this type of rash behavior was a sign of substance addiction. It would get much worse. One day we would look back at the BMX bikes as a minor financial blip, compared to the catastrophic damage he'd do to his and my mom's entire life savings.

Even at that age, I sensed something was *different* about my dad. He wasn't always around like Mom was. If there was an event after school, Mom was there, guaranteed, but Dad would turn up only once in a while. And often, if he wasn't present it was because he was off with his friends at a bar somewhere.

He had a volatile temperament. Sometimes he'd be the funniest, happiest man in the world, with fresh and exuberant energy. The next moment he'd be in a dark, dark mood. I feared him when he was in these moods. I didn't want to cross him and bring his terrible wrath—and six-foot-four, 240-pound frame—down upon me. He was a giant, both jolly and fearsome.

He had his moments, though. I'll never forget the thrill of hopping onto my slick BMX bike that Christmas morning, and the proud, joyous smile on his face as he watched my brothers and me pedal around. Before that morning, during my bouts of restless wandering, I could only go as far as my feet could take me. With my brand-new bike, the world now lay at my pedals.

Despite my proclivity for getting lost, my parents gave me a long leash. I rode my bike everywhere, often with one or both of my brothers and sometimes a friend or two. Nico and I learned the streets near our home first, then we ventured farther and farther away, until our little legs couldn't pump any longer. We thought we'd reached the maximum distance we could travel from our home, limited by the feeble strength of our skinny prepubescent legs.

One day when we were ten, zooming past a city bus at a stop, we saw people attach their bikes to the front before boarding. Nico and I looked at each other and smiled. We didn't even need to say anything; we knew what the other was thinking.

We started learning how city buses worked—where the bus stops were and the different routes that crisscrossed the city.

When we were ready for our big journey, we invited our friend and classmate Marvin to join us. We rode up to the bus stop nearest our home, and when the bus pulled up, we brought our bikes to the front and put them on the rack, just like we had seen people do it before. We bounded up the bus entrance steps and surveyed the inside to pick out our seats. An arm extended before us, blocking the way. The driver pointed at a metal box beside him, with a coin slot on top. We had to pay to get on the bus? *Damn,* I thought. We didn't know and hadn't brought any money. Nico, Marvin, and I looked at each other sadly, resigning ourselves to climbing off the bus and halting our journey.

The bus driver spoke. We pointed at our ears and shook our heads. The driver raised his eyebrows.

"*Deaf?*" he asked. We nodded.

"*You don't have to pay,*" he said. "*Come aboard.*"

We couldn't believe our luck! We thanked the driver and climbed to our seats. It was the first time I got a freebie because of my disability. It's a nice little side benefit of having a disability—you can get tons of free or discounted admissions and stuff.

We rode that bus for a while, then caught more free rides on a second bus going another route, then a third, all the way to our destination: Texas School for the Deaf on South Congress Avenue, which was about ten miles from our home.

We snuck past the security guard at the entrance gate—it was summer and the campus was closed—and rode around the green grass of the school's football field.

In the distance, we saw a golf cart turn off the school road and onto the grass, barreling toward us. The security guard was at the steering wheel, pedal to the metal, shaking a scolding finger at us. We shredded grass toward the fence on the edge of campus, tossed our bikes over it, and scaled the chain link before the guard could reach us.

We were safe on the other side, but our excursion on campus was cut way short. With time to kill, we biked off to our next destination, a trading card shop. I walked right up to the front counter where the cashier was standing, unzipped my backpack, and poured out my Pokémon cards right in front of him. I pointed at my pile of cards and then at the store's cards behind a glass display. I pretended I was holding a card in each hand, one from my pile and one from the glass display, and moved my hands in a half circle, pantomiming a trade of cards between mine and the store's.

The cashier frowned and stared at me for half a minute as he tried to decipher my elaborate gesture. Then, light bulb lit, he patiently wrote out an explanation that the store didn't make trades; it could only sell cards. We groaned and grumbled and tried to convince the cashier to make an exception. We even upped our offer. But the cashier wouldn't budge. Disgruntled, Nico, Marvin, and I stomped out of the store.

We rode around without a destination until we came upon a movie theater. *Planet of the Apes* was showing. We parked our bikes at the bike rack without locking them. (Oh, the glory days of the 1990s, when bikes could be left at racks sans locks without sparing a worry about potential theft!) We went in and slipped past the ushers without buying a ticket. But by the time we'd taken our seats, we remembered that the movie didn't have captions and we wouldn't be able to understand it anyhow.

Our misdeed had been foiled by inaccessibility.

We walked out of the theater, saddled our bikes again, and, with nothing else to do, started pedaling home.

I rode side by side with Marvin, with Nico behind us. After a while, I sensed something wasn't quite right. I looked behind me and realized what it was: Nico was no longer trailing immediately behind us. I squinted my eyes and—there he was, way farther back, on his feet, running toward us. I waved to Marvin and we turned around and biked back to Nico. Up close, I saw that his pale face had turned deep crimson; his eyes were puffy and tears streaked his cheeks.

ME TRY-TRY WAVE-WAVE, YOU-BOTH NOT SEE!

He heaved and coughed and bent over at the waist to catch his breath. Then he explained that his bike chain had slipped off. He tried to get our attention, but we hadn't noticed his frantic waving, and of course had not heard his panicked yelling. He was terrified; he thought Marvin and I would leave him behind, lost and alone. I pulled him close and told him I'd never ever leave him behind.

YOU FINE NOW, I said, patting his back.

Nico wiped his tears away and his face slowly returned to its normal paleness. We helped fix his bike chain, then Nico and I parted ways with Marvin to head home.

Pumping our exhausted legs, we began to realize we had overestimated our strength. We were worn out and starving but didn't have any money. We were too exhausted to even try to navigate city buses to get back home. A few miles away from home, our reserves of energy had been completely tapped out. We rolled off the road and into an Applebee's parking lot. We fibbed to the hostess that we were lost and didn't know our way back home. She called the police, and moments later a cop car pulled up in front. We explained to the cop that we had gotten lost and asked if he could drop us off at our house. He nodded and loaded our bikes in the trunk, and we hopped in the car.

The police car parked outside my house and the cop escorted us to the front door. My dad opened the door. The way his eyes darkened at the sight of the cop by our side, I knew immediately that he was in one of his moods, and things were about to get way worse.

The cop, realizing my dad was also Deaf, didn't bother to communicate any further. He had completed his charge: two lost boys had been returned to the safety of their home and were now under the watchful eye of a parent. The cop drove away and my dad pulled us inside the house with rough tugs of our arms.

YOU-TWO-IN TROUBLE? he asked.

NO. I started to explain what had happened, but he cut me off.

BULLSHIT. WHAT DID-YOU-TWO DO WRONG?

NOTHING, I told him.

Whap. He'd swung his arm and smacked me upside the head with his open palm, hard. He stood over us, casting a menacing shadow. I knew he wanted to intimidate us. That was how he'd thought discipline and love should be shown, by creating fear. I winced at the pain on the side of my head, but I resisted the urge to shrink back from him.

GO UPSTAIRS.

When he was in this state of mind, I knew there was no point in trying to explain things. It would just make things worse. Once he saw a cop he automatically assumed that we had gotten into trouble and needed to be punished. There was nothing we could say to convince him otherwise.

My mom wasn't home. She was working with a group of local Deaf women to form a new nonprofit organization focused on supporting Deaf women experiencing domestic violence and sexual abuse. Her work required her to travel to Seattle periodically for organizational capacity-building training and workshops under leaders of Abused Deaf Women Advocacy Services, a model Deaf domestic violence and sexual abuse advocacy organization.

My grandparents lived with us, but they had a large bedroom that doubled as their living room and they mostly kept to themselves. Without our mom and grandparents around, Nico and I were left to endure the wrath of our father. I felt his heavy feet stomping on the stairs right behind us, following us all the way to our bedroom.

STAND THERE, he told us, pointing to the middle of the room.

STAY. THINK-ABOUT WHAT YOU-DID WRONG.

My dad walked out of the room, staring us down with a withering look, and left the door open.

We were left to stand alone, in the middle of our room, with nothing to do but stare at our bedroom wall and try not to think about the aching, trembling fatigue that slowly set into our feet, legs, back, neck, shoulders, whole body. The punishment was a military-style discipline that I think my dad had learned from his dad, a hearing military veteran and old-school hard-ass.

Once in a while he would walk by the room, checking to make sure we were still standing.

After about two hours, my dad finally came into the room to tell us we could sit down. He told us he hoped we had used the time to think about what we had done wrong.

I wanted to ask him what, exactly, we had done wrong, because I knew he didn't know the answer, either.

But I said nothing, because my feet and legs were on fire and my brain was a bit mushy from staring at nothing for so long. I was just glad it was over and the last thing I wanted to do was say or do something that would lead him to make me stand any longer.

I wish I had told him that all I had thought about for the entire two hours was what a dumbass he was, because I hadn't done a single thing wrong.

But I didn't, because I was scared of him.

I walked downstairs and out the front door and picked up my bike, my dad's impulsive Christmas gift. I went for a ride around the block. Despite my exhaustion from that day's ultramarathon bike ride and my dad's physically crushing punishment, it was refreshing to wander away for just a little bit, to feel the wind on my face and the bike's thick rubber tires treading the smooth asphalt, the world at my pedals.

# 6.

# Them Hearing, Me Deaf

I was running on the grass near the swings, under the cool shade of the big oak tree. Next to me was a boy whose name I didn't know, though I'd seen him at this park many times before. We played tag with my brothers and other kids. Nico crept up from behind and tapped me on the shoulder—I was it. I set my sights on this boy. He started running and I took off to chase him. He was fast, but I was faster. I closed on him after a few seconds and tapped him on the back. Now he was it. He reached to tag me back, but I dodged out of his reach.

Later, I found some sticks under the oak tree. The boy picked up a stick of his own. We danced around each other, swinging and jabbing and parrying blows with our sticks. In my head, we were the Teenage Mutant Ninja Turtles in battle training: I was Michelangelo, my favorite character, and my sticks were nunchucks. The boy was Donatello with a bō staff. I wondered if he was imagining the same thing in his head. We kept whacking our sticks to our endless joy. Eventually, one of my pretend-nunchucks snapped in two and our game came to a halt. We collapsed to the ground, laughing and panting.

WAVE-WAVE.

It was my mom, gesturing for us to come over. When we got to her, she mouthed to the boy next to me: "What's your name?"

*The boy frowned. He didn't understand why Mom wasn't using her voice. He tried to speak, but my mom pointed to her ears, shook her head, and mouthed her question again. The boy swiveled his head around. He was looking for someone, maybe a mom or a dad or a sibling, anyone who could help.*

*Mom tried again and this time the boy understood. He spoke, and she read his name off his lips. She started to gesture and mouth words: POINT-AT-KID "Your name" HANDSHAPE-B HANDSHAPE-I HANDSHAPE-L-WIGGLE-WIGGLE HANDSHAPE-Y "Billy."*

*The boy's frown faded away. He smiled and nodded and pointed at himself. My mom repeated the handshapes, and he mirrored her hand with his own.*

*Mom pointed at me. I tried to mouth my name but the boy doesn't understand. I took a piece of chalk and wrote my name on the sidewalk. The boy read out my chalk markings on the concrete and I saw my name on his lips. I taught him how to fingerspell my name, and then I saw my name on his hands. We smiled and nodded and laughed. He was Billy, my friend from the park.*

*Mom pointed at Billy. HIM HEARING, she signed. Then she pointed at me. YOU DEAF. I nodded. I knew this. She had said this many times before, with other friends I had met at the park. My friends from the park, who had been hearing, used their mouths to talk. Me, my mom and dad, my brothers, my family, who were Deaf, used our hands. To me, this was the only difference. I didn't feel sad about this difference. It didn't make hearing kids better than me. It was nothing. In everything else, we were equal. I saw this in the games we played. I could outrun Billy at tag, and he could snap my stick in half in our pretend battles. At the end of the day, we would go home, where we would tell our families over dinner about the new friend we made at the park. He would use his language, spoken English, and I would use mine, ASL. Our families would nod and laugh along with us, and we wouldn't miss out on any of the conversation.*

*Hearing Billy and Deaf me were equal.*

*I didn't yet understand the full weight of the difference between these two words Mom was trying to teach me. I was too young then, only six years old.*

*But I would learn, very soon.*

WHEN NICO AND I WERE around seven or eight, Mom and Dad signed us up for Little League baseball. We were the only Deaf kids on the team. Mom, especially, wanted it to be this way. Nico and I spent the majority of our time surrounded by Deaf people in our family and at school. An all-hearing Little League baseball team was a chance for us to step out of the Deaf world we lived in.

We didn't have an ASL interpreter. Instead, Dad assumed the role of de facto assistant coach. He helped out during practices and sat with the team on the dugout bench during games. Whenever the coach talked, Nico and I would first try to lip-read what he said, snatching a word here and there. After the coach finished, Dad would turn to us and sign to us a summary of what he was able to catch from the coach's lips.

This communication system was far from ideal—it sucked, really—but Nico and I didn't mind. Frankly, we didn't care enough about baseball to notice how much information we were missing out on. There were lots of other things we would have chosen over baseball: playing video games, trading Pokémon cards, or riding around on our BMX bikes.

Despite our obvious indifference to the sport, Mom and Dad made us play. Mom, because she thought we would benefit from socializing with hearing kids our age and broaden our view of the world. Dad, just because he was big into sports and wanted us to play ball. Our brother Neal was the jock of the family and shared his love of sports with Dad. Nico and I, while we were pretty good natural athletes, didn't have a whole lot of passion for organized sports. Dad hoped to change that through Little League.

Despite Dad's optimism, Little League didn't spark our interest. The few parts of the activity that Nico and I did actually enjoy had zilch to do with the actual playing of the game. We loved chewing up and spitting sunflower seeds all over the dugout and rattling the chain-link fence whenever our team scored a run. After games we were always the first kids in line when one of the parents passed out snacks.

During games, the coach often put me in the outfield, where batted balls very rarely reached. I killed time by picking strands of grass and kicking at dirt mounds, ignoring what was happening with the batter. When it was my turn to bat, I was even more hopeless. I swung at pitch after pitch that spat out from the spinning machine on the mound, but rarely made contact with the ball. The few times my bat performed a minor miracle by touching the ball, the ball would only dribble weakly inside the infield, and I'd get thrown out way before I got to first base.

Initially I didn't mind being a terrible batter. But then I kept seeing other kids on my team hit the ball and get on base. Their parents would cheer when they'd got a hit, beaming and clapping at their kids, who would smile proudly, flashing thumbs-up back at them.

Hey, I want that, I realized.

I got tired of rattling the fence for my teammates' hits. I wanted them to rattle the fence for *my* hit. I pictured what it'd be like to get a hit and stand on base and see my mom, dad, grandparents, and brothers all clap for me, and man, that scenario felt *good*.

I started trying harder during my at bats, but I still kept swinging and missing. The pitches that spat out of the spinning machine on the pitcher's mound whizzed by too quickly for me. I started to dread the slow walk of shame from home plate to my seat on the dugout bench.

One game, I couldn't take it anymore. After striking out on three swings and misses, I stomped back to the dugout and walked right up to the coach. I shrugged my shoulders, spread out my hands, and then mimed the swing of the bat, as if to ask: *How do I hit the ball?*

The coach nodded and began talking. My eyes quickly darted to his lips. He grabbed a bat, showed me how his hands gripped it, and demonstrated a swing. I adjusted my eye gaze to catch his demonstration but missed what he was saying because I couldn't read his lips at the same time. After the coach took a few demo swings, his mouth stopped moving.

I readjusted my cap and tried to piece together the few words I'd plucked from his mouth. They weren't helpful when put together: "*Bat . . . ball . . . swing . . . eyes.*"

The words floated meaninglessly in my head.

The coach patted me on the back and walked away, shouting instructions to the kid who was walking up to home plate, bat in hand. The kid nodded and walked away to start his at bat as the coach clapped.

I sulked to the end of the dugout, where my dad was sitting.

WHAT'S-WRONG? Dad asked.

ME WANT HIT. DON'T-KNOW HOW.

SWING-BAT ME KNOW HOW, Dad signed. COME-ON, ME TEACH YOU.

He pulled me behind the dugout. Like the coach, he grabbed a bat and demonstrated how to swing. But unlike the coach, he used ASL to communicate his instructions, and I could easily understand everything he said. I understood that I was supposed to spread my feet out for balance, keep my hands close together on the bat for better control, and lift my front foot up when the ball came for more power.

Dad formed a sphere with the fingers of one hand and pointed to his eyes with the other.

WHEN BALL COMES, WATCH IT, Dad signed. He moved his hand-slash-ball toward the bat. EYES LOOK-AT BALL, he said, moving his hand-slash-ball until it touched the bat.

He looked at me. ALL RIGHT? he asked.

I nodded again. He handed me the bat. SHOW ME.

I spread my feet and kept my hands close together near the middle of the soft handle grip like Dad told me to. I imagined the ball coming out of the spinning machine, lifted my foot and stepped forward, swinging the bat around.

GOOD! Dad signed. REMEMBER, KEEP EYE ON-BALL. UNTIL BALL-TOUCHES-BAT. IMPORTANT.

The coach came up to us—it was my turn at bat again. Feeling a surge of confidence, I stepped to home plate and crouched in the batting stance that I'd just learned from Dad. I kept my eyes locked on the pitching machine. My front leg twitched, ready for the lift and step forward. The ball exploded out of the machine. I lifted my leg and stepped forward, swinging the bat with my forward motion. In the palms of my hands, I felt a *crack* as the ball connected with the bat. The ball flew in a beautiful rainbow arc. It sailed farther and farther away and then disappeared behind the outfield fence.

I looked back at Dad in the dugout. He was hollering and signing "home run" repeatedly, forming the handshapes: *H-R! H-R! H-R!*

I tossed my bat aside and started trotting along the base path. From the dugout, Nico and my teammates cheered and rattled the chain-link fence. My mom and grandparents clapped and waved their hands from the side of the field.

But I didn't think about them as I ran. My mind had rewound to a few minutes before, to the moment when my coach was trying to teach me how to hit. I knew the coach was hearing and that he used his mouth to talk. But it hit me then what that really meant when I was trying to learn directly from him. I could only catch a few spare words from the coach's lips. It wasn't enough for me to learn how to hit the ball.

My foot touched first base.

But just because I couldn't speak and hear didn't mean I couldn't learn. My quick hitting lesson in ASL with Dad was proof of that. I could understand Dad's ASL clearly and easily. I could try my best when lip-reading my coach or other Deaf people, but it was never going to be equal to communicating in ASL.

As I tapped second base with my cleat, I swelled with pride. Like the coach and most of my Little League teammates, the vast majority of the world was hearing, and they used their mouths and ears to talk. I couldn't avoid the hearing world—I would always need to adapt and work with hearing people. But I had ASL. It was *my* language, perfectly designed for someone like me.

I touched third and rounded the corner.

Through ASL, I could communicate with other people, learn new skills, and understand more about the world. Without ASL I probably would have kept whiffing at the ball for the rest of the baseball season. But with ASL, I learned the right way to hit and knocked the ball out of the park.

I looked up at the crowd of teammates that had gathered at home plate.

THEM HEARING, ME DEAF. *They speak, I sign.* Once empty of meaning, the weight of these words started to grow within me.

My feet landed on home plate and I ducked under my teammates' outstretched arms.

DURING THE YEARS WE LIVED in Austin, dozens of Deaf adult softball teams from all over Texas and the surrounding states came every summer for a tournament hosted by the team my dad played on. Neal, Nico, and I eagerly went along, but not to watch Dad play—no way. The sport was already boring as heck to play, let alone watch. No, we were excited to go because there was a humongous playground next to the softball fields. And all day, while the adults played softball games on the fields, my brothers and I and other Deaf kids scurried around the playground to our hearts' content.

I imagine that at first, the hearing kids at the playground were genuinely baffled by the hordes of Deaf kids on the monkey bars and going down the slides, our hands flying as we chatted to each other. But if there was any initial shock, it wore off quickly, because it didn't take them long before they started to mock us. They pointed at us, threw up their hands to create mocking nonsense signs, and cackled at us. Derision and condescension painted their gleeful laughing faces.

The first year this happened, I was bewildered. Why were these hearing kids, who were strangers we'd never met, making fun of us? We hadn't done anything to spark their bullying other than just be ourselves. After our confusion subsided, we became angry. The hearing kids' mockery was mean and uncalled for. And it hurt. I had only recently hit that home run, had just started to claim ASL as *my* language. Mom had planted that seed, and it was sprouting into a sapling of pride in ASL. At the playground, this sapling had come under fire from these bullying hearing kids.

Despite my anger, I didn't respond. None of the other Deaf kids did, either. We didn't know how—gesturing or mouthing words didn't feel like they would deliver a strong enough rebuke. We tried to ignore them, but that didn't work; they kept on making fake signs and laughing at us. That day all the Deaf kids played among ourselves, quietly seething in our humiliation.

The next summer, we were ready. I was a year older, and that small sapling of ASL pride had grown strong roots. It could withstand a beating—and deliver punishment when threatened. Early in the morning, my brothers and I huddled up with the other Deaf kids at the playground next to the softball fields. We settled on our plan of battle, and then we spread out to make preparations.

As the sun rose above the trees, the hearing kids came. They saw our flying hands and, as expected, started making fun of us. As planned, the Deaf kids climbed up to the high platforms of the playground, where we'd brought our armaments: rocks collected from the fields around the playground. The Deaf kids looked at each other, nodded, and opened fire.

We were merciful in our assault, aiming for the ground at the hearing kids' feet, intending only to ignite fear. The hearing kids hopped and skipped like scared rabbits as they fled far away. We raised our fists in jubilation.

For one day, the Deaf kids were kings and queens of the playground. No hearing kid would dare make fun of our language.

AS I GOT OLDER I learned other ways to handle cruel and heartless treatment from hearing kids—methods not quite as physically violent as throwing rocks, but just as effective and a great deal more vulgar.

One summer, our family went to a large camping gathering for

Deaf families in upstate New York. Hundreds of Deaf families from the Northeastern United States were attending, and we knew many of them from our time living in New York City. Neal, Nico, and I also made new friends with Deaf and CODA kids our age. CODA, or child of Deaf adult(s), is what we call hearing kids of Deaf parents. Some of the Deaf and CODA kids we hung out with were a couple years older than Nico and I, and we thought they were the coolest and looked up to them. We followed them as they snuck around the forest surrounding the campground and lifted our eyebrows in surprise as they lit up cigarettes. They took deep pulls and gently blew smoke so it hung around their face. Nico and I gaped at them, in awe of their utter badassery.

Some local hearing kids were at the campground, too, and they mocked our signing. They looked like a cat had dragged them in from a hick town nearby. They wore baggy black cargo pants with chains that extended from a front pocket to a back belt loop. Streaks of greasy black dyed hair swept over their faces. They moved together in their own clique, giggling and throwing up fake signs anytime they saw us. Their harassment didn't faze the older Deaf and CODA kids we hung out with. They knew how to handle it.

An older Deaf girl, the leader of our Deaf/CODA pack of kids, approached the emo kids. She was attractive and she knew it, and she put on her best, flirty smile when she talked with them, with the help of a CODA kid interpreting.

"Hey, do any of you guys want to learn how to sign?"

One of the emo kids stood up, taking her bait. He told the Deaf girl that his name was Mike.

"Okay," she answered, and the CODA kid interpreted. "Here's how you sign 'Hi, my name is Mike.'" She demonstrated the phrase in ASL for Mike, but slyly substituted the kid's name for another sign.

Mike didn't suspect a thing as he repeated the signed phrase. Neal, Nico, and I clapped our hands to our mouths, our cheeks ballooning with the laughter we fought to keep inside. Mike started smiling in an arrogant way that seemed to say of the signs he'd just learned: *See, this is too easy.* Desperately, we held down the giggles that threatened to overflow the fingers at our mouths, and agreed with the boy whole-heartedly: *Yes, this is too easy.*

We led the kid to an area where many of our Deaf parents were seated in a circle of lawn chairs, socializing.

"Go on," Our Deaf pack leader goaded Mike, with the help of the CODA kid interpreter. "Show them what you just learned!"

The kid stood at the edge of the circle, every Deaf parent's eyes on him, and, with a great deal of smugness, introduced himself, signing:

"Hi. I am a dick."

The Deaf parents looked at the kid with faces that ranged from perplexed to disgusted to incensed. Some of them shifted their eyes at the older Deaf and CODA kids, the real culprits of this prank. They cackled and sprinted into the forest, their safe place. Neal, Nico, and I ran after them, our faces streaked with tears of sweet, sweet laughter that we'd let out, finally.

After we returned to Austin from the New York camping gathering, I took a page from the older Deaf and CODA kids' playbook and added my own twist. At a local park, I stared deadpan at a hearing kid as he made fake signs and laughed in my face. I said nothing until he was finished, and then I wrote down on a piece of paper: *Do you know what you just signed?*

The kid frowned and shook his head.

*You said, "I have a small penis."*

I put down the pen and paper and walked away. I didn't look back, but in my head, I pictured the other hearing kids reading the note and then pointing and cackling at the bully.

NOT ALL OUR INTERACTIONS WITH hearing kids were all-out battles with bullies. We met far more nice hearing kids than we did bullies. We made friends with them at the park and in Little League.

The truth is that hearing kids mostly intrigued us. Through our limited interactions with them, we learned enough about hearing kids to know that Deaf kids were different. Language was a big difference that we were well aware of. But we didn't know a whole lot about how hearing kids lived, and, especially, what their schools were like.

All Nico, Neal, and I knew was the Texas School for the Deaf (TSD). We existed and thrived with Deaf classmates and teachers who (mostly) could sign. TSD was familiar, comfortable, and safe.

The schools that hearing kids went to? They were a mysterious other world to us, shrouded in secrecy. Hearing schools might as well have been on Mars, for as little as we knew about them. That was the case until Neal entered the fifth grade. That year, while Nico and I were in the third grade at TSD, Neal took half his classes at a local public elementary school. In the mornings, Mom would drop him off at the public school, where he and a couple of his TSD classmates were the only Deaf students, and at lunchtime they rode a bus to TSD for the rest of their classes.

For half a day every school day, Neal disappeared from our familiar, safe world and explored this unknown other world. I itched with jealousy. Anything either of my brothers got to do, I wanted to do the same, or better.

Aside from my jealousy, curiosity gnawed at me. Every day after school, I pestered Neal with questions about the public school. Did they learn the same subjects as we did at TSD? What did the classrooms look like? Did they have physical education and recess? In class, were the kids good and angelic or did they engage in mischief?

GO-AWAY, Neal told me.

Neal is soft spoken and quiet. He doesn't talk a lot in general. And if it was his pesky little brother asking, well, he was content to shove me out of his bedroom and close the door in my face. I eventually gave up pestering him for more information and decided to wait for my chance.

Neal's foray into public school lasted one year, and he returned to full days at TSD the next fall. I learned nothing of his trips into the strange other world of the hearing, yet my curiosity remained white hot. But my opportunity finally came when I entered fifth grade. Now it was my turn.

There was one small difference between Neal's and my mainstream school experiences. While Neal had Deaf friends with him, I
went alone; nobody else from my class at TSD was enrolling at the
mainstream school. Nico refused without even a second thought. He
wasn't going to mess up a good thing at TSD and start spending half
his school days at a place where nobody shared his disability or communicated in his language. It was a risky endeavor he was fully content to turn down.

*No big deal,* I thought. As twins, Nico and I spent practically
every minute of every day together. It even mildly annoyed me that I
didn't get to have a birthday to myself; I had to share that with him,
too. But at public school, it'd just be me. I looked forward to being
on my own.

The first day of school, my mom pulled up to the front doors of the
public school, kissed me, and told me she loved me and to have fun. I
stepped out, butterflies churning in my stomach. The sidewalk leading up to the school teemed with kids; there were so many more than
I was used to seeing at TSD. I shouldered my backpack and merged
with the crowd streaming into the school. The hallways were long and
labyrinthine, and there were so many lockers and doors. The sheer
size of the school building and the density of the kids filling up its
halls mesmerized me. I wandered until I found my classroom.

*Wow,* I thought as I entered. *Even the chairs are set up differently
here.* At both Deaf schools I'd attended, Lexington and TSD, the chairs
were always arranged in a semicircle facing the front of the classroom.
This was so we could see both the teacher and our classmates as we
signed to each other. In this classroom, there were four long rectangular tables sitting perpendicular to the front wall of the classroom;
seats ran along each long edge of the tables. There were also a lot
more chairs in this class than at one of my classes at TSD, more than
three times as many.

The teacher approached me. Next to her was an interpreter I recognized from TSD.

"Hi, Nyle! I am so excited to have you in my class this year," the

teacher said. She pointed toward a chair to the far left of the classroom.

"We've set up your seat right there," she said. "Right across from
the interpreter."

Another chair sat across from mine, facing it. The teacher said
this arrangement would give me an unobstructed line of sight to the
interpreter while still being able to see the teacher and the whiteboard. Sitting there did make it easier for me to follow along in class,
but it still felt weird—I had never been assigned a seat before in the
Deaf schools I'd attended.

As I sat down, I made eye contact with the other kids. They
smiled, but none tried to communicate with me. I wasn't an ordinary
new kid—I was the new *Deaf* kid, who communicated with his hands
and had an adult person by his side at all times to help with communication.

The teacher started the class, and I shifted my attention to the
interpreter. The teacher wanted to start with introductions and asked
the students to take turns sharing their names.

I quickly noticed another difference between TSD and mainstream school classes. At TSD, I was able to directly listen to each
individual—the teacher, my classmates—as they signed. This way, I
sensed the color and vibrance in their communication: personalities,
emotion, tone, unique signing styles, accents, sign choices, use of facial expressions—eyebrows, eyes, mouth, cheeks. I had never realized
how interesting, how much of a luxury, it was to be able to listen to
each person directly as they expressed themselves until I entered a
mainstream school classroom.

The interpreter was a skilled signer with years of experience
working at TSD under her belt. But despite her above-average skill,
it was difficult for me to follow the discussion. As an interpreter, she
was an avatar for everyone in that classroom—the teacher and thirty
students—and thus superimposed her style on every single voice. And
so, to steal a metaphor from the hearing world, instead of the beautifully distinct and varied melody of thirty different voices, I experi-

enced each unique voice as filtered through the droning monotone of the interpreter's signing. Most of the emotion, humor, nuance, *personality* of each voice was stripped away.

Not only was it unexciting to watch, the interpretation made it difficult to follow who was saying what. The interpreter would spell out the name or point toward who was talking, but there were too many students to remember who was who. I was used to being in classes of ten students or so at the Deaf school; now I was in a class of thirty, and they were seated all around the classroom. I had to swivel my neck and lean in all directions to see the speaker.

Additionally, it was difficult to look away from the interpreter to read whatever the teacher wrote on the whiteboard; I'd miss important information that was being interpreted at the same time. It was like trying to track a pinball while also trying to focus on the discussion and whatever visual cues the teacher was using. At times, I gave up trying to follow who was saying what and just kept my eyes on the interpreter.

With information coming to my eyes in a monotone, I found it incredibly difficult to focus. Like never before, I started to zone out.

There's a sign made with both index fingers, each repeatedly jabbing past the eyes on both sides of your head, fingers pointed toward the space behind you. Roughly similar in meaning to the English idiom "in one ear and out the other," the sign indicates information slipping past your eyes. You don't catch, understand, or remember the visual information that comes and flies past. WHOOSH-PAST-EYES. That was how I felt in that first mainstream school class, and in many classes after.

When class ended, I picked up my backpack and quickly slipped out of the classroom. I was suddenly conscious of the interpreter and didn't want to have her follow me, like a conspicuous shadow, to my next class. I wanted to look and feel independent. Plus, I didn't really have any friends to chat or joke with in between classes. So I speed-walked to the gym for my next class, PE, and stood around waiting until the other kids and the interpreter arrived. It felt so different from TSD, where the brief time spent in between classes in the hallways were cherished moments of pandemonium: yelling, teasing, pranking, roughhousing.

After the second class ended, it was time for recess. I followed my classmates down the hall toward the exit doors that led out to the school's playground area. As I walked, the interpreter tapped on my shoulder to let me know she was going on break. I nodded and kept walking until I was outside, then I stopped to take in the view before me. Just ahead, the ground dipped at a row of rocks, and beyond lay the playground and a wide, grassy field. Hundreds of kids, all of them unfamiliar to me, ran and yelled and laughed on the field and playground. If I walked past the dip at the rocks, I'd be alone in a sea of strange kids; without an interpreter, I would be asking for a communication disaster; beyond the rocks, incomprehensible speech, misunderstandings, and humiliation awaited me. I retreated to the school building's brick wall. A teacher aide nearby noticed and gestured for me to go and play. I shook my head. *No, ma'am,* I thought, *I'm fine right where I am.*

I stayed for fear of embarrassing myself if I tried to play with all those hearing kids. But staying put didn't make me feel much better. I hated the feeling I had when standing there, left behind, *alone.*

At midday, when my half day at the public school had ended and I was on the bus back to TSD, I was giddy with excitement. I missed my TSD classmates and the ability to communicate with everyone directly. I also felt sad: the mysterious other world I'd waited so long to see had fallen well short of my expectations.

Things didn't get much better the rest of the school week. At the end of each school day, I was exhausted, mentally drained from working extra hard to focus on the interpreter and follow along with class discussions. I hadn't made any new friends in the public school, and a bit of my freedom had been stripped by having the interpreter follow me around. And every recess period I stayed by the school building, hoping I could somehow hide by sinking into its brick wall.

While I was at the public school I didn't feel like myself—like Nyle. I felt as if I was seen just as the Deaf boy.

At the end of the school week, on Friday evening, I tapped on Mom's shoulder. I told her how I felt at the public school. I laid it all out, all my frustrations and feelings. As I finished, I asked:

ME QUIT MAINSTREAM SCHOOL, GO-BACK TSD FULL DAY, CAN?

It was only one week into the year; surely it would be easy to make the change now.

Mom smiled. There was some sympathy in her smile, but I also saw a hint of knowing and—strangely—happiness.

ME GLAD YOU HAVE-THIS EXPERIENCE, she told me. VERY IMPORTANT, DEVELOP SKILL INTERACT-WITH HEARING PEOPLE. MANY-OF-THEM, FEW-OF-US.

I listened with apprehension; I still held hope she'd be on board with my request to abort the public school experiment.

YOU-NEED FINISH WHAT YOU STARTED. WE DON'T QUIT. YOU STAY-AT PUBLIC SCHOOL, LEARN. GIVE-IT TIME. IT-WILL GET-BETTER.

I knew there was no point in arguing; Mom held the final word. I suspected Neal's previous experience wasn't doing me any favors; he had lasted the entire year in mainstream school, and I think my mom thought that if Neal could do it, I could too. Never mind that Neal had some Deaf buddies with him at the mainstream school and that I was going solo—I knew that argument wouldn't fly with Mom.

She understood that the first weeks at a new school could be tough. If I gave it more time, she was confident that I would find ways to adapt and become more comfortable in this strange new environment.

OK. ME WILL TRY, I said. Then I ran off to play with Nico. The weekend had already started and I didn't want to waste a single moment more before it ended.

ON MONDAY MORNING, I WORKED up the courage to climb out of bed and start a new week at the public school. Mom dropped me off, and I walked the winding hallways of the public school alone, took my assigned seat opposite the interpreter, and endured the first class. It did not go any better than it had during the first week.

Next was physical education. One small silver lining from the first week had given me hope: PE class. I loved physical activities and was a natural athlete. The week before, I had noticed that few other kids could run as fast as I could. This athletic advantage gave me a self-esteem boost and the confidence that I very much needed. I looked forward to going back to that setting in PE class, where I could show my hearing classmates my athletic talents.

That day the PE teacher organized a foot race relay. We had to run the length of the gym, tap an orange cone, then run all the way back to tag the next runner. When my turn came, the other team had a large lead—about half the length of the gym. I ran like my heels were on fire. I had the opposing team's runner in sight, and by the time I touched the cone, I was only a half step behind him. On the way back, I hit the gas and left him in the dust. When I tagged the next runner, I'd turned a half-gym-length deficit to a half-gym-length lead. A few runners later, our team won. My teammates clapped me on the back and gave me two thumbs-up. The teacher mixed up the teams before we ran the race again. My new teammates cheered when they saw that they'd wound up on the same team as me.

Reader, let me tell you: I was on top of the world.

Unfortunately, I didn't stay up there for very long, because soon it was recess and I was outside by the brick wall once again, watching my classmates horse around on the field and playground beyond the dip at the rocks. I stood there, frustrated. It felt as if I'd had a break-through in PE class, but at recess I was right back where I started. I wanted to break out of my recess period paralysis, to start connecting with my hearing classmates. But how to take that first step without feeling I was making a complete fool out of myself? I thought about PE class, how my athletic ability had helped me earn my classmates' respect without my saying a single word. How could I replicate that feat, here in recess?

With a smile I thought about another physical talent of mine. At home, we had a trampoline in our backyard. Neal, Nico, and I jumped on it for hours at a time. We practiced all kinds of tricks: front somersaults, backflips, even double somersaults. There was no trampoline here at the schoolyard, but I could do many of the same tricks I pulled on a trampoline on flat ground with a running start.

I pushed off the brick wall and started jogging. When I got to the dip in the rocks, I leaped across, and as soon as my feet hit the grass I started an all-out sprint. I aimed for a small open spot on the grassy field. When I got there, I took two rhythmic steps, and, simultaneously, exploded off both feet and drove my head downward. The earth turned all around me; when it was just above my head I reached out and pushed off. When the earth was underneath my feet again, I shifted into a cartwheel, then another one-handstand flip, and finished the tumble with a full no-handed backflip. I bent my knees sharply as my feet pounded the grass. Stuck the landing!

As I stood there, panting, I could see heads turning my way. I sprinted into another tumble, pouring hot sauce on it, combining several one-handstand flips, front and back, and culminated in a flourish with a front flip.

Several kids walked over to me, their eyes and mouths open wide in amazement. They extended their arms, palms up, and shrugged at me. *"Wow!" "How did you do that?" "Teach me!"* I read on their lips.

My fall was short lived; I was back on top of the world.

For the rest of that recess, I demonstrated tumbling movements for the other kids, observed their attempts at tumbling, then provided feedback by gesturing with them. Communication with the other kids was still rudimentary, but I had finally started making a connection with my classmates.

The public school became more bearable from that point on. I looked forward to every PE and recess, where communication transcended through sports. Eventually, I met a few kids in my classes who knew how to fingerspell, and I started fingerspelling my way through an occasional side conversation during classes. I taught some of my more curious and engaged classmates some basic signs.

I later learned that two of my hearing classmates lived only a couple blocks from me. One afternoon after school, I grabbed Nico and told him I was going to bike over to meet my hearing friends from school, and he should come with. Nico happily hopped onto his bike.

Nico and I had lived in the neighborhood only for a couple years and didn't know it as well as our new hearing friends did. While we were riding with them, they unexpectedly slipped off the sidewalk and wheeled into a heavily wooded area through a barely there trail Nico and I had never noticed before. We followed the trail until the woods opened up into a clearing. Old, beat-up objects lay all around the clearing: an empty oil can, a few rotten wooden fence barriers, even a tree house. Bright colors were splotched on the objects; the area had been used (or was still being used) as a paintball battlefield. We rode a trail around the clearing, climbed up the tree house, and played pretend army battles.

One of the hearing friends came up to me and Nico and asked: *"What's the sign for 'horseshit'?"*

We taught them how to say it using the *h* and *s* handshapes. They roared with laughter, and we ran around the clearing, gleefully cussing with our hands: *H-S! H-S! H-S!*

I felt proud of myself, gaining entry into this cool new circle of friends from the public school, and pulling my brother into it too. Nico and I hung out with the group of hearing kids often. Most times, we'd go biking around the neighborhood or the hidden trail in the woods. Sometimes we just milled about in each other's front yards, gesturing, teasing, playing.

A few times we slept over our friends' houses. Inside their homes, we saw that our hearing friends were more similar to us than not. They had video game consoles hooked up to TVs in their bedrooms or living rooms, just like we had in our house. They took shoeboxes and binders from under their beds and proudly opened them up to show off their collection of Pokémon cards, and when they came over to our house we returned the favor.

The mystique of the strange other world of the hearing slowly dissipated. The more ordinary my hearing friends appeared to me, the more comfortable I became around them. I began to show them more of my true nature, in particular my mischievousness. I teased them and played pranks, and sometimes I went too far. One time, a friend who lived in our neighborhood showed us his thick binder of Pokémon cards, neatly tucked into clear nine-pocket trading card protector pages. Turning the pages over, I spotted a holographic Charizard. A card I *coveted*. I waited until the friend wasn't looking, then slipped the Charizard out of its slot and into my own pile of cards, and nonchalantly walked home with it. Nico's eyes bulged when he saw me do it, and when we got home he said, with a face that was both impressed and appalled, "I can't believe you did that!"

The lights in our house flashed on and off and my mom answered the call on the TTY. It was the boy's mother, explaining to my mom that the boy's Charizard was missing and asking if we knew where it was. Mom gathered me and Nico and asked us. We flat out denied knowing anything. She let us go, but later, when I wasn't looking, she pulled Nico up to a bedroom upstairs to speak privately.

SERIOUS. WHAT HAPPENED? Mom asked.

Nico immediately caved and told my mom the whole story.

Just like the time I swiped the candy bar from the grocery store, my mom dragged me by the ear over to my friend's house and forced me to apologize and give back the card. Deservedly, I was grounded from sleepovers for a good while.

Later, another act of mischief would serve as a stark reminder of an important difference between hearing and Deaf people. It happened at a friend's home, a popular hangout spot because he had a homemade quarter pipe ramp and rail—perfect for skateboarding practice. After school, a bunch of us, hearing and Deaf kids, often hung out there. One afternoon, we were horsing around, teasing each other, and got a little too rowdy. At one point, I started screaming in a high pitch at the top of my lungs and noticed that the sound made my hearing friends wince.

*Aha.* I'd hit a sensitive nerve. I wanted to see how far I could push it. I screamed louder, and louder, and their winces got more and more exaggerated. The sounds of my own screams barely bothered me and Nico, and yet they were making our hearing friends press their palms to their ears and screw their eyelids tightly closed. I felt like I had a superpower to be able to do something that affected my hearing friends so much while Nico and I were impervious to it. I'd found the hearing kids' kryptonite. Caught up in the excitement of this discovery, I pushed a little further.

I went up to one girl in the group of hearing kids, a girl. Leaning in close to her ear, I cupped my mouth, gulped down a lungful of air (or, as my kid brain thought of it, scream fuel) and let loose a blood-curdling shriek. It was so screechingly high-pitched and teeth-rattlingly loud it probably made the windowpanes of my friend's house shake. From inches away, I'd pointed my maximum-decibel flamethrower gun of a voice box straight into this hearing girl's ear canal and pulled the trigger.

The girl snapped her head away from me and clutched her ears.

I let out a loud belly laugh. *I got her good,* I thought. With what hearing I had left, I knew the odd sensation the girl was probably feeling in her ear, a weird fluttering and tickling of the eardrum. It'd take a few moments for the strange sensation to pass. And then I expected her to pop back up and chase me down for a playful punch on the shoulder, payback for the prank I'd pulled on her.

But she didn't get up. Moments passed, and she kept still on the ground, her knees pulled up to her chest in a fetal-like pose. The deep frown on her face showed something more than just minor discomfort, something more like genuine pain. Her hand hovered over her ear, as if it would be too painful to even touch.

Another hearing friend, one of the boys from my public school classes that lived in the same neighborhood, walked over and knelt at the girl's side. He looked up at me, his head shaking.

"*Not cool,*" I read on his lips.

Guilt washed over me. I had only intended to pull a prank, not inflict actual pain. I thought the high-pitched screams were merely annoying, a nuisance to the hearing folks. The louder the screams, the more sick of it they'd get. But I didn't think my screams would actually cause punctured-eardrum-level pain.

I knelt down to the girl, to try to apologize. She only glanced at me and briefly nodded, too consumed with the pain in her ear to talk with me.

A hearing friend pointed at his ear and mouthed: *"Her ear is ringing."*

I got up and tried to get in a few runs on the ramp, but my heart wasn't in it. I kept looking over to where the girl was still sitting in the grass, holding her head to one side. Eventually I gave up skateboarding for the afternoon—there was no fun playing while guilt weighed me down. I walked over to the girl and apologized again. It took twenty minutes after I unleashed my banshee scream for her to feel better enough to get back to her feet.

I was relieved that she seemed to be recovering. But I still felt terrible overall.

*Man*, I thought. Deaf people and hearing people were still alike in most ways, as far as I could judge. But that year, spending all that time at the public school, immersing myself in the strange other world of hearing kids, I had learned so much about how different Deaf and hearing people could be. And every day I was still discovering new things, like how loud noises could actually inflict intense physical pain on hearing people.

I also learned I needed to adapt to settings based on whether they involved Deaf or hearing people. It was more like I *sensed* having to do this, because I didn't consciously change how I acted in the hearing school setting compared to how I acted in a Deaf school setting. I just did it without thinking. In Deaf schools, I was the wild, mischievous, smart kid in class, always goofing off while whizzing through math problems. At hearing schools, each interaction was so laborious that most of the time I defaulted to a quieter version of myself. I still found ways to bring out the real Nyle, such as in PE classes and at recess, where physical activities and sports flattened the communication playing field, and after school while playing with my friends. But I never felt fully myself in the other world.

The year at the mainstream school was exhausting. I had zero clue what I was getting myself into from the very first day, and then I had to grind it out the entire year because my mom, rightfully, wouldn't let me quit. It was also exhilarating, because I'd gotten to explore a strange new world, one where nobody really knew me. I made new friends. I learned what it was like to have all conversation funneled into a single voice, the interpreter's, and how to force myself to stay mentally focused. It would be an important skill that I tapped into again and again the rest of my life.

By year's end, I had had enough. When Mom asked if I'd like to go back to the mainstream school the next school year, I said no. It was time for me to become fully immersed again in that familiar and comfortable Deaf school world, which felt like home.

It's a good thing I made that decision, because I would soon have much bigger problems to worry about. I didn't know it then, but a massive storm was on the horizon, waiting to engulf our family.

# 7.

# Storms

S ome ASL signs are lines straight outta poems.

Take "memory," for example. Form a v with the index and middle fingers, place it to the side of the face, and touch the middle finger to the cheek just below the eye. And then you move the hand past your head, leading with the tips of the two fingers making the v.

The fingertips are eyes, looking at the space you left behind, peering into your past.

"Trauma" is another one. Make a hook with the index finger—the x handshape—and bring it across the forehead.

The fingertip, dragging on the skin, leaves behind a scar.

COTTONY SNOW SWIRLED AND FELL onto a thick white blanket on the central Pennsylvania highway blacktop. A school bus rolled by, leaving behind parallel black lines in the whiteout. Inside, the driver leaned forward and squinted to see through the thick flurry.

The back of the bus was filled with noise: visual (hands waving above seats and flying across the aisle) and audible (shouts, claps, laughter, fists pounding on seats, and boots stomping on the floor).

The driver probably wished he had brought along earplugs. These Deaf kids in the back were making a racket.

The bus carried the high school basketball and cheerleading teams from the Scranton School for Deaf and Hard of Hearing Children and Lexington School for the Deaf on their way to the Western Pennsylvania School for the Deaf for a basketball tournament. In the front row sat Neal, a skinny snot-nosed thirteen-year-old, the youngest and scrappiest player on the Scranton team. Near the back sat my mom, Donna, a seventh grader on the Lexington cheerleading squad.

Snow kept piling up on the highway. The bus tires lost their grip on the blacktop and started skidding. The driver eased his foot off the gas, but he was too late. The tires slipped on a patch of hidden ice, and the bus careened off the road.

Dad banged his head in a bad way in the crash. Mom was unharmed. She first locked eyes with Dad in the hospital lobby, a giant white gauze pad wrapped around his head. My mom felt sorry for the poor, skinny boy.

A few years later, Mom's and Dad's paths crossed again at another Deaf school basketball tournament hosted at Lexington. The basketball tournament was hosted every winter, but since the bus crash, which had seriously injured two other students in addition to my dad, Scranton School had declined all out-of-town sporting events. It was too bad for the Scranton students, because these tournaments were the highlight of the school year, a rare chance to gather with other students from different states, communicate in ASL, make new friends, and compete against one's peers. Eventually the Scranton School overcame its hesitation and decided to resume participation in the tournaments, much to Dad's excitement.

A friend tapped Mom on the shoulder and pointed at Dad.

REMEMBER HIM?

Mom looked at Dad, a tall, broad-shouldered teenager with glittering blue eyes and dark hair. He was familiar, but Mom couldn't place him. She shook her head.

Dad brushed his hair aside, showing her the scar on the side of his head.

YES, Mom said, memories coming back to her, of the blizzard, the crash, and Dad in the hospital, short and skinny and fragile.

YOU LOOK DIFFERENT, Mom said. Dad smiled.

Dad looked older, much less scrawny. His arms were no longer skinny; they had muscle packed on 'em. He was taller than most people at the Lexington gym.

They talked for a little while, then said their goodbyes.

The tournament ended, and their paths again diverged. They finished high school, Mom graduating first and Dad a year later.

In college at the National Technical Institute for the Deaf in Rochester, New York, Mom and Dad bumped into each other in the cafeteria. This time, Dad didn't need to show his scar; Mom remembered him instantly. Dad cracked jokes and Mom giggled along. Then Dad asked if she would like to go out to dinner with him. He had a car, he said. Mom said yes.

They dated for six months, and then started going steady. The rest, as they say, was history.

FAST FORWARD A FEW MORE years, to a hospital room in Queens, New York. Dad held my older brother, a newborn, in his arms. He beamed with pride down on the child, to whom he had passed on his name. In this moment, he felt joy. His mind was a clear, sunny sky.

But somewhere on the horizon lurked a dark cloud.

*What if . . . my son is like me?* my dad thought to himself. He looked up; the doctor had come into the room.

The doctor told my parents: *"Your son has hearing loss."*

Dad looked down at his son and his heart shattered. He broke down and cried. Confused by this reaction, Mom asked Dad what was the matter.

"He will be like me," Dad signed. "He will experience constant struggle and frustration. He won't learn to read and write well. Opportunities will always be just out of his reach."

Dad never wanted his child to be Deaf like him.

TO UNDERSTAND WHY DAD GRIEVED at the news of his first son being Deaf, we have to go back to the 1960s in Athens, a slumbering borough in northern Pennsylvania. There, Dad was born the only Deaf child to hearing parents; his father was a career military man and his mother, a CODA.

Dad's grandparents on his mom's side were Deaf, but their Deaf genes skipped a generation. His mom had mild hearing loss but retained enough of her hearing that she functioned essentially as a hearing person. The Deaf genes had a far greater impact on Dad's hearing ability, leaving him with very little residual hearing.

They enrolled him at the Scranton School for Deaf and Hard of Hearing Children, a two-hour drive away from Athens. It was a boarding school, so he slept in the dorm during the week and shuttled back to Athens for the weekend.

Like Lexington and many other Deaf schools and education programs influenced by the Milan Conference, the Scranton School followed the oral education philosophy. The teachers and students interacted primarily using spoken language. The use of sign language was actively discouraged and often looked down on. Students caught using sign language were scolded and at times punished with a swift and painful rapping of a wooden ruler on the backs of hands.

In defiance, the students continued to sign—outside of class and out of teachers' sights. They signed with Dad, and he learned quickly. Signing came naturally to him.

Speaking and listening weren't effective communication methods for Dad. He struggled to make out words with what little hearing he had and had difficulty articulating words. When he began school, his language fluency was already delayed because of the limited language exposure he'd had at home. As he grew up and struggled through his oral education classes, he fell further and further behind.

Despite the fact that his Deaf grandparents primarily communicated in ASL, Dad's parents did not teach him sign language at home. Instead, they wanted him to learn to communicate in spoken

English. His mom, the only other person in the family and the entire town who had any level of fluency in sign language, signed poorly. She mostly used the Rochester Method, a communication modality consisting solely of fingerspelling every letter of every word communicated. This method lacks the facial expressions, signs, and body movements of ASL; it's just fingerspelling at lightning speed. Dad's mom had learned the method from her own Deaf mother. His dad, a rigid and dispassionate military man, never learned ASL. Dad had two hearing brothers, and their signing skills maxed out at the ASL handshape alphabet; they communicated with Dad in a slo-mo version of the Rochester Method—spelling out each word, letter by letter, in painstaking fashion. Their inability to communicate was a main reason why Dad never developed a strong relationship with his dad or his brothers.

Kids need a language-rich environment for their brains to acquire the rhythm and pattern of language. My dad never had that. He grew up bored and lonely, restless for people to talk with and aching for the ease of accessible conversation. It wasn't until early in high school that my dad and the other students were allowed to sign freely at school; even then, classes were still conducted strictly using the oral education approach.

Summer gatherings with extended family members became Dad's only outlet while growing up. He had a couple Deaf cousins on his Deaf grandparents' side of the family tree, who lived up in Rochester. At home, Dad's cousins used the Rochester Method to communicate with their Deaf parents, but at the school they attended, Rochester School for the Deaf, they learned ASL. They were smart, too—because of the strong language foundation they'd developed with sign language, they picked up English, math, history, and other school subjects easily.

Dad desperately looked forward to these family gatherings. He enjoyed hanging out with his Deaf cousins and learning new signs from them. These get-togethers were among the few times each year he was able to communicate effortlessly.

Each summer, as Dad reunited with his Deaf cousins, he saw marked improvements in their intellectual capacity. They used many new words, both in ASL and English. Their signing became quicker and quicker. They talked about stuff that he hadn't the slightest clue about. Each summer when they reunited, Dad could see that his cousins had grown and matured, as he fell further behind.

Dad grew frustrated. He became angry at his mother, who knew some signs but never made an effort to communicate with him in ASL; at his father, for never even making the effort; and at the Scranton school, for cramming ineffective oral education into his useless ears. Seeing how his cousins flourished using ASL only made it worse. He knew that things could have been better for him. He just never received the opportunities and access to language that his cousins did. His self-esteem sank lower and lower as he grew up.

Language deprivation had not only slowed the growth of his mental capacities, it stunted his social and emotional development, too. Since he wasn't highly fluent in either ASL or English, he didn't have the words to share the frustration and anger he felt. So he kept these emotions bottled up inside him, and they brewed and brewed through the years. Over time, his pent-up feelings became a permanent raging storm of anger and hate and violence lodged deep inside him.

When he graduated high school, he bolted from Athens to the place he knew he would have access to sign language: Rochester, where his Deaf cousins lived. He enrolled at the National Technical Institute for the Deaf, where, as I mentioned, he and my mom met again. There he was introduced to many more Deaf people like his cousins—self-assured, knowledgeable, intelligent. He was thrilled to be surrounded by Deaf people and empowered with the ease of communicating directly with peers in sign language. But he also saw how far behind his classmates he was. He worked to make up ground, but he would never quite get there. It was a monumental challenge to undo the damage of an entire childhood of language deprivation, ineffective education, and deep social and emotional trauma.

My father carried this burden all the way to the hospital room where my older brother was born, and there it spilled out of him, tears pouring down his face as he looked at his Deaf son.

Luckily, Mom was there to push back the storm, if only for a little while. She took Dad's hand.

"Look at me," she said. "Our son has you and me. We will shower him with love. We'll teach him ASL and English and read him books. With ASL, our son will be able to talk with us about anything, at any time. We will tease, fight, disagree, and say 'I love you.' He will grow up to be smart and independent and successful. It will be different from when you were growing up. I promise."

At first, Dad had his doubts. Then he watched Mom with my older brother and saw how easily my brother absorbed the ASL and English languages from Mom, my grandparents, my uncles, and all the other Deaf family and friends surrounding him. Eventually Dad began to see and understand how rewarding life could be for a Deaf child. His boy was smart and would be independent and successful.

Dad put his fear and frustration aside and became a loving, funny, video-camera-toting dad. By the time Nico and I came along, Dad had fully bought in. When the stammering doctor confirmed that, indeed, their twin boys were Deaf, Dad roared with delight, fully ready to welcome two more Deaf children to his house of love and sign language.

Every once in a while, though, the anger and frustration Dad had internalized throughout his childhood needed an outlet. He resorted to drinking alcohol and doing drugs to ease the pain and feel better. The alcohol and drug habit turned into an addiction that he would battle for a long time.

When I was four years old, Mom sent Dad to a rehab center in Minnesota. He had to go that far away because the Minnesota center provided services directly to Deaf people in ASL. At the time, as far as we knew, it was the only rehab center to do so, and it drew many Deaf people from all over the country. But services supporting people rehabbing from addiction aren't one size fits all. If one rehab program didn't work for a hearing person, as long as they had the financial resources, there were other places to choose from to try again. If they wanted to find a rehab center close to home, they had that option. But if a Deaf person struggled in the Minnesota rehab program or it was too far away from home, they didn't have any other choice.

The Minnesota center worked well enough for Dad to kick his habit. He came back sober to our home in Queens and kept it up for a year and a half, until we moved to Austin.

We had clear, sunny skies for a while. Occasionally, there were brief violent and angry outbursts, like the time Dad smacked me upside the head and made me stand in my room for hours after the police dropped Nico and me off from our day of bike riding. These outbursts were like short thunderstorms that raged in the night but quickly passed when the sun came up again. Aside from those times, we were generally happy.

The beautiful weather didn't last very long.

THE STORM TO END ALL storms started with unexpected news.

One day Dad came home from work and told Mom that he had quit his job at the post office. Mom was floored. Dad always complained about his job and had often talked about quitting, but Mom let him talk. She knew he needed to let off some steam and thought that his talk was just that—all talk. She couldn't fathom him actually quitting his job. His income and benefits supported the family.

And now all of a sudden, Dad had just up and left his job, without even talking with Mom beforehand. After her initial shock subsided, Mom was furious. She rained down questions on Dad. What about health insurance, for them and us boys? How could we afford the house we lived in now? What was his plan? Did he even have a plan?

Dad had no answers.

QUITTING HIS JOB WAS FIRST. Next came the extended disappearances.

Dad started spending a ton of time with his friends. There were some bad eggs in that crowd, and Mom didn't like it when he hung out so much with them. But now that he was unemployed, he had all this free time on his hands, and he decided to give it to his seedy friends. At first he'd be out for a night here, an afternoon there. Usually he'd go off to a bar with his friends and come home out of sorts. I could tell something was off with him. He was chronically exhausted and had an even shorter temper than usual, and his communication was disjointed.

The length of his disappearances gradually got longer. Soon, he started going AWOL for a few days at a time, without warning.

Mom and Dad started fighting. Mom asked him what he was doing when he disappeared like that. He shrugged off her questions and told her to leave him alone. But Mom knew the answer.

ALONG WITH THE DISAPPEARANCES CAME sudden bursts of irrational, violent behavior. Minor transgressions committed by me and my brothers were met with savage physical punishments. Open-palm swings, belt whippings. He lorded his physical presence over us. I was afraid—of course I was; he was a giant compared to me. But I didn't back down, so he found other ways to get to me.

One time, we were in the kitchen, and Dad was pissed off at me.

WHY YOU DO THAT?! he yelled at me. I don't remember what I had done. At that point, it felt like he was making up reasons to get angry. But I do remember exactly what I felt at that moment: paralyzed.

It wasn't that I didn't know what to say, or that I was too scared to say anything. I knew nothing I could say would make it better. It wasn't like my brain was consciously aware of this fact. It was more an instinctual reaction from my body. I just knew, deep in my bones, that once Dad was mad, he was going to be mad no matter what I said or did. I couldn't go looking for Mom either, because she was in Seattle again for a training for her Deaf domestic violence advocacy organization. I stood there, stared at Dad straight in the eyes, and said nothing.

TELL-ME! he screamed, leaning in, his nose inches from mine. TALK! TALK!

I stared back into his angry eyes. I wouldn't talk; there was nothing I could say to make this situation better. There was no way out. My hands remained at my sides, limp, handcuffed to silence.

Dad's eyes shifted to my right, where Nico was standing next to me. Nico hadn't done anything wrong; I knew that for sure. He just happened to be there.

OKAY, FINE. LOOK, Dad said, inviting me to watch him as he wrapped both his large hands around Nico's neck and tightened his grip. Terrified, Nico started screaming and crying and flailing his arms, but Dad was too big, too strong. Dad looked into my eyes, his expression beckoning me to talk, or else.

I had been defying Dad's orders by refusing to answer his questions. He knew I couldn't let Nico get hurt like that.

NO, NO, NO, I started walking toward Dad.

TALK! TELL-ME WHY! Dad signed, returning his hands to Nico's neck as soon as he'd finished talking.

OKAY, OKAY! JUST STOP!

At last, Dad loosened his fingers from Nico's neck.

I ran to Nico, tore him from Dad's grip, and we got out of the kitchen, and as far away from him as we could.

THEN CAME THE HIT TO the family piggy bank.

One day, Mom checked her and Dad's joint investment retirement account—which held their entire life savings—and found it had a balance of exactly zero dollars.

Mom confronted Dad. Where was the money? What had he done with it? she asked him. Put it back! she ordered him. He just shook his head. Mom knew she would never see that money again.

Though Dad never told her what had happened to the money, Mom heard stories. During one of Dad's multiple-day disappearances, he'd gone on a massive bender. Drug use was already an expensive addiction. Had he decided to tell all his friends that everything was "on him"?

His friends were exploiting him. They knew his weak spots: his insecurity and intense desire to be liked. They took advantage and preyed on him.

Just like that, he'd burned through his and Mom's future financial security, every penny of tens of thousands of hard-earned dollars.

FINALLY, THERE WERE THE EPISODES of catatonia.

COME-ON, HUG YOUR FATHER UPSTAIRS, Mom ordered us. It was early morning and we were ready to head out the door for school. I groaned. Why couldn't Dad come down to say goodbye? Why did we have to go upstairs?

But then I saw the deep concern and sadness in Mom's eyes, and I knew something might be wrong. We followed her up to our parents' bedroom.

Dad was lying flat on the floor, his arms and legs limp and his head lolling a bit to the side. His body sagged; it looked like it was going to sink into the floor. His eyes, ringed with dark circles, were open but there was no life in them. They stared, unfocused, at the opposite wall.

Mom nudged us closer. We walked up to him and pressed ourselves into him. His body gave no response as I wrapped my arms around him. His arms didn't move to close me into a hug as they typically did. He was so lifeless, he might as well have been a sack of raw meat, just lying there. I detached myself from him and walked out to catch the bus to school.

On the way to school, the image of Dad lying flat on the floor, immobile, almost comatose, haunted my thoughts. Dad looked so out of it, I wondered if he would still be alive when I returned later that day.

When I came back home that afternoon, he was.

DAD BEAT ME, OPEN HANDED, all over my body. My head, shoulders, arms, torso, thighs: I caught his swings everywhere. I writhed out of his grasp and sprinted downstairs to my mom.

DAD HIT ME, I said. She frowned sharply, not quite believing me at first. All the times Dad had been physical or doled out excessive punishments, Mom had been out of town. None of us boys had complained about how Dad treated us. I think we weren't sure if it was normal and okay for a dad to act that way. But that day I had had enough.

WHERE HE HIT YOU? Mom asked.

I pointed to my neck, chest, back, legs. ALL OVER.

Something changed in Mom's eyes. She knew I wouldn't lie, not about something like this. And I had confirmation, from the look on my mom's face, that a dad hitting his kids was *not* okay.

YOU NEED-TO DIVORCE DAD, I told Mom.

I was all of ten years old, and I'm not sure why I felt compelled to say this. Maybe I thought Mom felt like she needed to stay with Dad for her boys' sake, to keep our family whole. Maybe it was my way of telling her that I was done with him, that things had gotten so bad that we'd reached the point where we'd be better off without him. Maybe I was also telling Mom that we were going to be all right. We'd stick together, Mom and me and my brothers, and Mom's mom and dad and her brothers.

Out of my two brothers and me, I think I had to be the one to tell Mom that message. Neal and Nico had different relationships with my dad. Neal and Dad bonded over their love of sports; Neal was the most dedicated athlete of us three boys. He played football, basketball, baseball; was good at all three; and was committed to getting better. Being older, he might have been more ready to appreciate the bond between a dad and son.

Nico and I were different from our older brother. We were natural athletes but traditional sports rarely held our interest for very long. Instead we rode around on our bikes all the time and later picked up skateboarding. We loved Pokémon and video games. Dad couldn't relate with us over those interests.

And Nico, being the good, kindhearted soul he is, had a greater capacity for forgiveness. He was willing to put up with more of Dad's storms and still love him despite all the pain he'd caused us. Because, well, he was Dad.

I was different.

I had a rebellious streak, and I caught most of the brunt of Dad's storms. I found it tough to bond with him, so I wasn't as attached to him as my brothers were.

I was detached enough to ask Mom to put an end to it. Before it got any worse.

IN THE END MOM NOT only decided to divorce Dad; she decided to move her family to a new place for a fresh start and a new Deaf school for her kids. Of course, my grandparents came along. The choice was Maryland School for the Deaf, in Frederick, Maryland, an hour's drive north of Washington, D.C.

So we uprooted our lives once again in earnest pursuit of a better, brighter future. Austin and the Texas School for the Deaf had been good to our family, but Maryland School for the Deaf was another excellent Deaf school, one of the best in the entire country. It was an exciting new challenge for my brothers and me.

After the divorce, Dad moved to Pennsylvania, and we didn't see much of him. Mom got a job at Maryland School for the Deaf working with kids in the after-school program, and with my grandparents pitching in, she was able to support our family, independent of Dad.

We were finally free from the storm. I moved on quickly. Worried about her boys after the divorce, Mom set up counseling for us. I went a few times at her request, but I stopped after the third session; I didn't feel like I needed to continue. I didn't feel any anger toward him. I didn't miss him or cry for him, either. I was indifferent. Life was going well without him. I felt a sense of peace. I didn't see the point in trying to dig up the past, so I didn't spare too many thoughts about him.

As I grew older, I came to better understand why Dad was the way he was when I started having more conversations with Deaf adults. As a kid, all I did was play with other kids; talking with adults was boring. With that natural distance, I grew up assuming that all adults attained a certain level of intelligence. When I entered into actual conversations with them more often over the years, I found that that was not always the case. Some Deaf adults that I talked with severely lacked basic language skills and knowledge.

WHY? I asked Mom.

GROW-UP, LIMITED ACCESS-TO LANGUAGE AND EDU-CATION, Mom said. SAME YOUR DAD. She told me about Dad's childhood—about Athens, his parents not using ASL, the oral education at the Scranton School. She told me about the damage his upbringing caused him—mentally, socially, emotionally.

The circumstances of his childhood didn't absolve Dad of everything he had done. But he was the way he was, in large part, because of the language deprivation and limited education he'd endured as a child. By the time he'd become an adult, I don't think he had matured enough mentally and emotionally to fully recognize that his behavior was wrong, let alone develop the ability for introspection—to be able to look at himself and realize that he wasn't processing his emotions the right way and was instead wrongly taking his frustrations out on his boys. His stunted socio-emotional development was probably why I found it so hard to try to reason with him growing up. He didn't have enough self-confidence and capacity for rational thought to be able to sit down and have discussions about what he thought I had done wrong and hear my side of the story. It was why he had such a *you're wrong, I'm right, period* mentality, and why I had clashed with him so often.

The world, and my dad's parents, had failed him. Coming from Athens, such a small town, where the nearest Deaf person was hours away, he had the odds stacked against him. Instead of counterbalancing the poor hand Dad had been dealt by providing him with accessible language, my dad's parents had tilted the scales *against* him.

All this time, the storms weren't just inside my dad. They had been raging all around him, damaging him to his core, until the space inside him *was* a storm, too, reflecting the world he lived in.

By the time I figured all this out, the divorce was far behind us. I did see my dad once in a while; he even came to live in Maryland for a short time. But we didn't reconnect in a meaningful way—we still haven't, to this day.

But I do forgive him, for everything. The storms weren't all on him. If he'd had access to language and education while growing up, who knows?

As a Deaf person, I don't have time to be upset at my own people. We can't stop and point at each other. We have to be vigilant; we have to continue to look outward and battle the storm, created and imposed on us by larger society, that continues to rage all around us.

FROM BIRTH UNTIL THE TIME we set foot on the Gallaudet University campus, my brothers and I carried our dad's family name. It felt empty, lacking the weight of a name that had true significance to me. The relationship between Dad and my brothers and me had faded since the divorce ten years prior.

My brothers and I were raised by our mom, grandparents, and aunts and uncles of the DiMarco family. That was the name we wanted to carry with us.

My brothers and I gathered the paperwork, filled it out, and mailed it in. Sometime later a letter came in the mail, addressed, for the first time in my life, to Nyle DiMarco.

The name felt just right, as if I'd carried it with me my entire life.

# 8.

# The Kitchen Light

'm lucky. I was born into a world in which ASL and other sign languages are generally recognized for what they are: languages. It wasn't always so.

Once, signs were exclusively viewed as rudimentary systems of gesture—pantomime. Outsiders assumed there was no complexity to the signs used by Deaf people; that sign language was nowhere near as sophisticated as languages communicated by sound and couldn't be used to express abstract concepts. Some said ASL was a bastardized, simplified version of English. Few were willing to lend sign languages a single shred of legitimacy. Then Dr. William C. Stokoe changed everything.

I learned the story of Dr. Stokoe, a hearing English professor at Gallaudet University, and his two Deaf assistants, Carl Croneberg and Dorothy Casterline, while in high school at Maryland School for the Deaf. Ironically, Dr. Stokoe was actually not very fluent in ASL. But as he watched his Deaf students sign, he spotted patterns and a structure. Somewhere in what initially looked like a beautiful chaos of hands, faces, and bodies was a set of rules that held it all together.

In the late 1950s, Dr. Stokoe and his two assistants set out to understand these rules. They filmed Deaf people signing, analyzed the

*film, and identified the linguistic elements they were searching for.
There was a syntax—a specific, acceptable order for signs to be used in
sentences. There were rules for how signs could be formed—the handshape, location in relation to the body, and palm orientation. They
discovered how facial expressions—movements of the eyebrows and
mouth—altered the meaning of signs and sentences.*

*The evidence was unmistakable. The signs that Deaf people used
were not simply gestures or pantomime. They followed a complex
system governed by rules, just like English or any other language in
the world. Dr. Stokoe, Carl Croneberg, and Dorothy Casterline published their findings in the 1960s. They named the sign language of the
United States Deaf community American Sign Language.*

*Their findings set off a seismic paradigm shift in the Deaf com-
munity. For the first time, our language had legitimacy. A sense of joy
and pride in this language, our language, blossomed in our community. Possibilities opened up. Deaf people started to think in terms of
literature and poetry and linguistic research in relation to ASL. Oral
education was dealt a powerful blow, and educators started to imagine bilingual classrooms in which ASL and English were used equally
as languages of instruction.*

*This last detail is important—if not for the research of Dr. Stokoe
and his assistants, I might never have tasted an ASL-led classroom.*

THE CULTURE AT MARYLAND SCHOOL for the Deaf was unlike anything
my brothers and I had ever experienced. High expectations were the
norm in and out of class; no student was coddled or pitied because
they were Deaf. Teachers moved classes through lessons rapidly and
doled out a constant stream of challenging assignments. Our classmates were whip-smart and carried themselves with an easy, almost
arrogant, confidence. In quiet amazement, I watched our peers as
they exceeded our teachers' expectations, chiming into lively classroom discussions with intelligent arguments and insights and breez-
ing through worksheets before class ended. With a competitive spirit,
our peers built up their knowledge from one another.

At first, this new educational environment felt like a dog-eat-dog world. Unused to the brisk educational pace and substantial workload and intimidated by my overachieving classmates, I fell behind. But I adapted soon enough to my new surroundings and found enjoyment in the school's rapid educational pace. I appreciated the high bar my classmates set for me—it made learning more fun, and in a way, made me feel more alive.

The athletics program at the school was one of the best, if not the best, among Deaf schools across the country. The school regularly won the national Deaf championship in different sports—volleyball, football, basketball, and so on. We whupped hearing teams, too. Over my four years as a high school student at the school, the football team won forty-two games and lost only one, and the majority of the teams it played against were hearing high schools.

Many students, like me and my brothers, came from ASL-fluent Deaf families. They benefited from the same language access and cultural pride that my brothers and I did while growing up. And at this school, the Deaf parents took a special, almost competitive, pride in their children's academic and athletic accomplishments.

Pushed by our intelligent and creative Deaf peers and the competitive and challenging environment, my brothers and I grew and flourished in different ways.

Neal, the jock of the family, was a star three-sport athlete through all four years of high school. While we were growing up, he had been two grades ahead of me and Nico. He had been the youngest in his class, and had he stayed there, he would have graduated high school and enrolled in college at seventeen. In high school, however, he repeated a year, so he ended up being only one year ahead of Nico and me. This do-over helped his high school athletic career, allowing him to play his last year of high school sports at the more physically mature age of eighteen.

Nico and I played football and basketball for just a couple years, but we played volleyball, our favorite sport, for all four years. I was the setter, the quarterback of the team. We consistently overwhelmed our hearing opponents en route to four consecutive league championships.

Over our high school years, Nico and I grew our hair long, started carrying our skateboards with us everywhere, and hung out with a motley crew of cool outcasts. Nico also discovered a passion for music, and he purchased a stereo system and set it up smack dab in the middle of the living room. The walls of our home constantly pulsed with the booming beat from the subwoofers, and nobody in our family was bothered by it—though our next-door neighbors didn't like it very much, going as far as to call the police when it was too noisy late at night.

Despite being in a new school and making new friends, I never lost sight of who I really am—the mischievous rebel that Mom dubbed her little devil.

The first day of my freshman year, the principal recited the rules in the school handbook to the student body. One of the rules, the principal said, was that students couldn't sport a mohawk. I was incredulous. Mohawks were commonplace in both cities I'd lived in before moving to Frederick, Maryland. Austin didn't have the motto Keep Austin Weird for nothing, and I'd seen many high school students at Texas School for the Deaf sport mohawks. It was only a hairstyle, merely a form of individual expression that never hurt anybody. The rule was stupid—and I considered it just a way for the school and its administrators to exercise power and control over us students.

That night I grabbed the hair clipper from the bathroom and buzzed off the sides of my hair. I hadn't started to grow my hair long yet, so the mohawk was barely an inch tall. The high school punks at Texas School for the Deaf would have laughed my ass out of the school's front doors if I'd shown up with my itty-bitty 'hawk. I wondered if it would even make a blip on the Maryland school administrators' radar.

I didn't wonder long, because the next morning in the very first period the principal walked into my classroom and waved for me to go with her. In her office she told me I was in violation of the school's rules and that I was going to receive two days of in-school suspension.

FOR MY MOHAWK? I asked her, feigning ignorance of the school's rule. ME JUST TRY EXPRESS MYSELF, THAT'S-ALL.

She didn't buy it, and I had to sit at a desk in a small room for two days to serve out my suspension. I relented and shaved off my baby mohawk—but I wasn't done challenging the school's boundaries.

From November through March, the school prohibited students from wearing shorts; they insisted that boys wear pants through the winter months. I bristled at this rule; I disliked wearing pants and wanted to wear shorts on days when I thought it was warm enough. To make matters worse, during these same months, the school allowed girls to wear skirts. It baffled me. Why did the school allow girls to wear clothing that left their legs exposed but not boys?

I complained to a friend about the gendered injustice of the rule, and he asked a very good question: Who decided that only girls were allowed to wear skirts?

On an unusually warm mid-November day, my friend and I strutted into school with skirts on, proud as peacocks. Before the first period even began, the principal pulled us out of class and informed us that we were going to be suspended from school for a week for breaking the school's policy.

WHY? THESE-ARE KILTS, I protested. KILTS, MEN WEAR OFTEN OVER-THERE SCOTLAND!

The principal took one look at the skirt I wore, a tacky blue denim skirt I'd borrowed from a female friend.

THAT NOT LOOK-LIKE KILT TO ME, she said, and sent me home.

Immature and naive as I was back then, wearing a skirt was a joke to me, a funny way to challenge the school's authority and society's norms. But nowadays I wonder about the damage gender norms inflict on folks that don't fit neatly into a neat gender box. I'm glad that I broke the rule and pushed back against the archaic and stupid gender norm the school applied to it, and am even prouder of the one-week suspension I served.

DURING OUR TEEN YEARS, A favorite pastime of my brothers and me was hosting parties. The basement of our house was the perfect space. Down there was my grandparents' bedroom, a kitchen, a living room, and a bathroom. My grandparents often went out of town for long periods, staying with my uncle Charles and his family in Staten Island, New York. My grandparents would leave the door to the basement locked, but we found that we could pick the lock and open the door by inserting an ID card into the gap between the door and the frame and undoing the latch. After we slipped into the basement, we'd close the door behind us, still locked. If my mom happened to walk by, all she would see was the closed and locked basement door.

As for the alcohol supply, Neal worked his network, which extended all the way to Gallaudet University. A black-haired former Gallaudet student had an Arizona driver's license that didn't expire for fifty years. That ID had passed through the hands of many underage dark-haired Deaf guys on the Gallaudet campus before Neal's turn with it. The ID allowed Neal to buy all the booze we wanted at the corner liquor store and walk out the front door without raising suspicion.

The parties rocked and rolled, and Mom never suspected a thing. But when our grandparents were in town and we couldn't use the basement, we had a problem. We wanted to host a party on the main floor of the house, but we needed to figure out what to do with Mom. We knew she'd laugh in our faces if we asked, so we had to find a way to do it without her finding out.

Our biggest worry wasn't the noise, of course. If anything was going to give us away, it was the light. Specifically, the kitchen light, which shined down the hallway and crept beneath the gap under Mom's bedroom door. If we were partying it up in the kitchen late at night the light filtering into her bedroom from the kitchen would undoubtedly wake her up, and she'd come out and bust us.

We came up with an inelegant but effective solution: roll up a towel and stuff it into the gap under Mom's door to block the light.

At one party sometime during Nico's and my freshman year, we tested out our solution. After Mom went to bed, our friends came over, hauling bottles of Bacardi rum and Smirnoff fruit-flavored vodka, and we knocked back shots all night long. The next day, Mom said nothing. It worked! We hosted party after party, and Mom slept soundly through them, never suspecting a thing.

THE FALL OF MY SOPHOMORE year, the school put on a play, *Little Shop of Horrors*. It was delivered entirely in ASL—even the songs, which was probably my favorite part of the play. When it came time to break into song, usually when the story reached a moment of suspense, a chorus group of three girls would slip onstage. Their bodies moved in time with the beat, and their hands whipped out the song's words in a chanting rhythm, punctuated by devious sneers and sinister side-eyes.

LITTLE SHOP,

LITTLE SHOP,

LITTLE SHOP OF-HORRORS!

The naughty way the chorus girls signed the songs looked sexy as hell, and the sexiest girl was the one in the middle, Hannah. Every time the chorus girls popped onstage, I fixed my eyes on her. *Damn, she's hot*, I thought.

Hannah was one of the most popular girls in school. She had long locks of wavy brown hair, a beautiful smile, and an easy, sparkling laugh that made my heart skip a beat. Besides stealing the stage in the school play, she led the school's cheerleading squad and looked gorgeous in her uniform. She had a picture-perfect image at the school, but I knew she had a naughty side, because I saw her often at our parties. Like me, she loved animals, especially dogs. That's how we bonded at parties. If there was a pup around, we would find each other by its side, rubbing its ears with one hand and sipping a beer with the other.

Our romance started during a party in the basement of my house, on my grandpa's favorite armchair. I didn't drink much that night; I'd gone out to the garage with some friends for a few hits of weed off a pipe we passed around. Back in the basement, I noticed that Hannah was pretty blitzed, giggling and drunkenly slurring signs as she talked with her friends. When she saw me sitting on my grandpa's armchair, she hopped onto me, her legs straddling over my hip. She started nibbling my neck, then my cheek, then her lips closed in on mine. I wanted to kiss her, but I gently pushed her away.

WHAT'S-WRONG? she asked.

YOU-ARE DRUNK. WAIT UNTIL YOU SOBER.

ME FINE, ME FINE, she said, leaning in again.

NO, STOP, I insisted.

FINE, she said, as she climbed off and went back to her friends. I groaned. I did want to kiss her, but I knew telling her no was the right thing to do.

The next day her screen name popped up on my AOL Instant Messenger.

Your loss, she wrote.

I didn't want to take advantage of you, I responded. I told her I wanted to wait until she was sober.

My pubescent chivalry won a few points with Hannah; she began to see me as a respectful young gentleman, someone who might want something more serious with her. We started exchanging furtive flirty glances in the school hallways and slipping clandestine notes in each other's lockers. Once we started openly flirting, it was game over. We became inseparable.

We had one class together at the time, math. For the first time in my life, I had something more interesting than my favorite academic subject to occupy my time and attention during class. Every day I would walk into the classroom scanning for Hannah and grab the seat next to her. Through entire class periods, I barely paid attention to the teacher, instead flirting with Hannah, keeping my hands low and moving slowly, in a sign-language whisper. The teacher would catch us anyway; it isn't tough to notice when Deaf students aren't paying attention—our heads were turned and our eyes were drawn elsewhere instead of the front of the class. Knock it off and pay attention, the teacher would scold us. We'd listen to him for only so long before we started flirting again. I especially liked to draw little heart shapes on Hannah's worksheets, making her smile at the corner of her mouth as she tried to focus.

One day, the teacher had had it with our flirting and decided it was time to separate us.

MOVE OVER-THERE, he told me.

Recall that desks in Deaf classrooms are arranged in a semicircle instead of rows to give us lines of sight to the teacher and our classmates. That day Hannah and I were sitting on one end of the semicircle, or one tip of the C shape. The teacher ordered me to move to the other tip of the C, which meant I sat directly across from Hannah. Our lines of sight toward each other were essentially a few degrees off from our lines of sight to the teacher. We didn't even have to turn our heads to see each other; all I needed to do was flick my eyes from the teacher to her. The teacher, however, was standing at the gap between the tips of the C, and which put Hannah and I far on the edges of his peripheral vision. It was easy for Hannah and me to see each other *and* difficult for the teacher to see us.

I brought my hands up to the surface of my desk and gave Hannah a small wave. It caught her eye; when she looked at me, we smiled mischievously.

WOW TEACHER ZERO-IDEA WE STILL TALK-TALK.

She giggled. SEE-SEE HOW LONG BEFORE HE CATCHES US.

I nodded. We kept our whispered conversation going, dropping our hands and flicking our eyes back to the teacher whenever he looked our way. We talked for nearly the entire period, until the teacher finally spotted my moving hands. He blew the roof.

The next week, Hannah wasn't in the classroom when I walked in. She'd been moved to another class. We'd flirted so much that the school could no longer allow us to be in the same class.

We still had time together in the hallways, at the cafeteria, and after school to flirt and talk. I felt like I could talk with Hannah about anything, all day long, every day. She was smart and headstrong, and challenged me to think twice about how I viewed things. She was a pescatarian and called me out for eating meat, saying I was harming the animals I said I loved. I didn't give up meat in high school, but she made me think hard about it.

Hannah matched my natural tendency toward mischief with an equal measure of daring and fearlessness. One night, way past our bedtime, I snuck over to her home. I didn't need to scale any fences or climb up a trellis to slip through a second-story window, like you see in the movies. While her Deaf parents snored peacefully in their upstairs bedroom, I strolled inside through the front door. Her yapping and yowling Mini Pinschers didn't even wake them up.

She took my hand and led me up to her bedroom. The walls were painted pink, and she had posters of Travis Barker by her bed. I sat down on the edge of her bed, and butterflies exploded in my tummy. I was nervous, not because I was fearful that her parents would wake up, but because I hadn't kissed Hannah yet. I'd been saving that first kiss for a special night. And in the early morning hours alone with Hannah on her bed, it felt like this was the night. She felt it too, and she let me know in subtle ways, leaning against me when she laughed, touching my hands and shoulders during lulls in our conversation. But I talked and talked, and kept on talking for *hours*. She didn't mind; she enjoyed my company. Slowly, I warmed up. When she leaned against me, I wrapped one arm around her shoulder. I took her hand into mine when she reached out. Eventually I closed in.

Her lips felt like big fluffy pillows in mine. I sank into them, my nerves melting away. When I drew back, she looked at me with that beautiful smile of hers.

PAH, she said, using an ASL word that means "at last."

Not so long after, Hannah returned the favor and snuck over to my home, also walking through the front door undetected by my dozing, Deaf-as-hell Mom. These secret midnight home visits became a regular thing, *our* thing. Sometimes we'd switch it up, and rendezvous at a park near our homes, one of us sidling into the other's car, where we'd enjoy each other's company under the starry night sky.

Neal and I took turns swiping Mom's car for midnight trips; it was easy since Mom left her keys on the kitchen countertop and couldn't hear the car as it pulled out of the driveway. Our late-night auto borrowing scheme required a high level of precision and attention to detail. We had to park the car back in the same exact spot on the driveway where Mom left it, and the interior had to be left undisturbed, every item in its same precise place as the moment we'd entered the car. We were careful to limit our trips to locations less than ten miles away, so the change to the gas tank wouldn't be perceptible and the increase on the odometer of Mom's car, which had more than a hundred thousand miles on it, would be negligible.

We'd kept up this scheme effectively for a while, but eventually Neal grew too careless. While he was out on a midnight cruise, a stack of files on the passenger seat had tipped over, and he neglected to put them back when he'd returned. A thing like that didn't slip past Mom. To prevent Neal (and, though Mom didn't know it, me) from taking the car in the middle of the night again, she started keeping the keys in the end table right next to her bed as she slept through the night.

COME-ON. IDIOT! YOU CLUMSY, NOT THINK CAREFUL, NOW BUSTED, I scolded Neal. NOT FAIR. ME NEED KEYS, MEET HANNAH TONIGHT.

JUST GRAB KEYS WHILE MOM SLEEP, Neal signed back.

When I hesitated, Neal asked, YOU SCARED? and laughed as he walked away.

That night, after the clock struck twelve, I opened Mom's bedroom door, tiptoed up to the end table, an antique, and grabbed the handle of the drawer. The handle grated roughly (and most definitely very audibly) in my hands as the bottom of the drawer scraped, sandpaper-like, against the warped brackets that supported it. I looked at Mom. She was dozing blissfully two feet away from me. I picked up the keys, shut the grating drawer, and walked out. Neal was right; I laughed at how easy it was. And when I came back at four A.M., I put the keys back in the drawer, my mom never the wiser.

After another late-night meetup I parked the car in the driveway, and as I entered the house, Mom was awake. She asked me what I'd been doing. I stammered that I couldn't sleep and decided to go out for a walk. She nodded and told me to try to go to sleep, as it was still too early in the morning. When she went into the living room I sprinted to her bedroom to slip the keys back in her drawer before I went back to my bed, my heart pounding.

HANNAH WAS A YEAR AHEAD of me, in the same class as Neal. When I entered my senior year of high school, she, along with Neal, was headed to Gallaudet University. We had a long talk that summer before the school year started and decided to call it off. It tore my heart apart, but I knew it was the right decision. Hannah needed to have the freedom to explore in college, and I needed to be able to live my own life as I finished my last year of high school. We cried a lot of tears during that talk, but we made the decision that was best for the both of us. We knew there was a chance our paths would cross again; if not, so be it.

Our senior year, Nico and I went all out. We hosted parties nearly every weekend. Sharing the same black hair as Neal, I inherited the fake ID from him and took on alcohol supply duties for the parties. I discovered that it was a sweet-paying gig—in exchange for my services, I got to keep whatever change was left. Kids would give me $20 for bottles that cost $17, and those few dollars added up when I was buying a dozen bottles or so for a party.

Midway through the school year, I achieved my magnum opus: a massive lunch period food fight. I got the idea from a friend who attended California School for the Deaf in Fremont. She'd described an epically fun food fight at her school to me over AOL Instant Messenger. The idea captivated the rebel in me, and I knew I had to have one incredible and glorious food fight before I finished high school.

The fight itself was over in a flash, a marvelous two-minute flurry of chicken nuggets, mashed potatoes, PB&Js, and deli meat slices.

But it had taken days of work and careful planning. I identified a few friends as designated food fight initiators, strategically placed them far and wide apart in the cafeteria; determined a start time and a subtle signal; and, when the time came, personally gave the signal and witnessed the flawless execution of the elaborate plan. As edible projectiles flew across the cafeteria, I basked in the beautiful chaos I had wrought upon the school. It was worth every minute of the one-week school suspension I received, though now revisiting the memory brings a twinge of regret as I think of the poor cafeteria staff. Belatedly, I thank them for cleaning up the terrible mess afterward.

THE FALL OF MY SENIOR year, the school had a new transfer, a good-looking guy from the West Coast who oozed surfer dude vibes. All the girls made googly eyes for him. I looked him over and thought to myself: *Mm-hmm, this guy is hot.*

Having such thoughts about a guy wasn't new to me; I had just always pushed them aside while growing up. But now, entering young adulthood and unattached to a girlfriend, I became more acutely aware of them. And once I allowed myself to consciously acknowledge these thoughts, they took a vise-like grip on me. No matter how much I resisted, I couldn't shake them off. So I let them linger in my head, giving them a space where they could hang safely, apart from *me*. After a while I got used to these thoughts and started wondering what would happen if I acted on them.

Once in my senior year, I came close to finding out. There was another guy in my class who was open about dating both boys and girls. During a party at my home, he asked me if I wanted to go out to the backyard and bong some beer. My gut told me that it wasn't just an invitation to drink beer; it was a hint to go someplace quiet and away from the crowd, to be alone. Curious what would happen if I gave in to those feelings in my head, I said yes, and we walked outside. When I handed him the beer bong, his hand brushed over mine and paused there. It was maybe a millisecond, but I could sense it—a wordless invitation. He took the bong and finished his beer, and I took my turn.

Then we locked eyes and I felt something rise up in my throat, something more than idle curiosity—a feeling of intensity, a longing. I searched his eyes and thought I saw that my feelings were reciprocated.

But then nothing happened. Neither of us made a move, and the moment passed. As I walked back into the house, I pushed my thoughts and feelings about guys safely back into their space apart from me, inside my head.

OUR LUCK DIDN'T LAST FOREVER. Nico and I should have known it wouldn't, that during one of the parties the clock would strike midnight on us. But we were young and riding a hot streak and thought we were invincible.

It happened deep in the early morning. Kids were taking shots of vodka and rum on the kitchen countertop, playing flip cup on a white folding table in the living room, bonging beer outside (somehow we never received a visit from the cops), and engaging in a spirited match of beer pong on the dining room table. The party was raging on at full blast.

As she probably had during many previous parties, Mom woke and went into the bathroom in her en suite. She was completely ignorant of the massive banger outside of her bedroom as she walked back to bed in the dark, the kitchen light securely blocked by the towel we always put under her door. But just as she got to her bed she stopped. Her mouth was a little dry, and she thought she could use a glass of water.

The kitchen light hit her as soon as she opened the door. She stared down the hall at the bunch of kids hooting, taking shots, roaring with laughter. She was dumbfounded. It was three A.M., and strange kids were in her house.

I was sitting in the living room when I saw a head of dark hair and a nightgown. My heart plummeted.

I looked over to Nico, at the beer pong table. I knew he'd seen her, too, because his eyes were saying what I was thinking. *It's over*. Our glorious run of parties was done.

Mom pointed at us. GET-OVER-HERE NOW!

WHAT-IS THIS? WHAT WERE-YOU THINKING? she yelled at us. The whole party, peaking at a banging volume a moment before, collapsed into a whimper. Noise is visual, too, and Nico and I saw hands dropping and eyes turning in our direction.

Nico and I immediately switched to damage control mode, saying we were sorry.

I DON'T CARE! HOW DARE YOU DO THIS TO ME?!

She turned to everybody and sign-roared at them to get out of her house.

WAIT WAIT WAIT, we signed, rushing to get back in front of her to get her attention.

DO-YOU WANT SEND EVERYONE DRIVE HOME UNDER INFLUENCE?

Mom simmered down a little at that. She shook us off and told everyone they could stay. But she was still pissed. ME SINGLE MOM, she scolded us. YOU DARE DO THIS TO-ME.

SORRY, we signed again, our hands and faces as meek as we felt.

Eventually the kids went home, and Nico and I were grounded, for a long time.

NICO'S AND MY HAIR FELL past our shoulders at graduation, flowing freely beneath our graduation caps as we swung our tassels from one side to the other. By the time we joined Neal at Gallaudet University the following fall, we'd chopped off our long locks, memorializing the end of an era and marking the start of a new one.

My freshman year at Gallaudet, I was free for my own year of exploration. Hannah, meanwhile, had a new boyfriend. As salty as I was, I knew it was my chance to maximize my first year of college, just as she'd done. I dated different girls and had my share of fun.

During my sophomore year, I got a text from Hannah. She had

rescued a twelve-week-old dog, a mixed breed she had named Foxy, and invited me over to her room to meet her. I fell in love with Foxy at first petting. She was adorable and had an intelligent look in her eyes. She was very visually perceptive, I would later learn; dogs generally follow visual commands well, and by age twenty weeks, Foxy knew multiple tricks commanded to her in ASL.

After introducing myself to Foxy, I saw that Hannah was on the videophone, chatting with her mom. She patted the seat next to her, and I sat down to chat with her and her mom. The moment felt comfortable and familiar; I was a junior in high school once again, hanging out at Hannah's house with her folks.

A few weeks after that, late on a weekend night, belly full of beer, I wandered over to Hannah's dorm room. When she opened the door I told her I wanted to see Foxy. And I did, but I wanted to see Hannah too.

Eventually the midnight visits to Foxy and Hannah turned into a regular occurrence—another thing we brought back from our high school days, only instead of swiping my mom's keys and driving to Hannah's house, I just had to take a short stroll toward her dorm room. We built up our feelings for each other again, and a romantic reunion felt inevitable.

In the meantime, I kept the thoughts and feelings I had about guys in their own special space in my head, securely hidden away.

# 9.

# Fighting Back

In 1990, President George W. Bush signed the Americans with Disabilities Act (ADA) into law.

It was a key milestone along a long, winding path (wheelchair-accessible, of course) that had been laid brick by brick, decade after decade, by disability community advocates like Helen Keller, Judith Heumann, U.S. Senator Tom Harkin, and thousands of others who courageously fought for the civil rights of those with disabilities.

Deaf people played a critical role in making the ADA a reality, too. The Deaf President Now (DPN) protest at Gallaudet University helped lay down a good number of bricks in the final stretch of the path toward the ADA. The DPN protest happened in March 1988; fifteen months later the ADA was signed into law.

What did the ADA do? Simple: It made discrimination based on disability illegal in many key areas, among them employment, transportation, public accommodations, communications, and access to state and local government programs, services, and resources.

Once, mall builders could laugh off requests for wheelchair ramps and employers could rip up a Deaf candidate's job application if they asked for an interpreter for an interview, without fear of consequence.

*The ADA gave people with disabilities the ability to bring down the hammer of the law on discriminators. The ADA turned access for the disabled from charity into a right endowed upon us as citizens of the United States of America. In a way it helped society change its perception of people with disabilities from subhumans to, well, regular humans.*

*But the ADA hasn't been perfect. Even with the law in place, people with disabilities still have to fight tooth and nail for accessibility. Businesses have sought legal loopholes and rejected requests for accommodations—and have gotten away with it if their action goes unchallenged. This was especially true in the early years of the law, and it's still true today.*

*The state of disability rights and equality in the United States continues to be unsatisfactory. The disability community keeps fighting for better access, treatment, and respect. Inch by inch, we continue our struggle.*

ONE EVENING THE SUMMER BEFORE Nico and I began our studies at Gallaudet, Mom sat us down for a talk after dinner.

Once upon a time, Mom had sat us down every evening after dinner, cracked open *Are You My Mother?*, and told us the story of the newborn bird who'd left its nest in search of its mother. That story, which she told beautifully in ASL and used to teach us English, had been one of her earliest lessons for her sons—one of the first bricks she'd laid in her boys' educational and linguistic foundations. And now, a dozen or so years later, Nico and I were about to depart her home—her nest—for college and beyond.

Before we flew the coop, Mom had one last lesson for us. It was a dark and somber lesson, but an important one. The world we were about to enter into was *tough*, especially on Deaf people like Nico and me. Growing up, we had learned that we were different from hearing people. We'd also gotten a taste of the cruelty of hearing people toward the Deaf when childhood bullies mocked our signing. As we ventured forth on our own, Nico and I would see how that cruelty could take more harmful and sinister forms: blatant oppression and discrimination. Attitudes—of condescension, malevolence, or indifference—all harmful, to varying degrees, to the Deaf. And somewhere woven into this pattern of violence, the message *You are not worthy.*

All our lives, Mom had been our bulwark against this cruelty. But now we were stepping out from behind her protective shield, and she wanted us to be ready.

She shared her lesson by telling us two stories. The first one was about my grandpa.

LONG BEFORE I WAS BORN, Grandpa stopped smoking. When my brothers and I were very young, Grandpa was a healthy and fit man. But one day in fall 1995, he tapped my grandma on the shoulder.

ME HARD BREATHE, he told her; his chest felt tight. Grandma immediately alerted my mom, and they thought the worst: Grandpa was having a heart attack. They rushed him to the car and sped off to the same hospital on Long Island where Neal, Nico, and I were born.

At the hospital, Grandpa was rushed off for testing. A thoracic surgeon called on my mom and grandma to explain the results.

Six years before, Mom had given birth to me and Nico without an interpreter. She didn't ask for one; that was just how it was. But this was 1995, and the ADA was five years old. She had every right to ask that the hospital provide an ASL interpreter to facilitate communication, and she did.

The doctor responded, point-blank, *"No."* He wouldn't even use a pen and paper. Instead, he started speaking, expecting Mom and Grandma to lip-read. Left with no choice in the middle of a medical emergency, they labored to understand him. The doctor pointed to his chest and Mom caught a few words on his lips: *"deflated lung."* Mom and Grandma were relieved it wasn't a heart attack, but they worried about Grandpa's lung. It wasn't clear how serious the issue was.

The doctor continued explaining, and at one point Mom thought the doctor said that Grandpa's lung issues were caused by my grandpa's height. He was tall, about six three, but Mom couldn't see a connection between his height and his lung problem. Mom thought she probably misunderstood the doctor, but he had moved on, and the next word Mom caught on his lips was *"surgery."* And then he waved, cutting off his explanation, and walked away.

All Mom and Grandma knew was that Grandpa had a deflated lung and that he was having surgery. They didn't know how serious the problem was, whether my grandpa's life was in danger, or the details of the surgical procedure the doctor was about to perform on him.

Frustrated, Mom went to the front desk and requested an interpreter from several nurses. Each person she asked denied her, until someone finally led her to the hospital's patient representative service. There she was asked to file a claim, which they promised to look into. It would be a slow process, Mom knew, and she had no time to waste; an interpreter was needed immediately. But she was exhausted after running around the entire hospital looking for a solution to the problem and reluctantly went home with Grandma to rest and check on her boys while Grandpa was in the operating room.

When it was time, Mom and Grandma returned to the hospital and went straight to the recovery area, thinking that's where they'd find Grandpa. But he wasn't there. Confused, they asked at the front desk, but no one there knew where he was. They stopped a nurse that passed by, but he didn't know, either. They checked different floors at the hospital but didn't see Grandpa anywhere. Confusion turned into fear. Where *was* Grandpa?

At last, they saw the thoracic surgeon. Gesturing and enunciating, he told them that Grandpa was in the ICU, which sounded like very bad news. Mom and Grandma sprinted to the ICU wing.

When they arrived, they saw tubes sticking into Grandpa's body everywhere—his forearm, chest, nostrils. The sight of Grandpa like this made Mom think he was dying.

From his bed, Grandpa was so relieved to see family. He'd been alone in the ICU all this time, without an interpreter. He hadn't been able to understand anything the doctor and nurses told him; the doctor in particular refused to use a pen and paper. He had no clue what was going on; he was scared.

Grandpa, too, thought he was going to die.

At last they found out why Grandpa was in the ICU. After the surgery, his heart rate was too low and his blood pressure too high; he was in the ICU so they could keep a closer eye on him.

Mom and Grandma were fuming. The doctor had given them very little information before the surgery. They hadn't received critical details: the possible outcomes of the surgery, the fact that Grandpa could be sent to the ICU if his vitals weren't at the levels they needed to be. The lack of accessible communication heaped unnecessary confusion and stress upon the situation. Grandpa's serious health condition was stressful enough; the additional problems caused by the doctor and hospital refusing to allow access to communication were not only discriminatory and robbed him and our family of dignity; they literally hurt Grandpa's chances of survival.

The doctor entered Grandpa's ICU room and gave a brief explanation of the surgery. All Mom and my grandparents were able to understand was that the medical team had inserted a tube into Grandpa's chest, through his rib cage, and into the deflated lung. Then they pushed air through the tube to help inflate the lung. The surgery was successful, and Grandpa's vitals eventually improved. After a spell in the ICU, he was moved back to the recovery room. The doctor ran a battery of tests, including X-rays, that confirmed that the lung had recovered near-full function. Finally, after a week in the hospital, Grandpa was allowed to go home.

Never once in his weeklong stay had he been given access to an interpreter. The patient representative service was still reviewing the case, and the doctor and everyone else kept telling Mom no.

Before releasing Grandpa from the hospital, the doctor gave another abbreviated explanation. Mom caught only a few words from his lips to take home.

At home, Grandpa seemed to be doing okay. Days passed and he went on about his business. He was eager for life to return to normal and to have his pasta dinner on Sundays.

But Mom and Grandma continued to monitor him, and after he'd been home about a week, they started noticing something was off. Grandpa was moving around slowly and labored hard as he walked.

Grandpa denied anything was wrong; he said he was just a little tired from the surgery, which was normal. Mom convinced him to let her take his temperature, to make sure. But the thermometer showed a fever. Not a good sign—one of the few things Grandma and Mom were able to snatch from the doctor's instructions was to bring Grandpa in if he had a fever.

HOW YOU FEEL? Mom asked Grandpa. HONEST.

Finally, Grandpa admitted he'd been feeling awful the past couple days. He'd kept it a secret because he was scared to go back to the hospital. He was traumatized, MIND-SCARRED, from his experience the first time. Without an interpreter and little access to communication, he felt there was little point in going to the hospital.

NO, Mom said. YOU SICK, MUST GO BACK.

They went to the thoracic surgeon's office. Again, he refused to provide an interpreter. Grandpa was taken in for testing. Afterward, the doctor explained the results to Mom, Grandma, and Grandpa. But without an interpreter, the communication was superficial. The doctor said *"infection"* and showed them the X-ray. There was a white cloudiness all over the afflicted lung. The doctor ordered them to take Grandpa back to the hospital immediately.

Grandpa, Grandma, and Mom were upset. Again, lack of communication access had contributed to the worsening of Grandpa's health condition. The doctor hadn't given them clear instructions for post-surgical care: things they should monitor, activities Grandpa should avoid, food he shouldn't eat. If they had received the instruction clearly via an interpreter, they might have been able to prevent this infection, or caught it before it had spread throughout his lung. And if they'd had an interpreter the first time, Grandpa wouldn't have hidden his illness for fear of returning to the oppressive, confusing environment at the hospital.

Grandpa had another surgery, this time to suction out the infection and clean up the inside of his lung. His second visit to the hospital lasted two weeks, and Mom, Grandma, and my two uncles took turns staying with him at the hospital. They wanted to have someone by his bedside at all times, to support him and help him communicate with the nurses and doctors.

Again and again, Mom followed up with the hospital patient representative service. When she was at the hospital she visited their office, and at home she made calls using the TTY. She would dial a relay service and connect with a relay operator, who would call the hospital's office and facilitate the conversation between the two. The operator read Mom's typed messages out loud to the patient representative and typed in the representative's response for Mom to read. During one call, she encountered a representative with a condescending attitude who brushed off her interpreter request, telling her to pay for her own interpreter or stick with lip-reading. When she tried to explain the ADA law and how it required hospitals to pay for accommodations for disabled people, the patient representative said under her breath, "Bullshit." The relay operator caught it and told Mom. By then the rep had hung up and Mom couldn't respond.

Mom never gave up. She kept calling and reaching out to the patient representative service. At last, Mom finally heard back from the service; they had relented and scheduled an interpreter. But the interpreter didn't show up. They booked another one, who showed up but signed so poorly that the family couldn't understand her.

Mom did her best to find other solutions to communicate. A teacher at Lexington who had taught Neal had a sister who signed fluently and worked at the hospital. She wasn't an interpreter, but she graciously helped out a few times. She wasn't always available, though, and anyway these band-aid solutions didn't fix the real problem: the doctor and the hospital's stubborn refusal to provide Deaf people equal communication access, a right protected by the ADA.

Eventually Grandpa recovered enough to be able to go home. He was overjoyed. Fortunately, his lung healed and the issue never returned.

To address the hospital's and doctor's illegal refusal to provide an interpreter, my grandparents filed a lawsuit. Legal action is one powerful tool that people with disabilities can use to combat discrimination.

Unfortunately, the lawsuit failed. The hospital was able to prove that they made attempts at providing us with interpreters (only two times in three weeks, both taking place during Grandpa's second stay at the hospital, was apparently enough effort). The ADA was young back then, and the courts were still trying to figure out how it would apply.

Grandpa's lawsuit may not have led to a positive outcome, but my family was far from giving up our fight against discrimination. In fact, as we received the decision on the hospital lawsuit, my uncle was in the middle of another one.

That was the second story Mom told us.

ONE WARM SPRING EVENING IN Queens, a neighbor walked up to my uncle Charles and handed him a piece of paper. The neighbor, an older man who was always friendly toward the DiMarco family, was a longtime employee of the New York City Department of Sanitation. The paper he handed my uncle was a job application.

*"You should apply. It's a good job. It pays well, and there are great benefits. You get health insurance. Full pension after twenty years,"* the neighbor said, my uncle reading his lips. He paused and his eyes flickered to Charles's ears. *"I don't know if your deafness will be a problem."*

With a shrug, he added: *"But I know you can do the job. It won't hurt to try."*

Charles thanked the neighbor and brought the job application inside the house to think on it a little more. It was 1990, and he had recently graduated from Lexington School for the Deaf—the same school my brothers and I attended a few years later. He had his eyes set on a career as a Wall Street investor. He was drawn by the mythos of Wall Street, propelled in the 1980s by the Oliver Stone and Michael Douglas film and other popular culture vehicles. He imagined himself wrapped up in the constant pulsing activity of a Wall Street investment firm, his hands waving and slamming along with those of the other traders, soaking up the adrenaline and energy that oozed from cubicle to cubicle, from desk to desk. The mental challenge of figuring out the financial markets excited him, too; he was dang good at math, a DiMarco hallmark that I would inherit. He would have no problem crunching numbers, analyzing and predicting the most lucrative stocks and bonds. Bottom line, he had no doubt he would kick ass on Wall Street, look super slick wearing the expensive suits he'd own, and make bucketloads of cash.

After getting his high school diploma, he took his first step toward his dream job by enrolling in the National Technical Institute for the Deaf (NTID) in Rochester. He had already started preparatory courses at NTID when he learned that the state financial aid he was counting on to help pay for tuition had fallen through. Without financial aid, he couldn't afford to stay in college. He packed up his car and drove five hours back down to New York City to move in with his parents until he figured out his next move. He found a job at a car wash working as an auto detailing specialist. It was an okay job but it felt temporary, not something he could build a decades-long career on. He still had his eyes set on Wall Street, but he wasn't sure how to get started in college without having enough financial aid. He felt like he was floating in the middle of the ocean, moving wherever the current took him, with little control over where he was going. And then the neighbor showed up and pressed that Department of Sanitation job application into his hand.

Charles wasn't sure if he wanted to apply. It was an opportunity to seize control of his life, his future—but a job driving a garbage truck on the New York City streets was a long way off from his dream of trading stocks and bonds on Wall Street. He asked his dad what he thought.

FOR DEAF, GOOD JOBS HARD FIND, Grandpa said. WON'T
HURT TRY.

My uncle filled out the application. Remembering the neighbor's
words, he made sure to write down that he was Deaf on the application. He offered this information up front; if there were any issues
related to his hearing ability, he expected to learn about them soon
enough.

Soon after applying, he received a response from the Department
of Sanitation. To proceed with his application, he needed to complete
three assessments: a written test, a physical evaluation, and a medical
exam. He took the written test and aced it, scoring 92 percent. He
did even better on the physical evaluation meeting 100 percent of the
requirements. Last, he went to the doctor's office. The doctor did a
typical medical check-up: he reviewed Charles's blood pressure and
other vitals, pressed a stethoscope to his heart and told him to breathe
deep, tapped a small hammer to his knees and made his legs jerk in-
voluntarily. So far so good. At the end, the doctor said he would need
to assess Charles's hearing.

*What do you mean?* Charles asked, using a pen and paper. He
read the doctor's response off his lips: It was a required part of the
medical exam. The doctor needed to test Charles's hearing and record
the results.

*But I'm Deaf,* Charles wrote in response. *You know that. The department knows it, too. I put it down in my application.*

The doctor shrugged; he was just following orders. With a sigh,
Charles went along with the test.

The Department of Sanitation received thousands of applications
every time they opened up positions. They couldn't hire everyone all
at the same time, so they had a waiting list. The order of applicants on
the waiting list was determined by how well they did on the writing
test. Charles's good score had earned him spot number 2,902.

There was nothing he could do but wait. He continued with his
job at the auto detailer and eventually gained managerial responsi-

bilities. The neighbor who handed him the application retired from his job at the Department of Sanitation. Never finding a solution to his financial aid need, Charles saw the prospect of college and a Wall Street job fade from his picture. As his name slowly climbed the 2,901 places ahead of him on the waiting list, Charles patiently waited.

Three years later, a letter from the Department of Sanitation finally came. He had grown bored working at the auto detailer and wanted a job that paid better and provided benefits. Then he could move out from his folks' house and get his own apartment. At twenty-three years old, he was ready for a career. The letter he held in his hands was his ticket to a better future.

He eagerly opened it and started reading. His heart sank.

The Department of Sanitation would not be offering Charles a job, the letter said. The reason made Charles feel even worse: they would not hire him because of his bilateral hearing loss.

Charles couldn't believe it. He showed my grandpa the letter, stabbing his finger at where it cited his Deaf identity.

REMEMBER ME WRITE-DOWN APPLICATION, ME DEAF? Charles asked.

YES, my grandpa responded.

THEN WHY?

My grandpa couldn't answer. Charles couldn't understand it. He had noted that he was Deaf on his application, and then the Department of Sanitation proceeded to tell him to complete the written test, physical evaluation, and medical exam. Then it made him wait three years, only to tell him, no, you're not qualified to work for us, because you're Deaf.

The decision was so profoundly unfair that it baffled Charles. He told his friends what happened and they said it wasn't right, the city couldn't do that to him—it was discrimination. Charles knew that, but he wasn't sure what he could do about it. A friend pointed out that the ADA was passed into law to prevent this very thing from happening. It made discrimination against people based on their disability—deafness, in my uncle's case—illegal. Charles should sue, his friend told him.

He found a lawyer to help him with his lawsuit, a man named Ralph Reiser. Ralph was hard of hearing, had Deaf parents, and could sign fluently. After collecting all the facts from Charles, Ralph filed the lawsuit. Shortly after, Charles learned the Department of Sanitation's rationale behind rejecting his application. The department determined that he could not operate garbage trucks and other vehicles required for the job because he was Deaf and would not be able to hear the sirens of emergency vehicles. He was deemed a safety risk by the department.

Charles found the argument absurd. For a counterargument, he had to look no further than the wallet in his own back pocket. Inside was a driver's license, proof that the state of New York trusted him, a Deaf person who was not able to hear emergency sirens, to drive. In fact, Deaf people had been permitted to drive for decades, probably for as long as anyone could remember, in the United States. If Charles could drive a car, why not a garbage truck? Charles and Ralph forged ahead with the lawsuit. Ralph was confident that they could win, but he warned Charles that it would take a while, probably years, before their case reached its conclusion.

Charles had waited three years for his name to climb the Department of Sanitation waiting list; he reluctantly resigned himself to even more waiting. He was laid off from his job at the auto detailer, but soon after, he got a teaching assistant job at his alma mater, Lexington School for the Deaf, helping to teach high school math. Working with numbers, he was right back in his wheelhouse. The job was fun, but as with the auto detailer, it didn't feel like a career.

Meanwhile, the case moved at a snail's pace. It played out via the postal service, with each side sending volleys in the form of letters. Months turned into a year, then two. As 1995 wound down, the case neared the time of trial. Charles and Ralph were close to the chance to present the case in court.

The city asked to meet in January 1996. They didn't want the case to see the courtroom. Charles was offered a deal: he'd get a job at the Department of Sanitation. He'd won!

The city said Charles would have to hold on until the next hiring cycle. When would that be? Ralph asked. The city said they weren't sure; it depended on how many employees retired over the coming months, and that it could happen as late as the following year, 1997.

Ralph said that wouldn't do. The department had made Charles wait long enough already. They had to hire him immediately, or Charles was going to leave them at the table without a deal.

The city reluctantly agreed, and Charles began his job training that April. Because the department wasn't ready to start hiring again, he was the lone employee in his training class. But he didn't mind, because it meant he received one-on-one instruction, and it was much easier to ask his instructors questions or to have them repeat something he hadn't understood.

After completing a three-week training, he began a week-long on-the-job training at the Department of Sanitation's Garage Q7 in Queens. On Charles's first day at Q7, there was a meeting of the borough bosses at the garage. In a hallway, he happened to bump into one of the bosses, on a break from the meetings. The boss stopped him. Charles recognized his face—he was the fourth-ranking boss of the entire department. Charles felt a twinge of fear creep up his spine.

*"You the one who sued the city?"* the boss asked as Charles read his lips.

Charles didn't know what to say. He wondered if the boss thought he was an asshole. But he didn't see any option other than to tell the truth. If he didn't, the boss would find out eventually—he was the *only* Deaf person at the entire department, after all.

Charles nodded. The boss squinted at him. Then he clapped him on the shoulder.

*"Good for you,"* the boss said, smiling. *"Welcome to the New York City Department of Sanitation."*

"YOUR FAMILY HAS FACED A long history of oppression and discrimination. You will, too," Mom said after she finished telling me Grandpa and Uncle Charles's stories.

"Don't let it stop you. Fight back. You have the law on your side. Chase your dreams down. Always remember, you *are* worthy."

It wouldn't be long before I faced the world's oppressive cruelty on my own.

# 10.

# Guatemala

**C**an Deaf people . . . *is a question I get all the time.* Can Deaf people drive? Talk? Read? Have sex?

*Whenever I am asked one of these questions, I groan a little inside. These questions are steeped in ignorance and loaded with patronizing assumptions. They imply that because Deaf people are unable to hear we are unable to do many of the things an ordinary member of society does. There's this sense that the hearing person asking the question thinks that Deaf people are helpless. And often that assumed helplessness is equated with innocence. We're viewed as babies—underdeveloped emotionally, physically, and mentally. Some people see Deaf people as being so broken that we cannot break the rules and get into trouble.*

*I swear some hearing people look at Deaf people and see newborn lambs.*

*Baaaaa.*

*When this stereotype is thrown my way, I laugh. From the belly I roar with delight, and not just because I know better. Of course I know that Deaf people are capable of so much more than is often expected from us. But I am filled with mirth, because I know that our capability includes mischief.*

*A good bit of mischief.*

*I declare now to such ignorant hearing people a correction and a word of caution: Deaf people can be wicked and devious and armed with all kinds of trickery. When we want to, Deaf people can be, basically, evil raccoons.*

*We get into trouble just like anyone else. And, occasionally, on purpose or not, we get into pretty big trouble.*

DURING WINTER BREAK OF MY sophomore year at Gallaudet University, I escaped the biting chill of the D.C. winter for the sunny beaches of Costa Rica. It was my first international backpacking trip, and I carried around a school backpack packed only with tank tops, basketball shorts, a single pair of swimming trunks, and a baseball cap that I wore backward. I traveled super light on the advice of my more experienced backpacking companions on the trip, Brandi, Millie, and Misty.

Their advice was wise; you don't need much clothing when you spend all your time basking under the tropical sun and floating on ocean waves. Costa Rica's pristine white sand beaches and tropical jungles were beautiful to behold, and our four-week trip whizzed by. Before I knew it, it was time for our flight back to the States; our spring semester at Gallaudet started in a few days. The first leg of our flight would take us from Costa Rica to Guatemala, where we had a three-hour layover before the second leg to D.C. We went to the airport extra early, breezed through security, and arrived at our gate with hours to burn before our flight departed.

We dreaded the end of our dreamy vacation and having to start school again so soon. Determined to squeeze as much fun out of the little time we had left and finish our trip with a bang, we set out to the duty-free shop and bagged a large bottle of dirt-cheap flavored vodka. We were only eighteen and nineteen, but with our feet on Costa Rican soil, drinking was legal. We passed the bottle around and took deep swallows straight from it, and soon the bottle was empty. We roamed the airport, floating on our buzz. Outside the duty-free shop we saw a lady holding out a tray of sample shots of rum.

LET'S-GO! Millie said, leading the way. As we reached to grab our shots, I spotted two elderly ladies making their way past. Their heads were topped with carefully coiffed white-gray curls, and they walked with the cautious steps of senior citizens.

I thought they made for perfect drinking partners. I hollered out to flag them down and pointed at the tray, then at them.

DRINK?

The ladies giggled and reached out for their little plastic shot glasses. We roared with delight and drained the round.

Brandi looked at her watch.

SOON TIME FLIGHT.

Millie: ME STILL THIRSTY.

Misty: BUY BEER, DRINK-ON PLANE?

Me: WHOO, LET'S GO!

We stumbled past the sample tray lady into the duty-free store and emerged with a six-pack of bottled beer. As we glided toward our gate, I felt content. We'd made the most of our trip, packing fun into every last minute. We boarded the plane, found it three-quarters filled with passengers, and took our seats. After the plane took off, we each grabbed a beer bottle, cracked them open, and clinked in a toast.

COSTA RICA! we cheered.

The flight attendant did a double take as she walked by us. She wheeled around, a stern look on her face, her mouth motoring away, a finger pointed toward us, and her head shaking.

Obviously there was an issue, but we weren't sure exactly what it was. The alcohol swimming in our heads wasn't helpful. It appeared the problem had to do with the bottles of beer we had in our hands, but why? We'd bought them in the airport and brought them onboard to drink, just like we'd done with bottles of water or sports drinks all the time. Were the rules different with alcoholic drinks? Or maybe they didn't think we were of legal drinking age?

That shouldn't have been a problem, right, because we were traveling from a country where the legal drinking age was eighteen?

As our foggy brains muddled through the possibilities, one of us had the sense to point to their ear and shake their head—the universal gesture for "I'm Deaf."

The flight attendant looked at us suspiciously. *"I don't believe you,"* we read on her lips.

We stared back at the lady, at a loss for words, gestures, or signs. What can you do or say to prove to someone that you're Deaf? We don't have special ID cards signifying that we're Deaf, nor is it clearly stated in our driver's licenses. In general, the formal documentation that Deaf people have of their deafness is an audiogram, a chart showing the results of a hearing test. The audiogram indicates, in decibels, the quietest sound we're able to hear in different pitches ranging from high to low. But the audiogram is something we keep locked in the filing cabinet along with our Social Security cards and birth certificates. We don't carry it on us at all times, to be brandished at any moment, like a police badge, at any doubters, haters, or naysayers off the street. *Whoosh.* "Bam! Peep the trend line in the nineties! In your face, doubter!"

(That's the quietest sound I'm able to hear, in decibels. Ninety decibels, the internet tells me, is about as loud as a roaring lawnmower.)

Alas, without audiograms to flash at the flight attendant, all we could do was weakly protest that we were in fact Deaf. The flight attendant purposefully ignored our appeals.

Our next step was to communicate in an accessible and adult manner. At the start of our trip, we'd brought along a travel journal to use for communication. All throughout the trip we filled up the pages of the journal with conversations with hearing people we met along the way—directions to the beach, flirtations with strangers we met at bars, exchanges of travel tips with fellow backpackers. By the end of the trip, the journal's blank pages had been exhausted and we'd tossed it out along with the bottle of vodka we'd downed at the airport.

Left with no choice, we gestured, as politely as we could, a request to the flight attendant to bring out a pen and paper so we could continue our discussion.

The flight attendant shook her head and spoke: "*I know you can read my lips.*"

Now this lady was straight up discriminating against us. First she refused to acknowledge our disclosure of our being Deaf, and now she was dictating to us how we were to communicate with her.

One funny thing about lip-reading: it leads you right into a quagmire. Most folks are able to lip-read the basics—for example, I've seen the words "*Can you read my lips?*" on a thousand different lips, and I have no problem reading those specific words. But if I answer yes to that question, the person speaking will then advance into a conversation that I can understand roughly only 10 to 20 percent of, if I'm lucky. Then I'm screwed. Yes, we could read those words off the flight attendant's lips, but only because they were so familiar to us. It was her next words that we were worried about being able to understand, and why we were so adamant that she bring out a pen and paper.

By this time our annoyance with the flight attendant had escalated into full-blown indignation. She kept talking; we frowned at her lips and shrugged. We refused to engage until she brought out a pen and paper. Buoyed by the spirits coursing through our veins and our reckless youth, we scoffed at this authority figure who was trying to shut down our party.

The flight attendant grew more animated, and probably raised her volume. I say probably because, though we couldn't hear her, we could clearly see the heads that were starting to swivel in the seats in front of us. The man sitting in the seat in front of me turned and spoke to us, his expression angry. I repeated the gesture: POINT-EARS, SHAKE HEAD. I asked him if he had a pen and paper, or if he could help us by asking the flight attendant for them. He shook his head and angrily whipped back into his seat.

My friends and I looked at each other.

THIS-IS RIDICULOUS.

WE DEAF, SHE LOOK-DOWN-ON US.

ALL WE NEED, WHAT? PEN PAPER. SIMPLE.

The flight attendant was still in the aisle, shouting and angry. I took a deep swig of my bottle of beer and gestured again: pen and paper.

It couldn't get any worse than this, we figured. So we dug in. We weren't going to cave in and engage in a discussion that we wouldn't have full access to. If our beer was the issue and this lady was going to make us pour them down the flight restroom sink because it was against the rules, we might as well make her tell us *our* way. We weren't going to let her dismiss the fact that we were Deaf and force us to communicate in an inaccessible way.

One part of me had another thought about how this situation might work itself out. This part—which you might call the evil raccoon in me—thought that if we stood our ground long enough, the flight attendant would give up and let this situation blow over. I'd seen it happen before, many times.

One time was when I was about ten, riding along in the back of our Dodge family van. Mom was driving and Nico and I were sitting in the last row. We got into a squabble, I forget over what. It escalated into Nico lying on his back on the seat, pummeling his feet into my sides. My mom, seeing us in the rearview mirror, reached back with her right hand to scold us. Her feet laid heavy on the gas while she was trying to play boxing referee from afar, and sirens flared behind us. Mom pulled over, and I was terrified, because I knew she was going to have it out for us. The police officer walked up, rapped on the driver's side window, and began talking as soon as my mom rolled it down. My mom put up a hand to interrupt him, pointed at her ear, and shook her head.

The officer paused. He spoke again, pointing at his mouth. My mom shook her head again: she wasn't going to read his lips. In a situation where a cop had just pulled her over, my mom didn't want to leave anything to chance. She asked for a pen and paper.

The officer thought about it for a beat, then apparently figured it wasn't worth the trouble. Now it was his turn to gesture. He put out his hands, palms down, and moved them up and down, up and down, like he was fanning out a fire in slo-mo: *slow down.*

My mom nodded and mouthed, *I'm sorry.*

The officer nodded, waved her forward, and started walking back to his car.

From the backseat, I was enthralled. Mom had broken the speed limit, but the police officer let her off without punishment. Why? *Point-at-ear, shake head, pen and paper.*

Fast forward seven years to me driving alone down the highway, clearing the speed limit by at least ten miles an hour. Sirens flashed, and I pulled over. I rolled the window down, put my hands to the steering wheel, and waited.

And waited.

And waited.

The cop was taking forever. I checked the rearview and noticed that there wasn't anyone in the police car behind me. Suddenly, from the corner of my eye I spotted the police officer just behind my car on the passenger side, his back to the freeway barrier and a hand on his holstered gun, his mouth moving, barking out warnings.

*Whoa.* I didn't even see him coming until he was nearly at my car's taillight. My lack of response to his shouted instructions apparently put him on full alert. I put up my hands and pointed to my ears, trying to defuse the situation quickly. As visibly as I could, I smiled and laughed, doing my best to show how much of a nonthreat I was. The cop cooled off and moved his hand away from his holster.

(Now, as I look back to this story, I'm acutely aware of the privilege I have as a white man. Because of my white skin, I was able to emerge from this situation unharmed, despite the initial alarm and panic the cop showed at my lack of response. If I was Black, the outcome would likely have been very different.)

The cop walked over to the driver's side and started jabbering away at me. Again, I gestured that I was Deaf. His motoring mouth slowed to a shuddering halt. I saw beads of sweat dotting his forehead.

The cop pointed at his mouth and asked *"Read my lips?"*

I remembered my mom in this exact scenario years before. I shook my head and gestured for a pen and paper.

The cop wiped the sweat off his forehead with the sleeve of his uniform as he considered my request. It must have been too much of an annoyance, because he mouthed *"Slow down"* and let me off with a quick gesture down the road. I drove off without even a warning.

It was as if authority figures were allergic to the pen and paper method. Though my mom and I had clearly violated the speed limit, the cop had let us off without a ticket after we'd firmly requested a pen and paper to communicate.

On the plane from Costa Rica to Guatemala, I figured the flight attendant had two choices. Either she would need to accept our request for a pen and paper, and thus provide us with an accessible way to communicate with her, or she could save herself the trouble and leave us alone to focus on the hundred other passengers on the plane. I was betting on the latter. Sure enough, eventually she walked away, shooting lasers at us with her eyes as she moved to the front of the plane.

It was finally over, we thought. We put our beers away, though—we didn't want to push our luck any further. We checked our watches: only a half hour more until we landed. We settled back and shared memories from Costa Rica, and the time drained away until the plane's wheels touched down at the Guatemala airport.

We got up to grab our bags and saw the flight attendant walking toward us. She motioned for us to sit back down. Not this again, we thought. I was about to protest and demand, once and for all, that she write down what was going on.

But then I saw the two men behind her. They were dressed head to toe in camouflage military uniforms and wore black bulletproof vests. When my eyes saw what they were holding, I felt the hair on the back of my neck stand on end.

Around the men's shoulders were thick black straps, which were attached to AK-47s.

*AK-47s.*

Every cell in my body froze in terror. *What the fuck was going on?* I thought. *Why were men with assault rifles waiting for us?*

Sneering, the flight attendant put up her hand, commanding us to wait in our seats. She stood there, flanked by her two armed henchmen, her eyes never leaving us until every other passenger on the plane had gotten off. And then, with a proud cock of an eyebrow, she stepped aside. The first of the armed soldiers pointed at us and gestured at us to come with him.

Confused and terrified, we obeyed. We walked behind the two soldiers up the aisle, lifeless as robots, afraid of making sudden movements that would give the men a reason to pull the trigger. I looked back at my wide-eyed friends, and I knew my face probably showed the same terror. When the flight attendant had walked away during the flight, we thought the problem was over with. But as we walked off the plane, we saw that our trouble had just started.

As we entered the airport, we saw that it was eerily quiet. Two rows of armed soldiers, about two dozen in all, every single one of them holding an AK-47, stood waiting for us inside. Our escorts led us in between the rows of soldiers, who regarded us with mild indifference on their stoic faces.

We approached the corridor and suddenly I realized why the airport appeared to be so quiet. Through the windows, we saw hundreds and hundreds of people standing *outside* of the terminal. The entire airport was empty save for me, my friends, and our military escort. The people outside stood near the windows, their noses pressed against the glass, trying to get a glimpse of what had caused the evacuation of an entire airport.

I glanced at my friends; the look on their faces now was a mix of horror and shock and utter confusion. The train of logic in my head was leading me down a terrifying path. Airports are evacuated when a terrorist threat is detected. Is that what was happening here? What heinous acts did our military escort and all these people think my friends and I had plotted?

My mind was spiraling out of control. What if they were accusing us of committing a serious crime and were planning to lock us up? How would we get help? My phone wouldn't work; international roaming wasn't a thing then. If I was lucky, they might let me connect to the Wi-Fi, but even then I'd only be able to communicate via email. With likely a poor internet connection, I wouldn't be able to call my mom on video and talk to her in ASL. I'd be forced to explain this terrible predicament using my second language.

*It's over*, I thought. *We are truly fucked.*

The military escort led us to a private part of the terminal and into a white room with a single bright light bulb hanging from the ceiling over a steel table. It looked like an interrogation room from the movies, one where cops brought criminal suspects for an ass-kicking. Our military escort gestured us to sit at the table.

We sat and waited a long time, dizzy with shock and terror. We were in a foreign country. Who knows how they did things here? What was going to happen to us?

Finally, the door opened and two officers came into the room. They seated themselves across from us and looked at us with serious looks of disapproval. One of them started speaking.

Not this again, we thought. How many times did we have to repeat that stupid gesture? We tried it one more time: *point-at-ear, shake head.*

The officer paused for a moment, then pointed at his lips, with a quizzical look on his face.

We shook our heads furiously, hoping that we could finally hammer our point home. We gestured for a pen and paper. The officer considered our request, and then spoke to a soldier behind him. The soldier left the room and soon returned with what we'd been requesting for the past couple hours: a stack of notepad paper and a pen.

At last, we had the tools with which we could communicate. We explained: We'd been on the plane drinking bottles of beer before the flight attendant descended on us. We were never really sure what she was trying to tell us, because she kept talking, and though we kept trying to inform her that we were Deaf and needed to communicate with a pen and paper, she never seemed to understand—or believe us.

The officers sighed. I don't know what story they had gotten from the flight attendant, but it must've been pretty dramatic for them to decide to evacuate the entire airport and send along a military escort. Whatever the story was, they were probably expecting more dangerous-looking folks, perhaps a scar or two, hardened eyes. Instead all they got were four buzzed college-age Deafies wearing the hard-worn clothing of backpackers who hadn't done laundry in more than a week.

Neither career criminals nor newborn lambs, but somewhere in between: evil raccoons.

The officer was ready to let us go, but unfortunately we'd been detained for so long that we missed the one flight back to D.C. that day. We didn't have lodging arranged, and because we would have already been on our way to D.C. if they hadn't gone Threat Level Orange on us, they agreed to put us up in a hotel—a nice five-star, at that—for the night. They also gave us vouchers to use for meals, and we went out to a swanky restaurant and made a night of it.

In four days, our spring semester would be starting, and in three the inauguration of the United States' first Black president in history would take place. We did not want to miss this historic moment.

The next morning we woke up, packed, and got ready to head out to the airport when an airport representative arrived at the hotel. He informed us that all flights from Guatemala to D.C. that day were fully booked. We would need to stay at the airport another night.

The next morning, the representative returned and told us that the flights were fully booked again. Another night at the hotel.

Early on the third day, the day of President Barack Obama's inauguration, the representative again told us that the flights were nearly all booked. Only first-class seats, which were going for thousands per ticket due to the impending inauguration, were available. We immediately objected—if we didn't get home that day, we'd miss the start of classes the following day. The representative nodded and offered us a choice: we could fly home in first-class that day, upgraded free of charge, or take a $500 voucher and wait for another day to fly back home.

In a few hours we plopped our butts into the first-class seats, finally on our way home after a dramatic three-day delay. This time, we did not bring bottles of beer onboard. We landed too late for President Obama's inauguration, but the streets were still full of people celebrating. A friend picked us up, and the drive from Reagan airport to Gallaudet University, normally a twenty-minute trip, took more than an hour. We kept our faces to the windows of the car, watching with envy as people danced, sang, and celebrated in the streets. We couldn't wait until our ride arrived at Gallaudet, where we would shed our backpacks, take a quick shower, and join the celebration.

# 11.

# Explorations

When I was five years old, my number one favorite show was Mighty Morphin Power Rangers. *My brothers and I watched it every single afternoon when we came home from school—we never missed an episode. These brightly colored Spandex-suited superpowered teenage ninjas who fought baddies amid showers of fake explosive sparks gripped our nascent imagination.*

*My brothers and I each had our favorite Ranger. Mine was the Pink Ranger.*

*When Nico and I turned six, our birthday party theme was Power Rangers. Mom and Dad asked us which Ranger we wanted to have on our cakes. Nico chose his favorite, Red Ranger. When I chose the Pink Ranger, my mom and dad looked at each other and smiled. They knew pink was my favorite color (I opted for pink anytime I had to make a color choice; heck, my hearing aid molds were hot pink), but they thought my choosing the Pink Ranger went beyond the color.*

*Dad squeezed my shoulder.*

*PINK RANGER YOUR GIRLFRIEND? He winked at me.*

*NO, NO! I protested.*

*Dad made a face that said "Yeah, sure."*

*Kimberly, the brunette character behind the Pink Ranger, was*

*cute. Too bad she was taken by Tommy, aka Green Ranger. Tommy*
*was cute, too, with his long flowing brown hair and dimpled smile. In*
*a recent episode, Kimberly and Tommy had had their first kiss.*

*I brushed those thoughts away and put my foot down.*

*PINK RANGER NOT MY GIRLFRIEND!*

*Dad laughed and said, OKAY, NEVER MIND.*

RAISE YOUR HANDS SIDE BY side at your chest. Close them into fists, as if gripping your heart, and squeeze them tight. Rotate both fists in opposite directions to twist the heart, inflicting unimaginable hurt and excruciating pain on it.

Visualize, also, like dirty water from a wrung dishrag, the hurt and pain spilling out of the heart—leaving it partially empty, perhaps to be filled with love once again.

That's how we say "grieve" in ASL.

Sitting alone on my hostel bed in Cartagena, Colombia, my heart was sore and empty—all wrung out. There was a giant lump in my throat, and tears spilled down my cheeks.

I replayed the conversation I'd just had with Hannah over and over again in my head.

US-TWO FRIENDS, ME WANT, Hannah had said to me.

The words weren't mean; Hannah signed them sincerely but in a straightforward manner, the way she always had. No bullshit, just the truth—no matter how painful.

FOR A TIME AFTER WE got back together at Gallaudet, I thought Hannah would be my forever love. She was my best friend and partner in crime. We had just as much fun staying in and watching a movie, snuggled together on a ratty dorm couch, as we did going out to a club for a night of dancing. I loved taking walks or spending time at the dog park with her and Foxy. Our physical romance was hot and passionate; we were incredible in the bedroom. Our relationship was a fun roller coaster; we kept things unpredictable and exciting. I held on to her tight, and very easily got jealous whenever I saw her hanging around with another guy. With her I felt like I had all I needed in life; I was content.

But that feeling didn't last. Over our college years, Hannah and I matured into different people. Our interests evolved; we spent time in different circles and didn't much like hanging out with the other's friends. It was a natural progression; we were two tree branches that grew at different angles. A small part of me knew this, but it gave way to that other, stronger part of me that clung to the memories that she and I created together and the once-fiery passion we felt for each other. Hannah was like a security blanket to me, and I didn't want to let her go. So we made our relationship work, tirelessly trying to find a way to force our branches to grow in the same direction.

When she was in grad school and I was in my senior year at Gallaudet, we decided to take a trip to Colombia during winter break. Our relationship was in a rocky place and we had grown uncertain about our future together. In Colombia, we would be alone together, away from our friends, school, and other distractions. We were giving the relationship one last chance.

In Colombia, our relationship issues persisted. We got annoyed with each other easily over the smallest things. Tension hung over us during the entire trip.

Hannah was set to leave Colombia before I did, to fly to Kansas for an internship at the Deaf school in Olathe. After that, her plan was to move home with her parents in Southern California. I was going to stay in Colombia for a few weeks more, then head back to D.C. for the spring semester at Gallaudet.

I should have sensed that it was time to cut the rope, to let our branches grow in our separate directions. Yet when it came time to drop Hannah off at the Cartagena bus station to catch her ride to the airport, I still stubbornly clung to the hope that we could somehow save our relationship. I'd been with Hannah for so long that I couldn't imagine life without her. I also know now that I was afraid of what I'd find out about myself—and my sexual identity, particularly—once I no longer had a girlfriend. *We could make this work*, I thought.

But as we made our way to the airport, Hannah turned to me and said, IT'S-TIME. I recoiled, every fiber in my being resisting the idea, but Hannah persisted. It was so hard to admit it, but I knew she was right: it was time to let go. We said our goodbyes, and with one last hug and kiss on the cheek, we cut the rope.

All alone back at the hostel, I felt a deep sadness wash over me. It was the end of a cherished chapter of my life. Hannah and I had been together for seven years, on and off, throughout my time in high school and college. Now I was on my own, without my security blanket.

On the fringes of my sadness, I felt relief. I'd known for a long time, in the back of my head, that we would need to move on from each other. I just didn't know when it would happen, and I kept delaying it. And now it had finally happened; whatever mixed feelings I might have had about our relationship, Hannah and I were finally, truly over. (Though I didn't know it at the time, Hannah and I would become very good friends, and remain so to this day.)

I checked out of the hostel and went to the bus station to catch a bus to my next destination, Tayrona Natural National Park in the northeastern corner of Colombia, near Venezuela.

At the station a small white van was waiting, which I guessed was my ride to the park. But there weren't any signs around to confirm my guess, so I decided to ask someone to make sure. I approached two women who were about to board the van. They understood my "I'm Deaf" gesture right away, and pleasantly nodded at the piece of paper I'd thrust toward them. Their friendly smiles were a welcome sight.

The women had funky seventies hippie hairstyles, one a mullet and the other a head of dreadlocks that was shaved away on one side. My gut told me they were gay. They sat behind me in the van and tapped me on the shoulder for my pen and notepad. We started writing back and forth in English. I was right: They told me, proudly, that they had just got married. They were from Argentina, and one of them was a lawyer. She wrote that she advocated for same-sex marriage in their home country and had finally succeeded only a year and a half earlier, in 2010. Argentina became the first country in South America to legalize same-sex marriage, the second in the Southern Hemisphere, and the tenth worldwide.

The topic of gay marriage rights struck a nerve I didn't know existed, shining a bright light on the fact that I knew absolutely nothing about gay people. I didn't realize so few countries allowed gay marriage; in fact, I was barely aware that my own country disallowed it at the time. The two women before me were inspiring figures in a worldwide movement for the human rights of a long-oppressed community. It was jarring to look at this happy newlywed couple in that moment and think that only eighteen months ago they were banned from marrying each other in their homeland.

Deep down I was aware it wasn't an accident I knew little about the LGBTQ community. Growing up, if I found a guy good looking, my brain would register it, but I would brush these thoughts aside, thinking it was impossible that I could be into men. I was taught the false and harmful stereotype that all gay men were feminine. The gay men I'd met in the Deaf community were also primarily feminine, reinforcing this stereotype. I looked at them and thought, that's not me. So I thought I couldn't be gay. I built up a wall in my head and sealed my mind against the possibility that I liked men romantically. As soon as the thought *Am I gay?* arose in my head, I suppressed it immediately. I had gay friends, but I kept them at arm's length and avoided conversations about their gay experiences. Anytime I saw an article or news clip about gay people, I'd ignore it. If I didn't learn more about the LGBTQ community, I thought, I'd stay straight. If I opened my mind, I'd slide down a path of no return. So I fought to keep all LGBTQ-related thoughts safely hidden away behind this wall in my mind.

But there were moments when thoughts and emotions—about my attraction to men—breached the wall. The house party encounter with my bi high school classmate was one such moment.

Over my last few years at Gallaudet, those thoughts came in waves, battering the wall. They started one fall semester a couple years before the Colombia trip, when Hannah and I were on a break. A new student had just transferred to the university. Tall and incredibly athletic, he was a star point guard for the Gallaudet basketball team. I watched him play and was blown away—he had a smooth handle and a silky jump shot and could jump out of the gym. He was *good*.

One day a whispered conversation reached my eyes: the new basketball player was gay. At first, I thought it was a lie, a harmful false rumor run amok on campus. This dude's appearance bled masculinity. He was handsome, with piercing deep-set eyes and a trim muscular upper torso that boasted tats everywhere: on his pecs, the side of his biceps, his shoulder blades. He didn't fit the profile of a gay man that a lifetime of social conditioning had created in my head. But later I received confirmation—he was going out with another guy I knew.

As soon as I accepted the fact that the star basketball player was gay, my mind started to run wild. It meant that I, too, despite my masculinity and affinity for sports, could be gay. I grew a little bit jealous: This guy had figured himself out. I didn't know how the hell he did it, but I thought maybe he could help me figure out myself, too. When I saw him at parties or at the cafeteria, I started to chat him up. I wasn't sure exactly what I was doing. Maybe his gaydar would go off. Maybe during a party one thing would lead to another, and we'd start hooking up. Or maybe I could confide my innermost thoughts in him and he could guide me.

I thought that he could be my gateway to the LGBTQ world.

But nothing ever happened between us. He never showed any indication he suspected I wasn't straight. Maybe I was too cautious and shielded in my interactions with him.

Instead something else changed for me. The discovery of a gay masculine man seemed to awaken something that had long slumbered inside me. Soon after I found out about the gay basketball player, I started having dreams. Sexual fantasies ran through my subconscious, scenes of me and other men going to bed. It felt so good, so right.

I woke up shaking with terror every time I had those dreams. I didn't know what to do. Desperate, I pulled up my phone and Googled: "What do gay dreams mean?" "Are gay dreams temporary?" But no search results helped me address my deepest fears. The dreams continued. The part of my brain that I'd kept sealed off for so long was growing restless and overwhelmed me with all those thoughts, like water overflowing a full glass, and I was powerless to stop it.

After a while, the dreams slowed. I reunited with Hannah and settled back behind my wall. The thoughts subsided, though that part of my brain never quieted completely. I could sense it there, waiting for the wall to crack.

When Hannah and I broke up in Colombia, I felt the questioning part of my brain jolt awake. And then I met the lesbian couple. It felt like fate. There was a purpose in this happy chance meeting; the universe was trying to tell me something.

The couple asked me if I wanted to join them at Tayrona Natural National Park. I said yes.

The two women and I went on a beautiful three-day, two-night hike in the national park. We walked all day and had long conversations on paper after dinner. When the sun set, we slept in hammocks tied to trees.

It was nice having company during the first few days after Hannah left. The two women filled that void with their carefree, chill manner. They were easy to talk to and were completely nonjudgmental. They asked lots of questions about my Deaf identity and experience. To them, my being Deaf wasn't something to be pitied; it was just a different way of living. They were curious and wanted to learn, which I thought was supremely cool.

When they asked me what my sexuality was, I saw a safe outlet. An opportunity to be honest, be truly myself without fear of judgment.

*I'm not sure,* I wrote back. *I know I'm not 100 percent straight. But I don't know what that makes me.*

I looked up at them. They nodded and smiled.

*That's cool,* they wrote. *Take your time.*

Their nonchalant response was like a cool breeze on a sunscorched, 110-degree day. I felt confidence blooming in me. Emboldened, I opened up a bit further. They didn't ask—they knew to let me share at my own pace. Talking with them was comfortable; I'd learned a lot about myself already and I wanted to seize the chance to learn more.

I wrote: *I've felt that I wasn't straight for a long time, but I never explored that question. I'm masculine and I love playing sports. I don't look, talk, or act like a gay person, based on the stereotypes I saw growing up.*

They nodded and told me that I wasn't the only one that ever felt that way. There were many others who were like me, uncertain and confused.

It didn't help that I came from a small community, the Deaf community. There were gay men in our community, of course, but in my experience they tended to present as feminine. Before the Gallaudet point guard came along, I had not met a Deaf person like myself—masculine—who was also gay. So I had always thought it was impossible I could be gay, despite the attraction I had to men.

The women wrote back that they didn't know what it was like in the Deaf community, but they promised me that there were many masculine gay people out in the world. They didn't push me, but they said that if I wanted to step forward in that direction, I would meet LGBTQ people of so many different personalities, backgrounds, and identities whom I could relate to.

That thought stuck with me for a while. The idea that there were many LGBTQ people out there, an entire community, reminded me of my Deaf identity. For my entire life I'd been so confident and sure of myself as a Deaf person because I'd been born into a Deaf family and had attended Deaf schools growing up. I belonged to the Deaf community, and that reinforced my powerful sense of being as a Deaf person. I was nowhere close to achieving that level of comfort when it came to my sexuality because I hadn't yet allowed myself to explore, to find people like me, and discover that part of my identity.

I tagged along with my new friends for a few more days after Tayrona, and then we went our separate ways. Before I left, they wished me luck on my journey, wherever it took me. Man, those were two cool dudettes. I felt indebted to them, though they had done nothing more than just be themselves.

My conversations with the lesbian couple fractured the wall I'd built in my head. For the first time in my life, I began to think, with an open mind and heart, about the possibility that I was into men.

I made a conscious decision to explore that possibility and see where it took me.

THE CLIN D'OEIL FESTIVAL IS a massive international gathering of Deaf people in Reims, France. The festival showcases sign language in all forms of art—film, theater, literature, sculpture, street art. Every two years, tens of thousands of Deaf people turn up in Reims to celebrate our shared love of sign language—and to party.

About six months after my Colombia trip, I descended upon Reims during a summer-long backpacking trip through Europe. It was a revelation to be among so many of my people—Deafies—from all over the world.

We didn't all share the same sign language; it's a common misconception that there is one universal sign language that all Deaf people communicate in. In actuality, there are an estimated three hundred different sign languages all over the world. At international Deaf gatherings like Clin d'Oeil, Deaf people communicate using International Sign Language. International Sign isn't quite a language in itself—rather it's a combination of signs taken from different sign languages and commonly known gestures. While at Gallaudet, I had my first conversations in International Sign with fellow students and visitors hailing from all over the world. At first, I found International Sign easier to understand rather than to express. It incorporates a lot more of ASL than of any other sign language, which I suspect makes it easier to learn for someone fluent in ASL than for someone fluent in any other sign language. The outsize presence of ASL in International Sign has also recently sparked discussions about ASL imperialism.

It wasn't until I started my European backpacking trip that I began using International Sign on a daily basis. By the time I arrived at

Clin d'Oeil, my International Sign fluency was improving rapidly, and at the festival it was spurred on by all-day use and crowds of literally hundreds of International Sign–fluent conversation partners.

A popular event at every Clin d'Oeil Festival was the theater production put on by Teater Manu, a Deaf theater group from Norway. Teater Manu was a well-run organization that received ample grant funding. Top Deaf thespians from all over Europe and other continents flew to Oslo to train and perform with this prestigious organization. At every festival, Teater Manu delivered a top-notch creative theater production that often thought a little outside the box and challenged the norm. This year their production was *Jack and the Beanstalk*, and they had a female actor playing the role of Jack.

I was told to arrive early to grab a spot in line if I wanted a good seat. Sure enough, after I'd grabbed my spot, the line eventually stretched down the block. I waited for the theater's doors to open with a few friends I knew from the United States, killing time chatting, meeting new international friends, and people-watching—especially the festival workers buzzing about, making preparations for the theater production. The festival workers wore horizontally striped shirts, and one of them caught my eye. He was tall and had dark skin and hair. His handsomely shaped face looked regal and French to me, and he wore square-rimmed glasses. He strolled over to near where I was in line, signing instructions to festival-goers to stay in our line and prepare to enter the theater.

I didn't want to take my eyes off him, but I forced myself to. I was afraid that my American friends would catch me gawking at him and suspect that I was checking him out. It felt strange, my compulsion to stare at this guy clashing with my urgency to stay discreet.

The guy walked on, continuing to sign instructions down the line past us. The line started moving, and as I entered the theater I wondered who the handsome dude was. I didn't think I'd get a chance to find out—after the play was over, he was nowhere to be found. At a festival attended by thousands of people, it'd be hard to find him again. Damn, I thought. I hoped I'd get to see him again; he'd sparked something in me, and I was intensely curious to learn who he was and to see if my attraction to him was real and if anything could happen between us.

That night was the last night of the festival, and there was a huge outdoor party in a clearing within a forested area in the outskirts of Reims. Booths were set up around the perimeter of the clearing, Deaf artists gave live performances from a stage, lights flashed, music pumped, and the alcohol flowed.

In a stroke of serendipity, among the thousands of faces at the event I saw square-rimmed glasses and a handsome smile. We said hi, and he told me his name was Alphonse and that he was indeed from France. The conversation didn't last long. I was afraid to let on that I might be interested and was wary of falling into a deep connection with him. I didn't know if I was ready to begin a potentially romantic interaction—to *flirt*—with a man, especially in such a public place.

I could tell that Alphonse was gay. He never said it outright, but it was obvious to me. I couldn't tell you what it was that gave it away, but the mysterious inner workings of gaydar perform just as well on Deaf people, too. Some of it was his sense of style—his glasses and the thick circular earrings he wore, which made his ears look like they'd been gauged. Some of it was his physical mannerisms and how he signed—there was a touch of femininity. Gaydar is one of these things that's notoriously difficult to describe to another person, but when I knew, I knew. And I knew that this dude was gay.

I played it cool, floated away from Alphonse, and got caught up in the sweep of people mingling about. I found some old friends from back home and from previous travels abroad, faces I hadn't seen in months and years. I made new friends from all over the world and chatted with them through International Sign about their homeland, culture, cuisine, and local Deaf community.

As I knocked back drink after drink and mingled in the crowd, Alphonse lingered at the back of my mind. At five A.M., the party finally died down and festival-goers started wandering away from the clearing. I stayed behind, grabbing last conversational moments with friends old and new. My train to the next stop of my European back-packing trip was set to depart in a couple hours, and I wasn't planning on sleeping until I got on the train. The sky started to brighten, and the clearing, once packed with a couple thousand people, was down to a few dozen restless, euphoric souls.

I felt a tap on my shoulder and turned around. Square-rimmed glasses, wide earrings, handsome smile. Alphonse.

YOU WANT WALK BAKERY NEARBY, GET PASTRIES?

I looked around. It was just the two of us. I felt my heart flutter at the chance to connect with Alphonse alone.

YES, SURE.

The city was still asleep, and we had the streets all to ourselves. We strolled side by side, chatting. Fueled by liquid courage and feeling sheltered by the fact that we were alone, I gave myself to our conversation. We talked about the festival, our lives at home, my travel plans.

I felt the urge to kiss him, but I wasn't sure how to take the first step. Should I ask him if I could? Or give him a hint? Maybe touch him on the shoulder, arms, hands? Playfully, but with enough physical contact I could maybe lead into a kiss? But we weren't even holding hands yet.

We stopped at an intersection and waited for the light to change.

ALMOST ARRIVE BAKERY, NEXT BLOCK, Alphonse said.

The moment was now. I had a choice: kiss him, or do nothing and always wonder what could have been. I grabbed him by the shoulders, turned him around, and went in for the kiss. Our lips met, and I felt him give in to the kiss. It lasted a few seconds before we broke apart. Anxiously I looked at his face, his eyes, studying him to see what he'd felt. I saw confusion, but no anger.

I THOUGHT YOU STRAIGHT? he said.

I had never once given him a hint I was into men, much less him. The kiss came flat out of nowhere for Alphonse. But I saw a slight smile on the corner of his lips.

I pulled him in and we kissed again, longer this time.

The kiss felt *illegal*. So wrong, but in a thrilling way. Like we were breaking a rule and hoping we wouldn't get caught. My heart pounded with adrenaline.

I don't feel like that anymore. That's a good thing. It means I'm a lot more comfortable with the idea of being with a guy, and that I don't perceive it as breaking a rule—it *doesn't*. I don't miss feeling like I needed to conceal my attraction to men and repressing my true sexuality—fuck that. But I do miss those first few moments of physical intimacy with a man, when the experience was totally new and made me euphoric, my mind spinning and my heart fluttering.

Eventually Alphonse and I resumed our walk to the bakery, as my heart pounded. We grabbed our pastries and sat down at a table to talk more. We didn't have much time. I looked at my wristwatch; I had to catch my train in a few minutes. We stood up from our table.

HEY, VISIT-ME MY HOME OVER-THÉRE NICE, YOU CAN, he said.

We hugged and kissed one last time, and then I left.

Despite not having slept in more than twenty-four hours, I didn't fall asleep right away on the train. I ran through the kiss in my head over and over again—my first romantic kiss with a man. It felt nice, I enjoyed it, and I wanted more. I wondered what would have happened if I hadn't had a train to catch. Would I be walking with Alphonse back to wherever he was staying? I thought about what the kiss meant. I'd known I was attracted to men, but I'd only ever looked at them, never touched. I didn't know whether I'd take pleasure in actual physical interaction with one—until that day. I'd felt enough to know I wanted more.

Eventually my mind stopped racing and I fell asleep on the train. But I yearned for someone to talk about all of this with. I wouldn't have the opportunity for a while; I was traveling solo. I pushed the thought to the back of my mind.

THE NEXT STOP ON MY backpacking trip was Sicily. I'd marked the region on my map when I planned out my trip, because it was where my Italian grandpa's family came from. Both his parents were born in a farming town in Sicily called Agrigento, where our Sicilian heritage dates back to the 1700s. My grandpa's mom emigrated to New York City at the turn of the twentieth century; his dad followed later, in 1916. They met in New York City and eventually had my grandpa.

In Sicily, I paid homage to my Italian lineage and soaked in the culture and the sights. One time I set out for a flea market in the city of Palermo. Vendors at the market sold everything: cheese, salamis, pastries, clothing. I stopped in the middle of the market, my humongous backpack weighing me down, a shameless tourist drinking in the sight of the market's hustle and bustle: people walking about, waving to each other, laughing, shouting, singing.

My eyes paused at the counter of a butcher shop, where a butcher and a customer were frowning at each other, confused. By lip-reading I could tell the customer, speaking English, was asking the butcher where his meat came from. The butcher, a tall, dark Sicilian with a bushy mustache and curly black hair, used pantomime to respond to the customer. He pointed in one direction, made a curve in the air with an open palm, formed a roof with his hands and arms, imitated different animals, and with open flat palms mimicked carrying something to the shop.

The English-speaking customer stared flatly back at the butcher. He slowly repeated the butcher's gesticulations, ambiguously pointing in a random direction. Then he blinked, swallowed, and repeated his question. I knew it was hopeless, that communication between the butcher and customer had broken down fully and there was a slim chance of bridging the gap unless someone intervened.

Maybe that someone could be me. Why not? I could clearly understand what each side was saying. And when you're on the road, it can get lonely. I was glad for a chance to interact with other people.

I took out my phone and tapped out my interpretation of the butcher's pantomime into the Notes app: *The butcher said he lives on a farm, somewhere up the hill that way. He raises different animals on his farm, and the meat comes from there.*

Comprehension lighted up the English-speaking customer's face.

A giant smile spread on the butcher's face below his bushy mustache, and both of them thanked me for my help. For once, the Deaf person had stepped in as an interpreter between two hearing people.

It's funny how communication can break down when there's a language barrier, and how bridges can be built using tried-and-true methods that we as a society are often quick to cast aside. I'd noticed how valuable pantomime can be as a tool of communication, especially during my travels. I gestured all the time, asking what time the train came, where the bus stop was, and so forth, all using my hands and face.

I looked up at the butcher at the Sicilian flea market; he handed me a bag of sausage links, on the house. It was a nice treat for a hungry and broke-ass backpacker.

My trip continued, and I visited Deaf friends in nearly every town I stopped at. About a quarter of my Deaf hosts were fellow students I had met at Gallaudet. These friends helped introduce me to other friends they knew across the European continent, who were more than happy to let me crash on their couches when I alighted on their hometowns. The interconnectedness of the Deaf community, a network tightly woven across oceans and continents, is one part of something I teasingly call #DeafGain—the many special benefits of being Deaf and claiming membership in the Deaf community.

Finally I descended on Sofia, Bulgaria. The Eastern European capital city was hosting the Summer Deaflympics, which is just like the Olympics, only with Deaf athletes. Most of the standard Olympic sports are competed at Deaflympics: track and field events, swimming, basketball, handball, volleyball, beach volleyball—you name it. Hundreds of the world's top Deaf athletes, from dozens of countries, come to compete at the Deaflympics.

I was excited to be at Sofia, and not just because I'd get the opportunity to see the world's best Deaf athletes compete. I was also expecting to see many of my friends from back home, and after traveling a while on my own, familiar faces would be a welcome sight. I also needed to find someone to talk to about what had happened in Reims. Before long, I found that someone.

Millie was one of my best friends. I'd known her since I moved to Maryland from Austin when I was in the sixth grade and we were in the same class, and we later enrolled at Gallaudet at the same time. She was one of my fellow evil raccoons in the misdeed that resulted in the airport evacuation in Guatemala. We had gone through a ton of stuff together, and I knew I could trust her.

While in a whirlwind seeing and catching up with old friends at the Deaflympics, I spotted Millie. I wanted to talk with her alone, to tell her everything. We went out with our friends to bars in Sofia, painting the town red. When the night was over, at four A.M., we were walking down the street alone, just us two.

I blurted out: ME MUST TELL YOU SOMETHING.

In the same beat she responded: SAME, ME MUST TELL YOU SOMETHING.

We told each other our news at nearly the same time.

I KISSED A BOY.

I KISSED A GIRL.

Our faces stretched out in surprise and happiness. I couldn't believe it—we'd been friends practically all our lives but hadn't the slightest clue that we both weren't straight until now. It reminded me, like the lesbian couple in Colombia had said, that I wasn't the only one embarking on this type of journey. There were lots and lots more like me out there who weren't 100 percent straight and were still trying to figure out their sexual identity.

I had been wracked with anxiety just before I told Millie, my heart hammering in my chest. I was about to reveal that I wasn't straight to someone who knew me from back home. What would happen? Would her perception of me change?

I needn't have worried. Millie was genuinely thrilled for me, and I for her. We peppered each other with questions, wanting to know everything about the other's experience. As with the women I'd met in Colombia, I saw zero judgment on Millie's face.

When we'd finished telling each other our stories, we asked each other: What does this mean? What did this make us, as far as our sexual identities? We stared into each other's eyes for a long time, then we broke out laughing. We had no clue. But we were on our journeys now, no turning back. And now we'd have each other as companions as we set forth.

I couldn't have picked a better person to reveal my secret to, and it made it so much easier and better having confided in someone who was going through a similar experience. A burden had been lifted off my shoulders. I was still nervous about talking about my LGBTQ identity, but now I had someone to confide in, who would back me up when I started exploring my new world in the United States. I hadn't yet immersed myself into the LGBTQ community or tried to introduce myself to my LGBTQ friends as one of their own. In that sense, Millie was my first LGBTQ friend.

I NEVER TOOK ALPHONSE UP on his offer to visit him at his home in France. I thought about it, but I was having too much fun backpacking across Europe, and I wanted to make the most of every minute I had abroad by seeing new places and meeting new people.

At the end of the summer, and after I returned to D.C. for my last semester at Gallaudet, my curiosity still burned. I thought often about the kiss with Alphonse and wanted to know if there was more there. Was it just a fleeting fancy, brought upon by the euphoria of an international Deaf festival, the romantic French countryside, and jugs of homemade vodka-spiked cocktails I'd chugged that evening? Or was the sensation genuine, a product of my own longing?

I wanted to continue to explore my sexual curiosity, so I downloaded Grindr and set up an account, taking care to keep my identity discreet—which meant using a photo of my torso only, with my head cropped out; giving my initials instead of spelling out my name in full; and blocking people I knew every time they popped up on my screen. I didn't use Grindr for very long. For one, it's an app primarily used for hooking up rather than for meeting and dating new people. And two, I didn't feel great about using the app while actively hiding my sexuality. It fed the conflicting feeling I had inside regarding my sexual identity—the sliver of doubt that lingered in the back of my head. So I deactivated my account and deleted the app from my phone.

That December I wrapped up my bachelor's degree at Gallaudet. When spring came, I floated around for a while, looking for a job, not sure what I wanted to do next. My brothers had their futures laid out with more certainty. Nico had graduated with a degree in information technology and started a career with a federal agency, and he was beginning to score some deejaying gigs on the weekends. Neal had graduated with a degree in physical education and started teaching PE at the school we'd all graduated from, Maryland School for the Deaf, and was working toward his master's degree in Deaf education.

While I pondered my future, I picked up a new activity: modeling. Taking photos and posting them on socials was something I liked to do as far back as middle school—I carried around a digital camera and posted my best shots on MySpace, LiveJournal, and so on. After I graduated from college, my hobby evolved into modeling, and— fueled by social media platforms like Instagram and Facebook—it gradually turned into a serious interest. I would post shots on my Instagram, and then I'd get Facebook messages (Instagram DMs weren't a thing yet) from local up-and-coming photographers saying they'd seen me on Instagram and wanted to do a test shoot. We'd agree on a place and time to meet up for the shoot, and while no cash was exchanged, both the photographer and I came away with photos to help build our portfolios. I'd post some of these test shoot photos on my Instagram, which attracted new followers to my account and a new round of photographers reaching out on Facebook for more test shoots. I'd repeat the cycle again and again, and my Instagram following picked up, slowly but surely.

As I dabbled in modeling and tried to figure my life out, I put less of a priority on understanding my sexuality. Things would stay that way for a little while more, because soon enough, I was going to get the opportunity of a lifetime.

# 12.

# Use Your Voice

For thousands of years, humans have continued to believe that the ability to move the mouth and activate the vocal cords to create specific sounds was what made humans special. Speech was, and continues to be, used as a dividing line between those who were intelligent beings and those who were less than. Throughout history, Deaf people who signed and did not use speech have often been viewed as unintelligent, even subhuman.

Sign languages have existed throughout human history, long before ASL and other contemporary sign languages were understood to be true languages. One reference to the usage of signs in ancient history can be found in Plato's Cratylus, in which the Greek philosopher Socrates states that Deaf people communicated with one another by making signs. Though Socrates acknowledged the existence of signs, he refused to endow them with the respect that he gave speech. In another work by Plato, Theaetetus, Socrates states that anyone "can show what he thinks about anything, unless he is deaf or dumb from the first."

The Code of Justinian, a complete compilation of Roman laws written in the sixth century, denied Deaf people citizenship and important legal rights and privileges. Well, unless they could speak. Then they were considered full citizens.

*Johann Konrad Ammann, a seventeenth-century Swiss doctor who devised a method to teach Deaf people how to speak, wrote: "The voice is a living emanation of that spirit that God breathed into man when he created him a living soul." Ammann one-upped Socrates and just straight-out said Deaf signers who couldn't speak were devoid of a soul.*

*For a long time—certainly as far back as Socrates's time—Deaf people were referred to as being deaf and dumb. The word "dumb" referred to Deaf people's inability to speak. The line of reasoning went: if Deaf people could not articulate audible words, then they were incapable of reason and forming intelligent thought. Never mind that signing Deaf people communicated in complex, fully realized signed languages, could read and write and solve advanced math problems, and could consider and discuss abstract concepts like love, God, life and death, and hope. Basically anything hearing people could talk about, we could, too.*

*Without the ability to speak, a signing Deaf person was valued little by general society.*


SCHOOL TODAY YOU LEARN WHAT? Mom asked me one afternoon when I was in kindergarten.

I thought about it for a minute. Then I pressed my lips together, pushed my tongue against a small air pocket inside my mouth, and opened my lips to release the air bubble.

"*Buh.*"

Mom stared at me blankly. WHAT? she asked.

It was the *b* sound, I told her. OH, she responded, using the *y* handshape sign that indicated understanding or interest.

GOOD, Mom said. WHAT ELSE?

I couldn't remember what I learned from any of my other classroom subjects. I just remembered spending a long time in the speech therapist's tiny classroom. She put my hand to her mouth so I could feel the soft burst of air when she made the *b* sound: "Buh." Then she had me practice pronouncing it. I tried, but I kept saying it wrong.

She told me to build up a balloon of air in my mouth, then push it out just as I opened my lips. She put my hand to her mouth again to feel the tepid gusts that came from her mouth. I tried again, my cheeks puffing out with pent-up air, then deflating with a *whoosh* as air escaped my lips.

ALMOST, she said.

Over and over I tried, until I finally got it: *"Buh."*

The speech therapist clapped in delight and gave me a piece of candy. I quickly chomped it down. She asked me to make the sound again. And again. And again.

*"Buh. Buh. Buh. Buh. Buh. Buh."*

*"Buh,"* I showed Mom again.

LEARN ANYTHING MATH CLASS? Mom asked. OR NEW WORDS, YOU LEARN TODAY?

I shrugged. "Buh" was all I could remember learning that day. I'd repeated that sound so many times that it was drilled into my head.

My response made Mom sad. It was so important to her that her boys receive a great education. As Deaf people, we'd needed a strong educational foundation to give us the tools to overcome the many barriers and challenges we'd face as we navigated the world.

Every single day, Mom wanted me and my brothers to come home from school bursting with new words, math concepts, or science lessons.

Instead, that day, I'd learned how to say "buh."

INTERVIEW FOR ANTM, THE SUBJECT of the email message read.

The email, sent in December of 2014, was from Rachelle, a casting director for *America's Next Top Model*, with whom I'd been exchanging messages for a while. In her email, she wrote that *ANTM* was narrowing down its list of potential competitors for the upcoming season cycle 22 and she asked to do an interview with me over video chat to help *ANTM* make their final casting decisions. The email told me, in essence, that I was knocking on the doorstep of a chance to compete on the show.

And yet the opportunity had very nearly flamed out before it began.

After discovering me on Instagram in September, Rachelle sent me a DM encouraging me to apply for cycle 22. I had received similar DMs from other strangers in the past, asking me to try out for some sort of opportunity. I rarely trusted them unless I could verify who the messenger was. I didn't know Rachelle, and I thought that her message might be a scam. So I ignored her DM.

A little while later, Rachelle sent a second DM. I started having second thoughts. *What if she was for real?* I asked myself. I went online to dig for more information and found a regional *ANTM* casting tryout representative's email address on an official *ANTM* website. I tapped out an email stating Rachelle's name and asking if she was for real. Indeed she was, the representative confirmed.

Cautiously, I answered Rachelle's DM. Right off the bat, I told her that I was Deaf. She responded that she had no idea and that she still thought I should apply and send in a video submission. She shared a list of things to include in the video.

*What the hell*, I thought, *I'll give it a shot.* I'd seen some other *ANTM* audition videos online; some of them were poorly made, with grainy resolution or recorded at an awkward camera angle because the applicant was holding her phone, selfie-style, as it filmed her.

If I was going to create a video submission, I would do it right. I called up a few of my Deaf friends: MJ, a talented videographer, and Jonaz and Derrick, whose opinions and advice I valued. MJ brought her own video camera equipment to make sure we could capture creative angles and perfect lighting, making for awesome, high-quality shots. I was still living near Gallaudet, so we used the university's field house and recorded film of me lifting weights and swishing three-point shots. For one shot, I even rose up for a dunk.

My friends encouraged me to share about my Deaf identity in the video. I shouldn't shy away from the topic, they said; rather, I should talk about my Deaf experience with pride. It would make me stand out from other applicants.

I hesitated at first. Did I really need to make my Deaf identity a focal point of my application to *ANTM*? It felt like a weak play, potentially setting me up as a token disabled guy in the competition. I didn't want to use the Deaf card as a way to get on the show. Anyone who is Deaf or has another disability shouldn't need to sell that aspect of their lives; they should be afforded the chance to qualify based on their merit. I wanted to earn this opportunity, not have it handed to me because I'd used my Deaf identity as a gimmick.

My friends understood where I came from, but they said that the flip side was true, too: I should be able to talk freely and proudly about my Deaf identity and experience because it was such an important part of who I am, and not have to worry about how it was affecting my chances of getting on the show. And the simple act of sharing about the Deaf community would do a ton of good—it would help shine a spotlight on Deaf people, who were often overlooked, misrepresented, or simply absent in mainstream media. By sharing my story, I could also be another type of model on the show—a role model who helped other marginalized people like myself develop their own stronger sense of self. The more my friends talked, the more I agreed with them. In the end I went along with their advice.

It was the first time I saw how portraying my Deaf identity could be a boon to my modeling prospects while also achieving a broader impact. MJ, Jonaz, and Derrick helped plant that seed, and it soon became a central aspect of how I portrayed myself. Being Deaf was different, unique, and damn cool—that was my banner, and I waved it with pride.

After submitting the video, I continued to exchange direct messages and emails with Rachelle. She kept asking me for different things, like a professional headshot, more background information about myself, and a summary of my modeling experience. Finally, she sent me the email requesting a video-call interview.

I needed an interpreter for the interview, so I asked Erin, a hearing friend from Gallaudet. She came to my home and sat by my side, facing my laptop screen and camera, during the interview.

Rachelle was super nice and had a fun, bubbly personality. She asked me different questions about my family, my modeling experience, and my Deaf identity, and she seemed genuinely interested in who I was and what I had to say. Before we started I was apprehensive and afraid that I'd screw up the interview. But Rachelle and I quickly settled into an easy rhythm, and I felt more and more confident in my chances of making it onto the show.

It was a relief to me that the interview was going well for another reason: I had a difficult question to ask Rachelle. I had decided that if I wasn't getting good vibes from the interview or sensed that the interest in me was weak, I was going to leave my question in my back pocket. However, midway through the interview, my fears had been sufficiently allayed, so I let my question fly.

"Is *ANTM* prepared for a Deaf model?"

There were certain things that needed to be in place in order for *ANTM* and me to make this work. At the top of the list was an ASL interpreter, and they weren't free. And, unfortunately, this cost has sometimes stood in the way of Deaf people getting the access they rightfully deserved, as my mom had taught me.

I wanted to be brutally honest and upfront. Appearing on *ANTM* was an incredible opportunity for me, but I knew that it came with some risk. I would be putting myself out there. If *ANTM* wound up being a poor partner, unprepared or unmotivated to work with me to ensure an equitable and accessible experience for me, the other contestants, and everyone else involved with the production, my time on the show would likely be a frustrating experience.

I needed to know: Was *ANTM* committed to working with me?

Not missing a beat, Rachelle smiled and said calmly and confidently that yes, *ANTM* was ready. They were excited about having a Deaf contestant on their show. Arranging and paying for an interpreter was no problem at all. They had a budget prepared and would work with me to find a talented professional interpreter who fit my communication style.

I felt somewhat satisfied by Rachelle's response, but I knew that talking about being prepared to work with a Deaf contestant was different from actually doing so. I would have to wait to see if *ANTM* followed through on their word. But at that point in the video call, I was reassured enough to accept an offer to appear on the show if I received one.

So far, Rachelle had built up a great deal of goodwill on *ANTM*'s behalf. I felt like I could trust her, and by proxy, the show. And then she asked her next question.

"Nyle, can you speak a few words for me?"

SURE, I responded. She asked me to state my name, my height and weight, my age, and where I was from. Simple.

ME NYLE. ME 6–2, 185. ME AGE TWENTY-FIVE. FROM WASHINGTON, D.C.

"Oh no," she said. "I want you to use your voice."

MY VOICE? I pointed at my mouth.

"Yes!" Rachelle giggled.

I paused. At that instant, all I could think of was the feeling of a soft puff of air bursting from my lips:

"*Buh. Buh. Buh.*"

It had taken me weeks to master that sound. Multiple sessions, a half hour to an hour each day, seated alone across my speech teacher. Endless repetition, rote training. And then, after all that time, I'd earned only the ability to push a ball of air out of my mouth in just the right manner, in order to produce a specific sound.

After mastering *b*, there would be a new sound waiting for me in the next speech lesson. And with this new sound was the old familiar drudgery. It started with staring fixedly at the speech teacher's lips as she made the sound again, and again, and again, until I had memorized every whisker of hair on her upper lip, every creased wrinkle on the corners of her mouth. And then the lesson turned from the visual to the tactile as the teacher held my fingertips before her maw, to feel the faintly moist bursts of air that moved from her lips; on her cheeks, jaw, and most often, her throat, to sense the different vibrations that rippled in miniature seismic waves from the depths of her voice box. When all the lessons from seeing and feeling were exhausted, it was time for me to attempt to replicate the sounds. From there, more endless repetition, interspersed by an occasional bribery of a candy bar or with the support of a tool in the form of a single piece of paper placed in front of my mouth as the speech teacher instructed me to make my lips move "just so."

Because I couldn't hear myself very well, I could barely self-correct when I was trying to pronounce. Wearing hearing aids didn't help very much—they just made the noises louder. I continued to struggle to identify and understand sounds, no matter how loud my hearing aids made them.

Learning a new sound was like trying to find a small metal key at the bottom of a dark, muddy lake. All I could do was dive toward the bottom and drag my hands along the silt, praying I'd somehow, miraculously come across the key. If I did so often enough and long enough, by sheer chance my fingertips would eventually strike cool, sharp metal.

I got a sound right!

Then there would come the fireworks—cheers from the speech teacher, more pieces of candy. Occasionally I scored a trip to McDonald's and a Happy Meal. Even though I was lured by the reward of an occasional meal of chicken nuggets and fries, my enthusiasm for speech lessons deflated year after year.

In second grade at the Texas School for the Deaf, speech lessons came with a twist: instead of learning speech alone with the speech teacher one-on-one, students shared speech lessons in a group setting. For the first time I saw that I was not alone in my frustration with the endless drudgery of speech lessons. My classmates also despised all we had to endure: the endless repetition, the feeling of stale air from the teacher's mouth in our palms, the continual sense of hand-dragging, without purpose or direction, across the bottom of the lake for a single, elusive metal key.

There was open rebellion. My classmates and I deliberately ignored the teacher. We used our hands to talk, the way that we were born to communicate. We stood up from our chairs and wandered around the classroom at our leisure. Whenever we did so, the speech teacher would suddenly pause the lesson and chirp "The chickens have flown the coop! The chickens have flown the coop!" At first I was startled by the teacher's strange behavior and odd turn of phrase. I jogged back to my seat, curious to see what would happen. The results were anticlimactic: she merely returned to the speech lesson. The next time, and dozens more times after that, we wandered around the classroom oblivious of the teacher's chirping, until the teacher, her voice box beaten down in more ways than one, mercifully stopped. The chickens had permanently settled outside the coop.

Just before third grade, I was in a meeting with my mom and teachers and administrators at the school. The topic of speech lessons came up. They notified me that due to scheduling issues, my speech lessons could only be scheduled for the time period in which I had my math class. I would have to choose which to take: math or speech lessons.

I recoiled instantly. Math was my favorite class. Math concepts came to me easily, and I genuinely enjoyed learning about and working with numbers. The teacher taught math in ASL, so I had complete access to the information I needed in order to learn and understand. Not only were the answers clear and concrete—two and two made four, period—I could also communicate the answer with ease. To answer two plus two, all I had to do was bend my thumb and put up four fingers.

I was good at math, too, and I liked letting my teachers and classmates know that I was good at it. Once in a while the teacher would distribute worksheets with about a hundred quick math problems—addition, subtraction, and multiplication—for us to zoom through in timed tests. I whizzed through mine, my mind spinning at a clean hundred miles per hour, the number 2 pencil buzzing and twitching in my hand as I knocked out problem after problem. I regularly posted the best, or near best, time of my class.

And now they were asking me to give up math class for speech

lessons? Swap the crystalline joy of numbers for the muddy black
waters of speech lessons? Nope. I immediately rose to object. The
administrators looked at each other and nodded. The principal explained to us that the speech lessons were a choice. I could choose not
to take them anymore.

My mom turned to me.

YOUR DECISION. WHAT YOU THINK?

I was still pretty young. Though speech lessons were a hectic bore
and a mighty struggle, there was still a chance I could make rapid
progress over the next few years. To decline speech lessons at that
point would be to essentially give up any shot at gaining passable
speech, ever.

But I wouldn't be giving up a slim chance at improving my speaking ability for nothing. If speech lessons were like searching the
muddy depths of a lake for a single key, then the rest of my classes—
math, language arts, science, physical education—in ASL were like
a cascading downpour of keys, landing on my head, shoulders, the
ground all around me. I merely had to open my hand and it would
overflow with them.

I was trading a slim, snowball's-chance-in-hell shot at speech for
a better, stronger educational foundation, one my mom knew I would
need in order to succeed as I grew up. I was swapping single-syllable
sounds for *more* fractions, algebra, geometry, and calculus; Dr. Seuss,
Lois Lowry, J. D. Salinger, and Shakespeare. I was conceding the ability to communicate in a specific way for an improved chance to maximize my mental dexterity, so I could think for myself—critically, openly,
widely—about any topic in the wide world.

SPEECH LESSONS NO-MORE.

Almost twenty years had passed since that meeting. In all that
time, I'd never had a single request to use my voice in a formal setting,
like an interview—until Rachelle asked.

Prior to her request, I had already explained to Rachelle that I'd
been Deaf my entire life, that I had little residual hearing, and that my

primary language and method of communication was ASL. Despite knowing all this, she still asked me to use my voice.

Rachelle probably didn't know, but it was an insensitive request to make of a Deaf person who communicates primarily in ASL. In fact, a lot of Deaf people would have found the request to be deeply offensive. First of all, the request implies that speech is a superior form of communication compared to signing. It completely disregards the Deaf person's ability to communicate in sign language, instead shifting the focus to whether or not the Deaf person can communicate the hearing person's way. It's a test to see if the Deaf person can pass as a hearing person. Second, it's humiliating and dehumanizing. Making that request is akin to holding up a treat and asking a puppy to perform a trick.

I thought about explaining all this to Rachelle, but I decided against it. If I had the opportunity to appear on the show, then I could work to build trust. Once folks on *ANTM* knew me better and had a stronger understanding of Deaf culture, I could try to address these sorts of issues. By then, I would be in a better position to make positive changes by—pun fully intended—using my voice.

So I tried another strategy: I explained to Rachelle again that ASL was my primary way of communicating, and that, to be quite blunt, I couldn't speak for shit. I hoped my stark honesty would make it clear that it wouldn't even be worth trying and cause Rachelle to withdraw her request. It was not to be.

"That's okay," she said with a beatific smile. "I just want to hear your voice." She leaned forward, rested her chin on her fist, batted her eyelashes. Her lips curled into a mischievous smile. It was an insensitive request, but she had made it in such a flirtatious way it confused the hell out of me.

I made an action in my gullet that I hoped was how people cleared their throats. I felt so conflicted, as if I was betraying my Deaf identity by attempting to speak. I brushed the thought aside and opened my mouth to voice the words that she asked me to. Uncomfortably, I moved my lips and tongue and activated my voice box. Doing these things felt deeply unnatural to me, and I was embarrassed doing them in front of someone I barely knew. The words bumbled out of my mouth like fat, croaking toads.

Rachelle's face remained frozen in her angelic smile. "Thank you! That was great," she said. The whole time, her face never changed; I couldn't detect what she really thought of my voice. We spoke for a few more minutes, and then we wrapped up the interview and hung up.

There was one more person who had heard my voice: my interpreter, Erin. I braced myself for the worst, but some small part of me held out the slimmest hope that somehow, my speech lessons up to the second grade had granted me enough skill to have spoken these few words passably.

"So. How was my voice?" I asked her. "Don't lie, please. Give it to me straight."

She winced and laughed. "You were terrible."

Sheepishly, I buried my face in my palms.

Two weeks later, I got another email from Rachelle. *Congratulations!* it read. *You're going to be on* ANTM cycle 22.

# 13.

# I'm Sold

In February 2015, at around the same time that I received the invitation to compete on America's Next Top Model, I was offered an acting role on the Freeform channel show Switched at Birth. Filming for both shows was to occur at the same time, and I could pick only one.

I was torn. Both were great opportunities. I had a passion for modeling that ANTM could help nurture, but I also had my eye on acting, and Switched at Birth could be my shot at Hollywood.

I talked with everyone I knew—my mom, brothers, my closest friends—but I didn't get any closer to deciding.

In the end I decided to leave the decision to Foxy, the inordinately intelligent dog Hannah had rescued when we were at Gallaudet. I took two tennis balls, wrote ANTM on one and SAB on the other with a Sharpie, and placed them on the grass ten yards away from Foxy. The ol' girl sat patiently until I shouted my command. Then she was off, galloping toward the tennis balls. She closed in on one, sniffed at it, opened her snout, and picked it up. For a moment she held that ball in her jaw.

And then she dropped it, picked up the other one, and gave it to me. I turned the ball around to read what it said.

ANTM.

ONE MORE STEP, AND THERE is nothing but fifty feet of empty air separating me from the packed dirt far below. I am standing on the edge
of a two-foot-wide runway supported by steel beams perched top of a
tower of shipping containers stacked five high. The wind blows warm
L.A. spring air in my face. I adjust my harness, which is attached to a
pair of cables leading to a crane high above me. On my next step, the
cables will determine my fate. If they hold, allowing me to walk on
nothing but air to the opposite shipping container stack, I am safe.
If the cables drop and lower me to the ground, I am eliminated from
the competition, which has barely begun. In the brief moment before
I lift my feet off the edge and attempt to make footprints in the air, I
am strangely relaxed.

I know, with absolute certainty, that the cables will hold.

I STOOD AT THE EDGE of a crowd of twenty-two handsome and gorgeous humans. Their bodies and faces buzzed with movement: bursts
of laughter, anxious tucking of hair behind ears, elbows playfully
thrown into ribcages. This was *America's Next Top Model* cycle 22 and
we were gathered in the large living area of the mansion where the
castmates were staying for the filming of the show.

A producer stepped in front of us and the buzzing movement
quieted.

"Hello, models!" the producer began. Right next to her was Ramon, an ASL interpreter that *ANTM* had hired. They were off to a
good start in upholding Rachelle's promise of accessibility.

My castmates hooted and cheered in response. Their energy was
contagious; I lifted up my fists and let out a holler. The curtains had
lifted on the *ANTM* competition, the cameras were rolling, and I was
amped.

A few days before, as a group of thirty, the competing models of
*ANTM* cycle 22 toured the heart of L.A. on a double-decker bus. In
the middle of the tour, the bus pulled over to the side of the street.
One by one, the models climbed to the front, stripped down to our

bathing suits, and posed for photos. Yu Tsai, the *ANTM* creative consultant, looked on.

From watching episodes of the previous *ANTM* season, I knew Yu Tsai was not someone I wanted to mess with. During photo shoots, he scrutinized the models with an intensely critical eye. He wasn't afraid to deliver scathing, brutally honest criticism to a model if he disliked something he saw—a weak pose, awkward limb placement, lack of emotion in the face. His criticism was delivered in a stream-of-consciousness manner, and he wove in references and nicknames, which injected humor but could make his message super harsh. Sometimes he toed the line. Later on in the show, he made a habit of referring to me as "hearing impaired," a term that I and many Deaf people consider offensive. The term stems from the medical view of Deaf people, focusing on what we lack. It frames us as broken, reducing the identity of our whole being to the ineffectiveness of our ears. Our community, our language, our culture—all of that is stripped away by that term. That's why many of us prefer "Deaf"—it's a word we rightfully claim as ours, representative of our way of life. (Others with hearing loss may have different preferred labels, like hard of hearing or late deafened. If you're uncertain which term to use, you can simply ask someone about their preference.)

The first few times Yu called me hearing impaired, it rankled me. I didn't know for sure if Yu was aware that I found the term offensive. I thought about approaching him and telling him to knock it off, but I wasn't sure that would be the best thing to do. I reminded myself that even if he knew, he was probably pressing my buttons and trying to get under my skin. And then I remembered watching many reality shows, like *The Real World*, and finding myself loathing cast members who were dramatic and kicked up a big fuss over conflicts. I also thought that I couldn't afford to make any mistakes. I worried that if I complained, I'd be removed from the show. In the end I just decided to start ignoring Yu when he used that term and set my eyes on winning the competition, which would ultimately make a far bigger impact.

Aside from his tendency to blatantly disregard political correctness, Yu had one gift in his art of delivering criticism that I could appreciate. He could tell you, with crystal clarity, just how he felt— disgust, contempt, impatience, deep disappointment, sometimes all of the above—using only his face. He didn't need to utter a single word. He had sharp, arched eyebrows, and he would send one up his forehead like a slingshot whenever he thought a model was doing something completely idiotic. Simultaneously, he'd bare his teeth in a lopsided sneer. When he made this expression, it felt like a whip-crack warning.

While waiting for my turn to model on the double-decker bus I kept looking at how Yu was treating other models as they posed in their bathing suits. I winced every time he delivered a verbal lashing or waved off a model with bored disappointment: "You're done! Get out of here."

I gulped. I had very little formal experience as a model. Yu was a pit bull and I was raw T-bone steak; he was gonna chew me up and spit out the bone and lick his lips afterward.

My turn was up. Woodenly, I walked to the front of the bus, undressed to my bathing suit, took a deep breath, and faced Yu and the camera. The next few moments flashed by, literally and figuratively, and then it was over. Yu gave me a thumbs-up and ushered me away, already turning his laser eye to the next model.

That first shoot was a blur; I wasn't sure how I had done.

YOU DID GOOD! Ramon, the interpreter, assured me. HE KISS-FIST [loved] YOU.

The bus then turned the corner onto Hollywood Boulevard, where a jam-packed crowd and a red-carpet runway waited for us. Yu Tsai introduced judges Kelly Cutrone and Miss J, who drew huge cheers. But no cheer was crazier than for Tyra Banks, the creator and host of *ANTM*. Her presence was the first thing that I noticed: an aura of cool confidence enveloped her.

Tyra strolled all the way down to the red carpet, where she gave a brief speech to the crowd. She spoke about how *ANTM* set itself apart

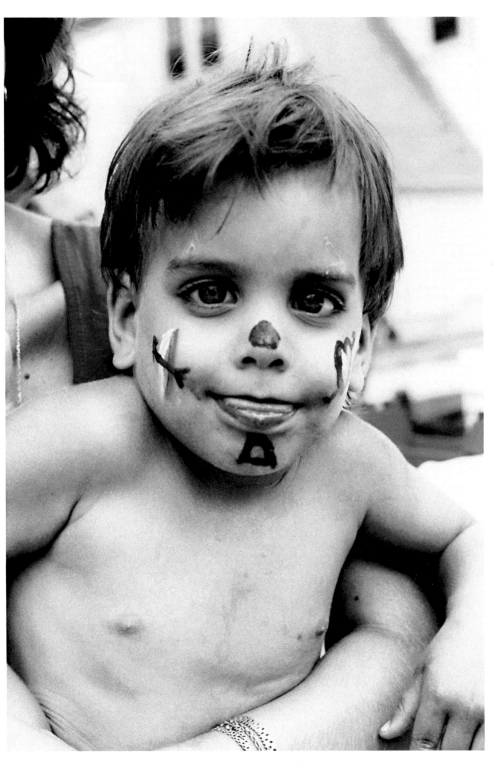

Getting my face painted at a block party!

My twin brother, Nico, showing me who's the boss.

Learning how to read with my mom! She helped me build a
strong language foundation in both ASL and English.

Giving my mom some sugar! In Queens, New York.

My mother reading aloud to me, Nico, and my classmates at
Lexington School for the Deaf.

My brothers and me in Montana, ready for some rough riding!
(Actually, with Nico driving, we probably went at a reasonably
safe speed.)

Three brothers under the scorching sun in Moab, Utah.

We rocked the tank top and short shorts look. (We still do!)

Gotta pose for the camera! Little League in Queens.

Back in the good old participant-award days: Me, Neal, and Nico in Austin, Texas.

When "Gangnam Style" went viral in 2012.

Cycling through the streets of Ghent, Belgium.

Out on an adventure with my childhood friends Brittany and Misella.

A gorgeous view in Bruges, Belgium.

Foxy preventing me from going to class at Gallaudet University.

My mom, Donna DiMarco, giving me a run for
my money on *ANTM*. Modeling with Mom was an
unforgettable experience!

Striking a pose on the beach during
*America's Next Top Model*. Yu is
probably just outside the frame, yelling
and gesturing out instructions.

Hanging out with my beautiful and talented dance teacher and partner, Peta, during a filmed *Dancing with the Stars* interview.

Tyra popped in for a surprise visit during a *DWTS* practice session. Between us is my ubertalented manager, Sami.

My mom holding my Mirrorball Trophy. I'm glad she was by
my side for two of the greatest moments of my life, winning
*ANTM* and *DWTS*.

Peta and me celebrating our *DWTS* win. The moment felt so surreal, and I couldn't stop smiling all night.

Rubbing my hands,
getting ready to share
more Deaf stories
with the world.

from other reality modeling competition shows. The other shows, Tyra said, "put beauty in a little circle, and say 'you have to look like this to be a model.'" But *ANTM*, Tyra proudly proclaimed, said "to hell with that."

In a way, I felt like she was speaking directly to me.

The challenge began. Two by two, we took on the red-carpet runway. The show had planted hecklers and protesters who stood in our way and waved signs and yelled in our faces, trying to throw us off. I barely remember walking the runway. My stomach was churning, the very tips of my toes and fingers were tingling, and my vision swam at the edges. I stepped off the bus and was back on it the very next moment.

Soon after, the judges made their picks and eliminated eight models; the remaining twenty-two moved into the mansion, where we stayed for the rest of the competition. I heaved a sigh of relief. We'd completed the very first phase of the competition.

And now the twenty-two of us, buzzing with excitement, were standing before the producer at the mansion as she began telling us about our next task.

"At the end of the day," the producer continued, "there will be fourteen of you." The buzzing in the crowd slowed. Eight more would be culled from our ranks.

"The decision of who stays and who goes will be made by Tyra and an executive in charge of reality programming at CW. To help them decide, you will have the opportunity to make the case for why *you* should stay. Today, each of you will go alone before Tyra and the CW executive to make your pitch. You will have two minutes."

One hundred and twenty seconds. That's all the time we would have to convince Tyra and the CW executive that we should stay.

As soon as the producer made her announcement, I knew exactly what I was going to say. The seeds of my pitch had been planted when I was filming my video submission for *ANTM* and my friends had encouraged me to share details about my Deaf identity. Ever since then, I had been thinking more and more about the topic. I thought about what my Deaf identity meant to me, and what it meant to others—both people who were Deaf and people who were hearing.

In the weeks leading up to the *ANTM* competition, I'd opened up my laptop and done some research. My first question was: How many Deaf people are there in the United States? I found a statistic from a U.S. census program that estimated there were around ten million Deaf or hard of hearing people in our country, a number roughly equal to the population of the entire state of Michigan. (Hard of hearing refers to people who have mild to severe hearing loss but generally retain enough residual hearing for some level of aural communication functionality.)

Now, how about the world? How many Deaf and hard of hearing people existed on earth? The World Health Organization gave me my answer: nearly 360 million people. That was way more than I had thought. Put one way, there were more Deaf people on Earth than there were Americans.

All those Deaf people . . . and they were experiencing life in similar ways as I did.

I thought about the biggest challenges that Deaf people face. An obvious example, one that my mom had taught me and my brothers to prepare for, was discrimination. Perception was another. The average hearing person doesn't know very much about Deaf people, so they rely on preconceived notions, stereotypes. So often, Deaf people are never given a fair shot. Because they usually find it difficult to communicate with us, hearing people write us off. They have low expectations of our intelligence and our capacity to learn.

I came across another important statistic, one that very few people are aware of: about 90 percent of Deaf children are born to hearing parents, and sometimes that Deaf child is the first Deaf person these hearing parents will ever have met. Many Deaf children grow up in households where they struggle to gain access to language; their parents may not sign, and the speech and listening methods they try with their child may not work. Due to lack of access to language, these Deaf children become language deprived—which happened to my father. By the time these kids hit middle or high school, their language acquisition is severely delayed: they're unable to express and comprehend either English or ASL as well as they should at their age. This impacts them in many other ways: they may struggle to understand key concepts of math, science, and history; they are unable to develop important basic social skills; and often their emotional development is stunted.

Reading about all this, I flashed back to when I was a student at Gallaudet, sitting in my dorm room with a beer in my hand on a Friday night, listening to my friend Barry tell his story. Barry was Deaf but had grown up without learning ASL. He wore hearing aids, had learned to speak fairly well, and had attended mainstream school all his life. His first day at Gallaudet, he walked onto campus with next to zero ASL fluency.

The signing environment on campus hit him like a fist to the mouth, and he busted his butt learning a new language while working on his college degree. Along the way he met and fell in love with a Deaf woman. By his senior year, when he was telling me his story, he had advanced his signing fluency enough to communicate in ASL without much difficulty. He was getting the hang of this new language that was 100 percent accessible to him, and it gave him a newfound swagger. He was getting cocky about his signing ability—until he started his internship at the Deaf elementary school on the Gallaudet campus, where he worked with a class of Deaf kindergarteners.

He shook his head when he started telling me about the kids he worked with.

"The first day, before I start, I'm feeling pretty good about myself. I'm a cool, funny dude, right? I figure I'll keep it light, crack a few jokes, and these kids are gonna love me. They're kindergarten kids; it doesn't take much to impress them. Right?"

I nodded along. Barry was indeed a cool dude, and I could imagine him being a hit with the little kiddos.

"I couldn't have been more wrong." He paused for a deep swig of beer. "I walk into class, and this kid walks up to me and signs something.

He's quick and sloppy, but his ASL's good, it's all natural to him. I understand none of it. It's too fast for me. I ask him to sign again, and he gives me this look and walks away. I watch the kid go up to another student, and they start signing to each other, and I still don't understand what they're saying."

I cracked up. Barry was suppressing a smile in the corner of his mouth as he told the story, fully cognizant of the humorous absurdity of the situation.

"It dawns on me: the kindergarten kids sign way better than me."

He took another drink and pounded his can down on the coffee table.

"It's bullshit!" He laughed. "I'm twenty-two, a college senior. I worked my ass off to learn ASL. I thought I was getting to be pretty good. But it turns out I'm not even on the level of a six-year-old signer."

I told Barry he must be exaggerating; he *was* getting better and better.

"Maybe. But I'm telling you, these kindergarten kids made me look bad. I wish I learned to sign while growing up."

I've thought a lot about kids who grew up like Barry but never had the chance to attend Gallaudet or learn ASL or develop meaningful connections with other Deaf people like themselves. Some Deaf children even grow up thinking they'll die before they become adults, because they've never seen a Deaf adult. They watch TV, but they don't see Deaf people onscreen. Deaf representation in media and entertainment is growing, but there are still so few Deaf people in entertainment that the odds of running across one on TV are ridiculously low. And so some of these Deaf children cannot imagine that Deaf adults *exist* in this world, let alone flourish.

At first I was disheartened when I put together all my research. So many Deaf people were struggling due to reasons entirely out of their control. But I felt a glimmer of hope that things could get better. And I believed appearing in *ANTM* was an opportunity for me to help bring forth that change.

I STEPPED INTO THE ROOM, a small auditorium. In the front row, Tyra Banks and the CW executive were seated next to each other. To the right of the executive was my interpreter, Ramon.

I walked over and turned to stand in front of them. I took a deep breath and began.

"Hi. I'm Nyle DiMarco. I'm Deaf. My whole family—my mom, dad, and two brothers, including a twin—are Deaf. I'm the fifth generation in my family to be born Deaf.

"American Sign Language is my first language. I love being Deaf. I'm proud of it.

"There are ten million Deaf people in the United States; 360 million worldwide. Deaf people are also part of the disability community; there are more than fifty-five million Americans with disabilities—equal to one in every five Americans.

"The world has very little idea of what Deaf people are capable of. We're often written off without being given a real shot. We are stereotyped as helpless and less intelligent. We are denied access to education and language. We face discrimination each and every day, and we have to battle to overcome barriers all the time.

"Being born to Deaf parents myself, I am in the minority. Nine out of ten Deaf children are born to hearing parents. These parents need more resources to better understand their Deaf children, and to believe that their Deaf kids have limitless potential. They need to see Deaf adult role models who show the tremendous successes that their Deaf kids can reach.

"Right now, on TV, there's so little representation of the Deaf and disability communities. We're not seeing ourselves reflected on the screen often enough, and the world is not seeing us for who we really are, and what we're truly capable of.

"I want to change that. I am starting right here and now, on *ANTM*. I'm here for them—the hundreds of millions of Deaf and disabled people in the United States and the world. I want them to know if I can succeed, they can, too.

"I'm here to win, not for myself, but for my Deaf and disabled communities."

My hands dropped, pausing my pitch. Ramon continued to speak, translating my final words from ASL to English. After he finished speaking, he titled his head slightly and jabbed a finger in the direction of the CW executive and signed to me: HE SAID, "I'M SOLD."

The CW executive had spoken under his breath to Tyra, and by all indications, had never intended his words for me. He most likely didn't realize that an interpreter's job is to interpret all spoken words and other sounds they hear. It's not the interpreter's responsibility to guess the intent of the speaker and filter out what should be interpreted or not. If a skilled and professional interpreter hears something, they will make their best effort to relay it to the Deaf audience. I mean everything, including cuss words. The interpreter is not there as a censor or a moral purifier of language.

It goes both ways, too—if a Deaf person mumbles something not intended for the hearing person, the interpreter should translate it into spoken English for the hearing audience present.

That's the way it should be. Unfiltered, no-barriers interpreting helps make access a little more equal for all involved, both Deaf and hearing.

The CW executive hadn't the slightest clue of how ASL interpreting works, and as a result, he had unwittingly tipped me off to his glowing assessment of my pitch.

I knew then that my path to the top fourteen on *ANTM* was pretty much guaranteed. I had more to say in my pitch, but I knew I didn't need to continue. I couldn't help the giant smile that had spread across my face. I thanked Tyra and the executive and walked off the stage.

"HOW DO YOU FEEL? WHAT do you think is going to happen? Think you'll stay or go home?" a producer asked me, just before I climbed up to the top of the shipping container tower and took my fateful step into the air.

"I feel good. I'm not worried," I told her. She must've thought I looked too calm; her face scrunched up into a frown.

"Aren't you nervous at all?"

"Nope," I told her. "I'm confident. The cables are going to hold, and I'm going to make it across."

The producer nodded slowly, faint confusion on her face, probably thinking that either I knew something I shouldn't, or I was the most overconfident, bordering-on-delusional bastard she'd ever met.

On the top of the shipping container, I pulled on the harness, strapped myself tight, and tugged on the cables. In the distance, the sun was setting, casting a warm glow on the packed dirt far below. I scanned the crowd of people: my castmates, the producers and production crew, Yu Tsai, and Ramon. They watched, anxious for me to take my first step into the air and see how the cables responded. I started walking on the narrow runway until I ran out of metal surface to lay my feet on.

Just before I stepped into the air, I felt little butterflies flare up in my tummy. It wasn't a last-minute charge of doubt. It was a feeling loaded with hope and sheer bright-eyed enthusiasm: I was excited to see what awaited me with this next step, and the rest of my *ANTM* journey.

I took a deep breath and lifted one foot forward.

# 14.

# War Heroes

In the 1970s, a Deaf scholar named Dr. Tom Humphries invented a new word: "audism." It meant "the notion that one is superior based on one's ability to hear or behave in the manner of one who hears."

Audism isn't just discrimination against those who are Deaf and hard of hearing. It's a belief that pervades our systems and people. It's the feeling, deep in the bones and seared into the consciousness of hearing people, that people who are Deaf are beneath those who can hear. That we're not worthy of people's time and attention. Of gaining access to language, education, information, entertainment, the world. Of the right to exist.

For as long as there have been humans, there have been Deaf people. And as long as there have been Deaf people, there's been audism. It's existed, all around us, for tens of thousands of years, manifesting in many different forms: Schoolteachers cracking wooden rulers on hands to punish Deaf children for signing. Parents hushing their child at the dinner table, saying, "I'll tell you later." Alexander Graham Bell discouraging Deaf people to marry and procreate, fearing they would form a so-called Deaf race. And today, the threat of CRISPR, a burgeoning technology capable of changing DNA sequences, editing and erasing Deaf genes before a fetus even forms.

*This hate, this anger, this deep disdain—it's swirled around us for all this time, starting when we were cavemen to the smartphone-wielding humans we are today. All this time, Deaf people have felt it, suffered, and endured.*

*All this time, we never had a word for what we were experiencing. We knew it was happening, but we could not explain it. We couldn't point to it and say, aha, that's what that is! We just knew it as frustration, anger, futility . . . and hurt. Deep, deep hurt.*

*After tens of thousands of years of existing as oppressed people, we finally corralled the source of our pain. At last, we gave it a name.*

*Audism.*

*Even before this kind of discrimination was named, Deaf people had fought against it, pushing back against the deep pain it inflicted on us.*

*Once it had a name, we started to learn more about it. We began to understand it better and figure out why it was happening, what forms it took, and how it evolved and adapted through the years.*

*And then we started learning how to defeat it.*

IN THE FOURTH EPISODE OF *America's Next Top Model* cycle 22 my castmates and I ride the *ANTM* party bus to a dirt clearing with field tents and camouflage armored trucks and tanks. Yu Tsai introduces us to a man and a woman wearing prosthetics. They are military vets who had lost limbs while serving in Afghanistan. They each tell their stories of heart-wrenching sacrifice, and my castmates and I tear up.

The camera cuts to me in a confessional interview. I share my thoughts: "Their stories were inspiring to me, because we have kind of a parallel life, you know? They have prosthetics, but they still go through life. They live life. And me being Deaf, I just truck through life, and I think we have a similar experience."

The scene switches back to the veterans. After they finish talking, the camera cuts to me and the male veteran. I've approached him, wanting to learn more about his story. We are both disabled, and I deeply empathize with him. A castmate says, "Have you met Nyle?

He's hearing impaired." I take out my phone to communicate; he responds using his voice, and I squint to catch the words coming out of his mouth. It is a brief conversation, a connection between two people who share a common experience.

Then I'm back in the confessional booth, confiding: "I think it really hit me that in this competition, I do feel more disabled. I'm the one person who hasn't been able to use my native language, American Sign Language, and I do feel lonely in this competition. I can front relatively easy, and I don't lose myself in public, but of course nobody wants to be invisible."

The camera cuts to me at the dirt clearing, standing alone behind a trailer. My eyes are swollen with emotion and I take deep breaths, trying to compose myself.

Next, my castmates and I take turns for our photo shoots, posing with the vets. My turn comes, and I nail the shoot. Yu is effervescent in his praise for my work, especially impressed by my ability to listen to direction and execute what is asked of me.

The success of the photo shoot is a jubilant rebound from my emotional breakdown mere minutes before in the episode. I have stared down loneliness and despair, brought upon me by my deafness, and have emerged resilient and victorious.

WHOA, WHAT A TEARJERKER OF an episode, one that gets you right in the feels. In ASL, the sign for that emotion is literally TOUCH—on your chest where the heart is. If anything, that episode was HEART-TOUCH.

Here seems like a good moment for a breather, so let's pause the episode, take a few deep lung-filling breaths, and get ourselves to a good, stable place emotionally. Trust me, you'll want to be on firm ground for what comes next.

You know the saying "Things aren't always what they seem"? In general, this is good advice to bear in mind; keeping a bit of skepticism in your back pocket is just a smart precaution as you go through life. It's especially effective when applied to certain situations, like, say, watching a reality show. Of course we know it isn't all reality— some of it is a bunch of cleverly edited fibs to craft a compelling narrative and draw eyeballs for ratings and advertising money.

Which is kind of what happened in this event on the fourth episode of *ANTM* cycle 22, which I had named in my head "War Heroes" in honor of the veterans. There were slivers of the truth there, but it was cut up and rearranged and manipulated, until the day with the veterans came out on TV looking completely different than the day I'd actually lived through.

The truth was, on that day I'd felt utterly oppressed as a Deaf man, which had happened very few other times in my life. The experience surprised and rocked me to the core.

When the episode aired, reliving that day pissed me off all over again. I had typed up drafts so I'd be ready to live tweet the episode, but I soon deleted them. What was being shown on the screen was far different from my actual remembered experience.

I felt cheated. Not because the episode had twisted the truth—I could deal with that. No, I was frustrated more because it missed a golden opportunity to share a critical lesson about the importance of access.

After seeing the episode, I told myself then that when the time was right and the ideal opportunity presented itself, I would tell the story of what really happened on that day. So let's go back to the beginning of that episode and press play again, this time with me narrating the true story of that episode.

The first fib is that the events shown in the episode were not from the fourth week of the competition—it was the fourth week only in reality TV time. In real life, we were only around a week and a half into the competition. My interpreter, Ramon, was fried. He'd been working nonstop at all hours of the day, for a week and a half straight. Even the best interpreters need a break, and Ramon was no different. The *ANTM* producers agreed to book another interpreter for the photo shoot. They told me not to worry, they'd take care of it.

The morning of the photo shoot, my castmates and I woke at

five A.M. and loaded onto the party bus to make our trip to the photo shoot location. The blinds on the windows of the bus were fully drawn; we were afforded no hints or clues en route to the shoot site. We were also "on ice," which, in reality TV speak, meant my castmates and I couldn't talk with each other. The producers wanted us to save the juicy bits—the poignant, relationship-building moments and spicy, dramatic catfights—for when the cameras were turned on. When they were off, which was probably about 90 percent of the time, we were on ice and left alone with our thoughts. We had a couple production assistants, or PAs, with us at nearly all times, whether at the house where we were staying or on the party bus. The PAs enforced ice time, and I called them our babysitters. At first I tried bringing a book to read when on ice during party bus rides, but the babysitters took it away. I guess they didn't want my mind escaping into a separate world, receiving nourishment and relaxation elsewhere through words, and perhaps making it easier to maintain a grip on my sanity. Most times we couldn't even enjoy the scenery when we were on ice on bus rides, because, remember, the blinds were often drawn to block us from looking out the windows and guessing where we were headed. We were left with two options: take a nap or have conversations with ourselves in our heads.

That morning, I'd chosen the former, catching a few moments of shut-eye when the bus rolled to a stop. My castmates slowly came to life. We stood up, stretched, and looked at each other in excitement. I could sense the tips of my castmates' tongues twitching, awaiting the moment ice time ended and they could blab their jolly mouths off. I held my Oppo phone, my main tool of communication. Oppo, the phone company, is based in China. The phone's keyboard was a little off—some of the letters weren't in their usual places—and I found it difficult to type on. Still, the phone was often my sole channel of communication with my castmates and I had it on me at all times.

My castmates and I were ready to get off the bus and check out where the heck they had driven us for the photo shoot. But before they let us out, a producer boarded the bus and pulled me toward the back.

He wrapped his arms around me, forming a football huddle, and handed me a note close to my chest so my castmates wouldn't see it.

*We were not able to schedule an interpreter for today*, the note read.

I looked up at the producer. He had a look on his face that said, *Don't worry, you're going to be fine.*

He started scribbling $x$'s on the piece of paper. There were two rows of $x$'s on one side of the paper. He pointed to one $x$ and then to me, indicating that I was the $x$. There were three more $x$'s on the opposite side of the paper. He pointed at them and wrote out that we were going to meet two military veterans. The $x$ in the middle was Yu Tsai. The two $x$'s on either side were Veteran 1 and Veteran 2. The producer wrote on: Yu was going to speak first, then bring out the two veterans. Veteran 1 would speak. And then Veteran 2 would speak. The producer didn't expound on what each veteran would be talking about. I assumed their messages would be brief, if the producer didn't think it worthy of further explanation.

*Short and sweet*, the producer wrote. He looked up, gave me a thumbs-up, and told me to keep this information to myself and not tell the other castmates.

Now, it probably should have seemed terrifying to me to be taking on a photo shoot competition without an interpreter. Nobody was going to be communicating in my language. I would be limited to catching a spare word here and there by lip-reading. I was going to miss nearly all of the information that would be shared.

But, strangely, I was feeling a lot more confident than anybody in that situation deserved to. A small part of the reason why was the way the producer had written everything down. I thought it was going to be, as he'd explained, short and sweet. The event looked simple enough that I could scrape by without an interpreter. I also didn't worry too much about the photo shoot. Ninety-nine percent of my modeling work in the past was with hearing photographers, with no interpreter. I was sure I'd be fine here, especially working with Yu Tsai, with whom I was starting to develop a strong rapport.

But the biggest explanation for why I was feeling an irrational, completely undeserved amount of confidence at that moment, while standing on the precipice of an accessibility nightmare and potential elimination from the competition, was what had happened in fifth grade math class the year I went to the public school in Austin, Texas.

You'll recall from earlier in this book that I was the only Deaf student out of dozens of hearing students in my math class. Every day we'd get worksheets from the teacher to complete for homework. The worksheets had all sorts of questions and problems—multiple choice, show-your-work, word problems. Each worksheet had at least twenty questions, sometimes thirty or even forty. Some questions were easy; some were difficult, but because of the number of questions, they often took a long time to finish.

When I received the first homework worksheet at the start of the year, I noticed that the teacher circled a few of the questions or problems. There were twenty questions in this worksheet, but the teacher circled only five. I assumed that the teacher expected us to answer only the questions that were circled. That's what I did, and I handed it in the next day. When I got the worksheet back, graded, I got high marks.

The next worksheet I received from the teacher, same thing. It had thirty questions in all, but only a few—eight this time—were circled. I finished the circled problems, handed the worksheet in, got high marks again. Every worksheet after that was the same: I always completed the circled questions and was never penalized for not finishing the rest of the questions on the worksheet.

I didn't sense anything odd about this practice. My guess was the teacher saw little value in having her students complete all of the worksheets' questions, instead preferring to select specific questions that related to her lecture of the day. Having only a few to work on was a relief to me, because these worksheets had a lot of questions and it would have required a ton of time to answer them all. Every day, I zipped through my math homework on the bus ride back home, and always got the problems done by the time the bus rolled up to my doorstep. With homework out of the way, I had plenty of sunlight left to go outside and ride my bike around with Nico and our hearing friends from our neighborhood until bedtime. I had no qualms with the situation with the circled questions, and I was sure that my classmates were of the same mind.

At least, that's what I thought, until one day in class when the teacher was handing out our graded worksheets and I caught a peek at the worksheet being handed out to the girl next to me. There were no circles around any of the questions; she'd answered every question. And the kicker was, she had gotten a lower score despite doing three times the work I had done.

Perplexed, the next day I kept my eye on the worksheets handed back to the kids on either side of me. Again, there were no circled questions on their worksheets; they'd answered every question and gotten lower scores than me.

I had confirmation: I was being asked to do less work than the hearing kids in my math class. Even as young as I was then, eleven years old, I knew right away the reason why.

One of the more common assumptions people make about Deaf people is that we aren't as smart and capable as hearing people. They set the bar lower for Deaf people—just like my fifth-grade math teacher did for me compared to the other students in my class. And they let you get away with stuff, like only answering five questions instead of the twenty that your classmates were assigned.

Fifth-grade me loved the different treatment I received. No way was I going to complain and demand, on principle, that the teacher assign me the same number of worksheet questions as my classmates. Every afternoon that entire school year, I finished my circled questions on the bus ride home and arrived home homework-free with plenty of time to play outside before sundown. I wasn't breaking the rules; I was acting on the teacher's instruction. I was being allowed to get away with doing less work because I was Deaf. In the board game Monopoly, there's the get out of jail free card. In real life for Deaf people, we sometimes get the Deaf pity card.

In a warped way, my being Deaf has occasionally tilted playing fields in my favor. Talking with the producer on the bus before heading out for the photo shoot, I felt a familiar vibe. For one, the producer was already giving me a head start by handing me advance information. He'd huddled with me with the express purpose of hiding this information from my castmates, which made me feel like he was giving me a leg up. And two, the show knew they had screwed up by not booking an interpreter—which meant they owed me.

I felt the field tilt into a downslope. And I was ready to sprint all out downhill, leaving my castmates in the dust.

We got off the bus and stood in two rows, and there was Yu Tsai, just like the producer had drawn in the secret message to me. He started talking, probably revealing today's theme and introducing our guests. On cue, the military veterans walked out.

Right off the bat I noticed the prosthetics the veterans wore. They weren't just veterans; they were disabled veterans—amputees. This detail was a key nugget of information the producer had failed to share. But I was still okay, because I could see that the veterans were disabled, so that piece of information was not lost on me.

Then Veteran 1 started talking. She talked, and talked, and talked. I squinted to read her lips, but I couldn't understand a word she was saying. This wasn't "short and sweet," as the producer said on the bus. I was missing out on a lot of information. I peeked at my castmates and noticed that their eyes were beginning to tear up.

The veteran was sharing a very emotional, heartfelt message, and I couldn't understand a single thing she was saying. She talked for probably ten minutes in all, but it felt like an eternity. Veteran 2 spoke next, and he, too, talked forever.

In the corner of my eye I noticed that one of my castmates, Ashleigh, was bawling. The veterans' stories were clearly striking a deep, emotional nerve with her and my other castmates. I started to get emotional, too, but for entirely different reasons.

The playing field was reversing its tilt; instead of a downslope, I was staring at an uphill climb that grew steeper by the minute.

It no longer felt like I was being handed a Deaf pity card. My arrogance, nurtured by my fifth-grade teacher and numerous other well-meaning but deeply audist hearing people, began to fade quickly. As I stood in the row of castmates, squinting to read the little I could from Veteran 2's lips and mustering up feigned anguish that, judging by my castmates' expressions, was appropriate for the occasion, rage started to well up in me.

My mind kept going back to what the producer had written down on the bus to prep me.

*Veteran 1. Veteran 2.*

That's it. The producer hadn't even mentioned their disabilities. There was so much more information that could have been shared. The producer could have provided me with full scripts that explained who each veteran was and the gist of the message they were sharing with the cast. I would have felt much better if they had at least made this effort. But they had chosen to withhold this information from me.

And to make matters worse, the photo shoot would begin soon, and we'd be posing with the two veterans. I knew very little of their stories, background information that would help me understand the emotional tone that I needed to set during the shoot, what poses to strike. If I screwed up the shoot, that would lead to low scores from Tyra and the other judges—maybe low enough for me to go home. My survival in the competition was at stake, and I was forced to compete with about 5 percent of the information that my castmates had access to. If I was eliminated now, my time on the show would end early in the season. I'd leave so many television minutes, each second a precious opportunity to showcase my story and the Deaf community's, on the table. I desperately wanted to stay on and capture every second.

The situation felt deeply unfair, and I felt more rage boiling up in me—the same fire that burned in my mom's belly as she dealt with the teachers and administrators at my schools when I was young. I felt deprived of information and access.

My memory flashed back to my preinterview with the *ANTM* casting director, Rachelle, before I'd been chosen to appear on the show.

I'd asked if the show was ready for a Deaf model. Rachelle had looked me in the eye and told me with absolute confidence that the show was ready. Yet only a week and a half into the competition, the show was holding an event without an interpreter and hadn't bothered to provide me with even a detailed written summary of the two guests' comments to help me fill in the gaps.

*ANTM* had committed to doing this right, for both me and the show. Now they'd gone back on their word.

After Yu Tsai and the two veterans wrapped up their introductions, my castmates dispersed quickly. They were processing the information the veterans had shared, adjusting their emotional tone, mentally and physically preparing for the War Heroes photo shoot. I stood there alone for a moment, frozen and unsure what to do with myself. My emotions welled up and bubbled over, until I couldn't take it anymore, I had to get out of there. I forced my legs loose and walked away to a private spot behind a trailer.

I felt overwhelmed by what was happening and started crying. I was worried that I would screw up the photo shoot, and that I'd have to go home, all due to circumstances completely out of my control. I didn't know what to do.

The producer noticed me alone behind the trailer and came over. I told him how I felt, tapping out messages on my phone.

*I'm sorry, man, I really am. We booked an interpreter, but they had to back out at the last minute,* he wrote. *Hang in there. You only need to get through this one day.*

He was trying to reassure me, but I felt angry at his words. He couldn't understand what I was going through, being left out without any access to information. But I was afraid to push back because I wanted to prove that being Deaf didn't matter, that I could win this competition no matter what.

*Don't worry. You're going to be fine,* the producer wrote.

Shortly after, Yu Tsai appeared, with a stern look on his face. Reflexively I winced inside, waiting for him to verbally smack me upside the head and tell me to toughen up and get myself together.

*"This isn't right,"* Yu Tsai said. His frown wasn't directed toward me at all, but at the fact I didn't have an interpreter. He patted me on the shoulder and looked me in the eyes.

*"You can do this,"* he told me. *"Forget about all of the other stuff. Focus. Just do what you have been doing."* He said I had absolutely nothing to worry about, that he would take care of me during the photo shoot.

Let's pause quickly here for some exclusive Director Nyle commentary. On the actual *ANTM* episode, this part was portrayed alongside a voiceover of me talking about how I felt lonely being the only Deaf contestant on the show. The message being sent was that loneliness was the reason I had been crying behind the trailer, triggered by the stories of the disabled veterans. The irony was thick, though, given that not only was I crying for an entirely different reason—being left without access during the day's events—but also that I couldn't possibly have been crying from hearing the disabled veterans' stories, because I had no idea what they had said in the first place. All of this aside, the part that frustrates me most about the episode was that it missed out on an important and useful lesson about ensuring access for every individual during any event, Deaf and hearing. That lesson, alas, was left on the floor of the film editing room.

Okay, let's press play again.

After the chat with Yu behind the trailer, I began to feel better, calmer. With a clearer head, I realized that I needed to prepare myself for the photo shoot. I didn't want *ANTM* to not eliminate me because they'd screwed up with the interpreter during the day's events; I wanted them to keep me in the competition because I kept kicking ass at photo shoots. Forget the interpreter blunder, and the overwhelming emotion I'd just felt. My job right now was to excel at my photo shoot and give Tyra and the judges every reason to give me high enough scores to survive that week and advance.

In a way, it was me telling my little fifth-grade self that it was time to finish the whole dang worksheet—not just the circled questions.

With my mind fully refocused, I set about on my important task:

to learn more about the military veterans and their stories. Any extra information I could learn now would help me set the appropriate emotional tone for the photo shoot. I found the male military vet under a tent and approached him, using my Oppo to introduce myself. I told him I could relate to his experience, being Deaf myself, and asked about his journey as a disabled person.

I thought that my using the phone was a clear indicator of how I preferred to communicate. The veteran didn't seem to fully understand, though, and began speaking rapidly. He avoided making eye contact with me, and his body language—especially how he laughed—made him appear impatient, condescending. I locked my eyes on his lips, trying to catch whatever I could, but it wasn't going well.

Mentally, I was saying *Fuck, this guy is an asshole.* Normally I wouldn't have even minded. I'm all for disabled people being whoever the heck they want to be, even an asshole. If that's how they choose to be, more power to them. Screw society and the tiny boxes imposed on people with disabilities.

But at that moment, when I was seeking more information to prepare for the upcoming photo shoot, I would have greatly preferred to have been conversing with a disabled nonasshole.

A castmate nearby, apparently trying to help, said, "Have you met Nyle? He's hearing impaired."

I wish I'd known what he was saying then, because if I had, I would've taken him to school. It was a week and a half into the competition and the castmate had been living in the same house as me the entire time, basically getting a crash course on Deaf culture. Yet he still used the offensive term "hearing impaired." He should have just said "Deaf," which I'd explained was my preferred term.

My attempt to make conversation with the veteran and gain some sort of understanding of the emotional tone needed for the photo shoot had failed spectacularly. The photo shoot was about to start, and I had no choice but to wait my turn and watch my castmates make their poses.

I sensed that Yu Tsai was turning it up a notch. He was laying into my castmates for the slightest errors during their shoots. He brought out his quick-raised-eyebrow sneer, and I didn't need an interpreter to understand that he wasn't very happy with my castmates. At this photo shoot, his fuse was shorter than I'd ever seen it.

Yu had told me earlier behind the trailer that he'd take care of me during the photo shoot; now I was beginning to worry he might not keep his word. But, to my great relief, when it was my turn to model, he changed up his approach. Clearly working hard to ensure that I understood what he expected of me during the shoot, he used his hands, face, and body to communicate with me. He gave me direction by modeling poses, pointed for slight adjustments, and used his face (softly) to express dissatisfaction or delight.

Throughout my time filming *ANTM*, I loved working with Yu. He was, and is, a great communicator. It always felt like we were on the same wavelength. He recognized my potential and nurtured it. Yes, he sometimes was a hard-ass and his criticism could cross the line, but I knew it came from his heart. He wanted the best for the *ANTM* models, to see us succeed, and he was powerfully direct in his feedback. Listening to him, I would learn, was the wisest thing a model could do.

My being Deaf was never even close to being a problem, from his perspective. The opposite, actually: he thought that it made me a better model. I was Deaf, but ironically I listened better than many models. I was able to take the direction that Yu and other photographers tried to give me and use it to turn good photos into great shots.

Communication between me and Yu (and many other hearing photographers) was simple but effective. To provide direction, Yu often put his hand to his cheek and turned his head along with it. All I needed to do was mirror his movement.

In a way, the simple communication method we used worked better than any spoken language. It was direct and uncomplicated, visceral and intuitive. Instead of Yu saying "Turn your head slightly down and to the left" and me needing to comprehend this sentence and follow its direction, he just did the movement himself and I copied him.

It helped, obviously, that I had used sign language all my life. I had thousands of hours of practice recognizing others' body movements and translating them into comprehensible instruction. I also had a heightened skill in using facial expressions and my body to communicate and convey emotions. Over time, I'd naturally developed a keen sensitivity to the visual and an awareness of the space around me, which helped me to strike creative, eye-catching poses. My facial and bodily control, honed by hours of ASL discourse, gave me the ability to make subtle movements and shifts of my body to capture just the right tone.

(It also probably didn't hurt that I had been a selfie-crazed preteen. Using a digital camera that my mom bought me, I'd strike poses and snap mirror selfies in the bathroom. I learned my earliest lessons about how to use light in photography with the fixture over my bathroom sink mirror. These selfie sessions would go on forever, until my brother Neal forced the bathroom door open. NOT AGAIN! he'd grumble as he muscled me out of the bathroom.)

"*We're done!*" Yu shouted, wrapping up my War Heroes photo shoot. He gave me a thumbs-up and waved me away with a wink.

I thought I had done well. I felt good vibes from the military veterans I posed with. Yu was generous in his assessment of my performance and was far kinder with me than he was with my castmates.

I didn't want to declare victory just yet. I wasn't truly in the clear until the judges turned in their scores on my photos. I had to wait a few more days; then it was time to film the judging.

Judging days were hell. On TV, the judging comes at the end of episodes, and they're often brief—maybe five or ten minutes at most. But in real life, judgings took six to eight hours to film. When each castmate faced the judges—Tyra, Miss J, and Kelly—to discuss their photo shoot performance, multiple takes were filmed, to capture different camera angles. And then each castmate faced Tyra alone to receive their scores, again in multiple takes, with multiple camera angles. The judging set was designed so the judges sat in three chairs on one end and the castmates stood in rows on the other. In many of the camera shots of a castmate facing the judges, the other castmates are visible in the background, which meant that for judging shoots, the rest of us also had to stand on the set the entire time—as long as eight hours. By the end of every judging day, our legs were jelly and our entire bodies felt exhausted. Add the emotional weight of awaiting our fate through the judging, and our souls were basically sad puddles by the time the last scores were handed out.

During the fourth episode judging, I was both mentally and emotionally drained. I couldn't wait to get it over with. When I faced the judges, they were kind with their comments. I hadn't blown them away, but I'd done well. Later, I got my score: I placed around the middle of the pack and was safe for another judging day.

The crisis safely averted, I went to the producers and told them how I felt about what happened. In total honesty, I didn't really believe the *ANTM* producers when they said they'd book a replacement interpreter for today's event. When communicating with them regarding interpreting arrangements for other events leading up to the War Heroes event, I'd noticed that *ANTM* would try to limit the hours Ramon worked. For instance, if there was an all-day event, the producers would book Ramon to work only specific hours of the day that they deemed I'd need an interpreter for. That forced me to communicate in other ways, like using the Oppo phone, for the noninterpreted portion of the day. I got the vibe that it was a budget thing, that the producers wanted to save on interpreting costs. So the fact that I didn't get an interpreter for the War Heroes event didn't come as a total surprise.

I told the producers that the impression they gave me, that they were trying to save money, was putting extra pressure on me. It made me wonder if the *ANTM* brass was sick of spending too much money on interpreting expenses. I was worried they'd decide they couldn't afford it and send me home just for that reason. This added to the stress I'd felt during the War Heroes event—in the back of my head I was thinking: *Is this it? Were they done paying for the interpreter? Am I going home soon?*

The producers said they completely understood my point of view.

They apologized and told me, straight out, that money wasn't an issue. They didn't want me to worry about that at all.

Their reassurance helped ease my fears. I thanked them for hearing me out and told them that's what really mattered to me, that they made their elimination decision for the right reasons.

"I don't want you to give me the boot just because of the interpreting cost," I said. "Now, if I suck at modeling, you can absolutely eliminate me. That's fair. I will have zero problems with that."

We wrapped up our discussion by setting clear expectations for how communication needed to work to be effective for everyone. And then I put the incident behind me. Yes, *ANTM* had screwed up, but it was water under the bridge, and I couldn't dwell on the anger and frustration I'd felt that day. I had more challenges to worry about, more photo shoots to ace.

You see, I realized that a playing field that could tilt one way or the other wasn't an apt analogy for the *ANTM* competition. It was more like one long chess match. And once I understood that, I began to play the game the way it should be played: one move at a time.

# 15.

# Tears of Joy

*In college, my plan was to become a math teacher at a Deaf school. It was a practical aspiration: I was good at math, I would enjoy a return to the Deaf school environment I'd thrived in growing up, and I thought I could make a difference in young Deaf people's lives. It'd be a worthwhile, rewarding career.*

*In 2013, right about the time my studies at Gallaudet were winding down and two years before I got the call from ANTM, I tweeted:*

"I wanna be a kid forever but there are kids that need me, to be inspired and to look up to. . . . They don't know me yet but they will."

*The tweet was written with my teaching career plan in mind. I got that part wrong, but everything else came true—in ways that exceeded my wildest dreams.*

M-I-K-E-Y . . . S-T-E-F-A-N-O . . . B-E-L-L-O . . . D-E-V-I-N . . . L-A-C-E-Y . . .

*Sigh.* It became tiresome to refer to each of my *ANTM* castmates by fingerspelling their names out in full every time.

Sure, Ramon and I could fingerspell quicker than lightning. But doing it again and again, it became tedious. That's one reason we have sign names in ASL—it's a quick and easy way to refer to someone. It's a cherished tradition in Deaf culture; practically everyone who uses sign language has a sign name (unless one's name is three or four letters or shorter; in some of those cases one might not have a sign name due to the brevity of the name). Some sign names are lexicalized, meaning they are made with the handshape of the first letter of one's name. Some sign names reflect a defining physical feature or trait, such as sticking the index finger into a cheek for a dimple or using the "laugh" sign for a good-humored person who cracks up easily and often.

My brothers and I have sign names. Neal's is the *N* handshape touching the upper lip just above one corner of the mouth—commemorating a small, near-invisible scar left behind by a dog who'd bitten him when he was two. Nico's is an *N* handshape too, flashing across the space in front of the forehead, in the same motion as one sign for "Italy," in homage to the Italian origin of his name. Mine is made in the space beside the face, begins with a bent number *3* handshape, moves backward past the face, and ends with the index and middle fingers and thumbs extended and touching at the tips. I was named that way because of my big bright eyes and their almond shape. I love my sign name. It's just as essential, if not more, to my identity as my English name, Nyle.

Because it's a big time-saver to use sign names instead of fingerspelling names, Ramon and I dubbed temporary sign names for my castmates. We based them on personality quirks, nicknames, or unique parts of their appearance.

Mikey was always talking about how he was going to hit it big and rake in the cash; he was, simply, MONEY. Justin's nickname became his sign name: J-SMOOTH. Bello had radiant ice-blue eyes, so he was dubbed GLOW-EYE.

The most idiosyncratic sign name belonged to Hadassah. On one side of her face cascading locks of hair fell down to her shoulder; on the other, her hair was shaved to a quarter inch above her ear. Her sign name, made with a fist grazing along the side of the head, was SIDE-SHAVE.

Hadassah didn't come into the competition with that hairstyle. It was given to her as part of the *ANTM* makeover. That day, my cast-mates and I loaded onto the party bus and headed over to a beauty salon, where we met Miss J, Yu Tsai, and a famous stylist to the stars. We gathered in front of them, and Miss J pointed at each of us and rattled off our makeover, machine-gun style.

"Devin, shaved damn near bald. Lacey, chic bowl cut. Ava, model mullet. Nyle, a cleanup."

My cleanup makeover was simple: just a trim of my hair and beard. I had no problem with it. Some of the other makeovers were quite a bit more drastic. Not all my castmates loved their makeovers, but everybody went through theirs without putting up much of a fuss.

Except Hadassah.

A tall African American beauty pageant veteran, Hadassah trea-sured her beautiful locks. Tyra's chosen makeover required her to shave off all her hair on one side of her head.

I pictured Hadassah's makeover, and I could see how she would rock the look. It was an *interesting* makeover choice, one that seemed to be an attempt to nudge Hadassah from her perfectionist beauty pageant contestant ways. A side shave was a fork in a path that had the potential to lead her modeling in a more adventurous direction—it broke Hadassah's mold. A bold change like this could do wonders for Hadassah on the *ANTM* competition, and for her modeling career.

But Hadassah only pictured her precious locks falling to the floor, the side of her head shorn to a quarter inch, and she did *not* like what she was imagining. On camera, she agonized over the decision whether or not to accept the makeover. Her emotions bubbled over, and at one point she leaned toward flat-out refusing the makeover and walking off the show. Eventually, after some counseling from Miss J, she relented and settled into a barber's chair.

Minutes later, Hadassah looked into the mirror to see the results of her makeover, and she despaired. She hated it; it was exactly as awful as she'd pictured in her head. She bristled at the decision she'd made and descended into a foul mood.

In the upcoming judging, she finished second to last, nearly getting eliminated. That night at the mansion, she aired out her feelings in front of all of the castmates, and the discussion turned heated. Some of my castmates supported her and others tried to help her see why a side shave was chosen for her, and how it might not be the worst thing.

It was late at night at the mansion and there was no event planned, which meant no interpreter was present. Following this impromptu discussion was tough, but a few castmates helped summarize Hadassah's thoughts for me by typing on their Oppo phones.

I could understand the emotion that came with the loss of Hadassah's hair. But it would grow back eventually, and I thought she was overlooking how this new look could be a step in an exciting new direction for her. Moreover, a key part of the makeovers was how the models responded to the changes that were asked of them. Tyra, the judges, the producers—they were all watching to see if we took massive changes to our appearance in stride. But it seemed as if Hadassah couldn't see the forest for the trees.

But because the discussion wasn't accessible to me, I was a few minutes behind in following it, and I didn't feel much like contributing to a debate over something that I found relatively unimportant. I settled back into my seat to observe Hadassah and my other classmates as they continued in their animated conversation.

Just then I felt a mild shock to my rib cage. I turned to look at the cameraman sitting next to me, who had just elbowed me in the ribs.

I saw this cameraman all the time, in the *ANTM* mansion and on challenges and at photoshoots. But it was the first time he'd actually interacted with me (if you can count an elbow to the ribs as in interaction). He pointed at me, gestured to my phone, and then repeatedly pointed in Hadassah's direction.

"*Go, go, go,*" I read on his lips. The entire time, he never made eye contact with me, keeping his eyes on the camera lens.

I didn't know exactly what I wanted to say, but I felt suddenly, imperatively spurred to send a message to my castmates. I pulled out my phone and started tapping. The cameraman peeked at my phone screen out of the corner of his eye. When I was done, I clicked the button, and my phone started voicing my message. Hadassah and the others swiveled their heads toward me. The cameraman already had the camera lens on me.

"I just want to say that you all are complaining about hair, hair, hair," the phone recited. "Am I complaining about my deafness? No, I am not. I feel like you guys are complaining about something so simple."

As soon as my phone stopped voicing my message, the room fell silent.

When the makeover episode eventually aired, my message became a key plot point. If not for the cameraman, it wouldn't have happened. What made it all the more astounding to me was that the production crew was strictly prohibited from communicating or interacting directly with the cast. We were around each other all the time, but we weren't supposed to talk to each other. When he urged me to jump into the Hadassah discussion, the cameraman had broken the rule.

That was the first, but far from the last interaction I had with the production crew. They broke that rule with me many times, and I was grateful for it. The truth is that these folks—people you never once saw onscreen during an *ANTM* episode but were around the castmates *all* the time behind the scenes—helped keep me going.

Soon after the Hadassah side-shave episode, I was walking down the hallway in the *ANTM* mansion when a cameraman happened to walk by. Just as he passed, he leaned toward me and signed:

HURRY WIN.

He had kept his eyes in front of him as he walked, giving his message major secret spy vibes. I did a double take. *Did I really see what I just saw?* I hadn't taught any ASL to the production crew. The cameraman either knew some ASL already or learned these two signs just so he could say them to me.

Either way, it gave me a massive morale boost. Over time the cameraman did it again and again: HURRY WIN. Then other people on the production crew started signing it too.

HURRY WIN. HURRY WIN.

It felt like I had a small secret cheering section for me at the mansion.

ONE PLACE WHERE I DID a ton of talking during *ANTM* filming was the interview studio. I spent hours there answering questions from Anita, the producer who led the interviews, sharing bits and pieces about myself and expressing my feelings and thoughts on what was happening on *ANTM*.

Often Anita asked leading questions—questions that had obvious answers that fit *ANTM*'s vision of what my storyline would be on the show. One storyline they tried to spin was that I was into Lacey, a fellow castmate.

In our interviews, Anita would say things like: "What do you think of Lacey? Is she modeling well? There seems to be an attraction between you and her."

In actuality, sparks never flew between us; we never had a thing. But by the latter half of filming the show, I had a good understanding that manufactured storylines were part of how reality TV shows like *ANTM* worked, and I played along with the Lacey storyline, to an extent.

But when the questions turned to my romantic life in general, I became more guarded in my responses. For one, all of their romantic questions focused on the female gender. They asked what type of woman I was attracted to, what I was looking for in my ideal woman.

I grew wary of *ANTM* portraying me as a straight person who was attracted to women only. By then, I had made important progress in understanding my sexual identity and knew with certainty that I was not straight. Allowing *ANTM* to portray me that way would be a harmful, damaging step backward for me, and it scared me to think about that happening. I'd earned each step I'd taken thus far; I didn't want to give up a single inch.

When I responded to these questions, I chose my words carefully. Intentionally, I used neutral "they" and "them" pronouns. ASL is ahead of the curve when it comes to pronoun usage—our pronouns are genderless. To refer to someone with a pronoun, we simply point at a designated space adjacent to our bodies. We do the same whether we intend to say "he," "she," or "they." When I signed these gender-neutral pronouns, I also mouthed "they" and "them."

Ramon caught on to this and pulled me aside.

"Which pronouns do you prefer me to use when I interpret: 'they'/'them,' or 'she'/'her'?" he asked.

I told him. On the same page as me, he interpreted my responses into spoken English using the gender-neutral pronouns whenever I was asked about my romantic interests during interviews. My responses threw a wrench into Anita's plans. My using "they"/"them" didn't neatly fit into the storyline they were building for me, as a straight ladies' man who was having fireworks with a fellow finalist, the gorgeous Lacey.

Eventually, one of my gender-neutral responses landed on Anita's final nerve. She had a storyline to build, and I was doing her no favors in her efforts. She stopped her line of questioning abruptly and asked me, point blank, to repeat my answer, with female pronouns. She recited the line she wanted me to say, word for word, replacing my "partner" with "woman," my "they" with "she," and my "their" with "her": "My ideal woman is someone who's independent and strong minded. She wouldn't be afraid to speak her mind and disagree with me. She'd always be honest with me, no matter what."

The moment felt like a test. I could play along with what Anita wanted from me, help *ANTM* build a false representation of my sexual identity that fit their storyline, and lose everything I'd worked for.

Or I could stand my ground and keep my forward momentum. I made my choice.

"I don't want to do that. I would prefer to use 'they' and 'them' pronouns."

It was a marketing strategy, I told Anita—I wanted to appeal to both sexes. The audience and following I wanted to build, during *ANTM* and afterward, included both sexes. I didn't say outright to

Anita that I wasn't straight—I wasn't ready to do that—but instead I hoped that my ambiguous response gave strong enough of a hint to Anita about my sexual identity.

Anita looked into my eyes for a moment, searching for something more. Then her eyes dropped, and with pursed lips, she accepted my refusal and moved on.

From that point on, we spent less and less interview time on my romantic life. Anita moved on to a bigger, more important mission: creating moments of intense emotion. Generally, she was a sweet and cheerful young woman, but in the interview studio she pursued her mission with a fierce passion equal to that of Yu Tsai's tongue-lashing his models toward creating the perfect photo. In interviews she lobbed question after question, digging deeper and deeper. Her questions were like a miner's pickaxe jabbing into me, dislodging stories from my personal history and probing for precious minerals: emotional, vulnerable moments.

The diamonds Anita was looking for were tears falling from the eyes of my castmates. She picked them off one by one, harvesting their emotion-choked footage to make prime reality TV. And then there was just me, the lone person who'd never shed tears on camera. She was gentle and I thought she was well-intended, but it was clear that she wanted nothing more than for me to cry during an interview.

As she asked me questions, I could sense her angling for a way into my rawest nerves. Her questions often focused on my Deaf experience and were framed in a way that suggested sad and negative responses.

"Is it hard being Deaf?"

"No, I love being Deaf," I told her.

Later, her eyes brightened when I told her I'd attended Deaf schools growing up. "That must have been tough!" she said. "Can you share more about that experience? Did you wish you attended 'normal' schools growing up?"

"I actually attended mainstream school for a year and hated it," I said. "I couldn't wait to go back to the Deaf school."

When I told Anita I was the fifth generation to be born Deaf in my family, her jaw dropped open, then her eyes seemed to fill with pity. I could sense her imagining how, with each generation that had been born Deaf, the levels of oppression and frustration grew and grew, until it had become a giant burden, a Mack Truck–sized snowball of futility that weighed on me.

She asked if being born into a Deaf family made being Deaf harder.

At this point I was saying, in my head, *WTF, calm down, woman.* Before she'd even met me, Anita had apparently painted this picture of my despair and helplessness as a Deaf person. It wasn't even her fault; it was the typical perception that mainstream culture had of Deaf people, one often reinforced by portrayals of the Deaf in media.

Sure, being Deaf isn't all good. But in the news and media, Deaf experiences are often shown in a negative, unflattering light. The focus tends to laser in on the bad parts of being Deaf: the absence of sound, how we become disconnected from the world, the barriers we face. Rarely do you see Deaf people just being shown for who they are—ordinary people doing awesome stuff, their deafness aside. And even more rarely do you see stories of Deaf people proud of being Deaf.

*That* was what I wanted to talk about. I didn't much like talking about sad, negative things, particularly when it came to my Deaf identity. I yearned to talk about who I was, and all the good things I had going on in my life. Being Deaf was 100 percent a part of that. In the interviews, I most enjoyed talking about my awesome Deaf family, including a loving, strong-willed mom and two handsome brothers, one of whom was a Deaf DJ. I explained to Anita how being born Deaf to a Deaf family and attending Deaf schools growing up were *good* things. In fact, I thought of my Deaf-centric life as utopian—the perfect mix of conditions for a Deaf kid like me. I'd been allowed to communicate freely and openly in my beautiful and unique language, ASL.

And at every chance I had in the interviews, I wanted to remind viewers how Deaf people were often underestimated, and how we proved people wrong all the time—which was my supreme mission as a Deaf competitor: to kick ass and win the *ANTM* competition.

As hard as she was trying, Anita was no closer to getting me to share a sad story, much less shed a tear. Undaunted, she continued to lead interviews down darker, bleaker paths.

During one interview, Anita started asking about my dad. I told her that I hadn't had any meaningful contact with him for more than a decade. Her eyes flickered as if she'd just caught a glint of a buried diamond.

"Tell me more," she said.

I told her about all of it: his drug addiction, his abusive behavior, how he'd been in and out of our lives until my mom and brothers and I left him for good, moving from Austin to Maryland.

Anita pressed on: What was my relationship with my dad like, and how did I feel about him now? How bad was his drug addiction? How did he abuse me and my brothers? Did I have examples? Any specific stories I wanted to share?

I answered her questions, and she continued to push hard on the topic, lobbing follow-up question after follow-up question. I kept answering her, but eventually I ran out of interesting things to say about my dad. Finally, I cut her off mid-question.

"Look, I can talk about how screwed up my dad was and how bad he treated me and my family all you want. You can keep asking me questions, and I'll keep answering them. But I've pretty much told you the important things to know. It's not going to get any more interesting from here on out. And, maybe most important of all, talking about my dad isn't going to make me cry."

Anita paused and said resignedly, "You're making my job so difficult."

Her mouth started quivering. Then she buried her face in her hands and her shoulders shook.

*Oh shit,* I thought. The goal during interviews was to get *me* to cry, not her. I held up a hand, meaning to apologize and let her know I hadn't intended to come across as harsh. She waved me off and told me the interview would need to pause for now, to be picked up another day.

I waited outside the interview studio until she came out.

I was going to apologize, but she started off by saying that she was sorry. Our interviews had become kind of stressful for her, but she hadn't meant to break down like that in front of me.

I pulled her into my side for a short hug and told her not to worry. Then I told her how I felt about the interviews.

"I really enjoy the interviews the most when we talk about positive things. My family. How I love being Deaf and all the cool things that come with it, like my community and ASL. I'd like to talk more about these kinds of things."

She nodded. I could tell that she understood how I felt, but that she also wanted me to show my emotions, to be more raw in front of the camera.

"I'm sorry I haven't cried," I said. (I'm amazed that this is an actual sentence that I have said in my life.) "Truthfully, I rarely cry because I'm sad. However, I do cry when I'm happy. Truly happy. Tears of joy. If I stay long enough in this competition, you might get to capture that moment."

Anita nodded, a touch of doubt in her eyes, then looked up the stairs. At the top was one of the cameramen, who happened to be her husband. He shot us a quizzical look. Anita told him what had just happened.

The cameraman sighed and waved to the door. I read his lips as he spoke to Anita: *"You're tired. Go home, babe."*

Anita was definitely tired, and so was everybody else: the production crew, my fellow castmates, and myself. Tired as she was, I hoped Anita would take my words to heart and stay patient.

THE HOMESTRETCH OF THE *ANTM* competition was a grueling, stress-packed sprint toward the finale. With about two weeks to go, we traveled to Las Vegas for some competitions and challenges. In one random moment, a producer walked into the room where the castmates were sitting around and chilling. He barked orders, and the production crew turned off the cameras. He started speaking, but there was no interpreter, so I had no idea what he was saying; he never made an attempt to ensure I would be able to understand him. After maybe ten minutes, he walked out. I asked one of my castmates what it was all about.

*He told us we that we need to create more drama when the cameras are rolling.*

I looked at the scrawled words on the paper and back up to my castmate. That was all? A ten-minute speech, squeezed into a sentence? Surely there had to be more to it.

Anger flickered inside me. We were months into the production. After the War Heroes interpreter fiasco, *ANTM* had assured me it would never happen again. It was made clear to all the producers, including the one who'd just spoken, how communication would work while I was around.

The producer had just blatantly tossed out the communication rules right in front of my face. It was an outright breach of the trust *ANTM* producers and I had long worked to rebuild after the episode with the veterans.

My brain flooded with questions. Did the producer have it out for me? Had I missed critical information to help succeed in upcoming challenges? The situation gnawed away at me, making me paranoid and suspicious.

During my next interview, I told Anita what had happened. She understood right away why I had been so upset. Shortly after, the producer who'd spoken without an interpreter approached me. This time we had an interpreter. He apologized for what he'd done, explained what he had said the day before, and offered his hand for a shake. I shook it, and the issue was resolved.

THE *ANTM* CAST GRADUALLY GOT smaller and smaller. Soon we were just five.

The photo shoot competition for the final five had a last-minute change. We didn't know what the original plan was, but they told us the new plan: a night shoot. Literally. We shot in the pitch black of night. I had no way of seeing my interpreter, the photographer, or Yu Tsai. I was supposed to strike poses when they gave me a visual cue, but it was tough to react in a timely manner when I was suddenly down to three senses. I felt completely disoriented. My competitors had the decidedly unfair advantage of being able to access Yu Tsai's shouted commands during the shoot, while I posed to a black void, utterly lacking direction and feedback. Predictably, my photos turned out awful. At judging, I scored so low I was in the bottom two. I stood in front of Tyra and prayed that she wouldn't say my name and eliminate me from the competition after I'd gotten so far.

To my endless relief, she didn't. I narrowly survived, advancing to the top four. Up to that point I was cruising through the competition, consistently finishing at or near the top during the judgings. High on my success, I had allowed myself to slip into the dangerous tendrils of hubris. I'd become an arrogant punk-ass who thought he'd had the competition in the bag.

Teetering on the verge of elimination snapped me back into focus. It reminded me that to win this competition, I had to be on edge all the time. I had to be ready to bring it during any challenge or photo shoot.

There was one issue, though. Staying on the top of my game constantly was hard as heck to do while spending nearly all my time with non-ASL-fluent people. I enjoyed the company of my fellow finalist castmates Mamé, Lacey, and Mikey, but the majority of my conversations with them had to take place through my Oppo phone; only rarely did I converse with them through Ramon, and even then the cameras were usually running and the conversation was unnatural. I had some fun private conversations via Oppo phone with those three about our family and friends back home, and about our dreams and aspirations. But after months in the mansion, I was exhausted not to be able to chat directly and informally in my language, ASL.

This continued communication isolation was eating away at me. Mentally, I was wearing out.

Fortunately, help was on the way, and when I found out, man, I was as happy as a little mama's boy could be.

One morning, Tyra surprised us by showing up unannounced at the *ANTM* mansion. She'd brought along her mother, Carolyn London, who'd been her photographer since she was a teenager and had helped jump-start her modeling career. Her mom had refused to photograph her at first, encouraging her to keep her focus on school. Eventually Carolyn relented, but still stuck to her guns with Tyra, instilling into her enduring values such as staying true to herself no matter what, telling her about modeling, "This is what you do, it's not who you are." Seeing them together, I was inspired and—to use an ASL phrase—HEART-TOUCHED.

My emotions were riding high and happy when Tyra told us she had a surprise for us at the door. I looked up and saw a couple older women whom I'd never seen before. Entering behind them was a familiar head of flowing brown hair—and then I saw my most favorite smile in the whole wide world.

I threw my hands up in the air and dropped them on my mom's shoulders, where I buried my face. I stayed there for a long time. I had missed her so much and was so glad she was here. When I looked up, a sweet and glorious torrent of ASL flooded my eyes.

YOU SURPRISED? Mom laughed. HOW YOU? I MISS YOU SO-MUCH. YOUR WHOLE FAMILY SAY HI, SEND MANY HUGS KISSES. THEY WISH THEY COULD BE-HERE. She looked around at the spacious living room. WOW! THIS-IS NICE HOUSE. She inspected my cheeks and arms. THEY FEED YOU ENOUGH?

I brought up my hands and paused for the briefest moment before I started talking. It'd been three months since I used ASL to talk directly to someone other than Ramon. Mom and I sat down on the couch and started chatting, in *our* language.

It was surreal seeing her in the mansion I'd spent the past couple months holed up in with just my castmates and the production crew to keep me company. I was bursting with pride, because now that my mom was here, she'd know I'd made it this far, to the top four. Privately, I was thrilled that *ANTM* cameras would capture my mom with me; it created an opportunity to show the unique family dynamic between a Deaf mom and a Deaf son.

After only a few minutes of chatting with Mom, I felt my depleted reserves of energy building back up. Her surprise visit couldn't have come at a better time. I was starting to slip and weaken under the pressure of my prolonged communication isolation. Just as I'd reached a low point, there she was, holding out a hand to help pick me back up.

Of course she was—she'd been there for my brothers and me our entire lives. She always had our backs. She was our rock. Now that my mom was around, I felt like I could take on the world. All doubts I had about winning the *ANTM* competition faded away.

Tyra and her mom told us to get ready: we were going to participate in a photo shoot. Each castmate would pair up with their mother, and Tyra's mom, Carolyn, would be the photographer. The photos of the castmates with our moms, Tyra told us, would be used for that week's judging.

I gulped. I wasn't sure how Mom would do on this challenge. It wasn't that she was uncomfortable in front of a camera. In fact, she'd told me about how in college she'd helped out a friend who was a photography major with a photo shoot assignment, dressing up in a beige jacket over a dark blouse and holding a pack of cigarettes as she struck poses.

But that had been long before I was born. I'd never seen her take serious model-type poses in front of a camera before. It didn't matter; all I knew was that I needed her to be ready to face this challenge. My chances at winning the competition depended on her.

I put on a brave smile, turned to face Mom, and started signing out instructions. Think about angles and how the light hits your face. Always keep your eyes on the camera. Don't smile, smize. I used a sign I'd created for the term, which is the same as "smile" but positioned next to my eyes, to convey its meaning: "smile with your eyes." I demonstrated a smize for her to see, and then she tried it out a couple times, improving with each round of feedback from me.

Heading into the photo shoot, I was so nervous my fingers trembled. My chances at winning this competition now depended on my mom's modeling chops. If she didn't have what it took, I could be going home.

I led my mom into the studio, and we stood before the bright lights, the cameras, and Tyra and Carolyn.

And then, unprompted, my mom lifted her foot and placed it on a large block, a prop.

Alarms flashed inside my head. *What are you doing?* I thought. *Oh no, this might go really poorly.*

But Tyra jumped to her feet, nodding her head, vibing Mom's pose. "I like that, I like that!" she said.

*Okay,* I thought. *Maybe this wasn't going as bad as I thought it was. Let's roll with it.* I followed Mom's lead and posed with her. Tyra and her mom hollered with appreciation.

For a brief moment, I broke my own rule and looked away from the camera and at Mom. Her smile was calm and regal, and her pose held all the fierce confidence in the world.

*Just trust her,* I decided. As I'd done all my life. I turned my eyes back to the camera and resumed my pose, following Mom's lead.

The shoots went brilliantly. Mom knew just how to pose in front of the camera. I didn't give her any instruction or feedback; there was no need. If I'm being honest, I started worrying that she was modeling *too* well and would outshine me in the pictures. She was killing it—and that pushed me to try to do even better.

It was a pressure-packed shoot. But even so, I relaxed for a brief moment to take in the scene: Carolyn on one knee, her camera in hand. Tyra right behind her, standing tall, flashing smiles, and shouting encouragement. Yu Tsai, Miss J, and Kelly behind them, looking on. My mom to my right, her back against me, her head raised and resting against my chest, showing her beautiful face in profile to the camera. And me, sitting there on a prop, my face and hair done in makeup by the best professionals in the world, the clothes on my back created by internationally renowned fashion designers.

I soaked in the moment, and then let out a breath and jumped back into my body, perfecting my pose for the next click of the camera.

WE HAD JUDGING THE NEXT day. Tyra called on each of us to go through the photos of the shoot with our moms. After yesterday's surreal photo shoot, I was excited when my turn came up to see if Mom's and my poses had created photos as good as I had imagined in my head.

The photos turned out even better than in my wildest dreams. Mom looked so beautiful—every bit the powerful, strong, proud, and gorgeous matriarch she was. In one photo, my mom cast a protective gaze over me as I held up her elbow on my shoulder—the perfect encapsulation of how she had kept a constant and careful watch over me and my brothers growing up, and how we repaid her by propping her up from time to time. In another photo, her head rested against mine and my arm wrapped around her, an embrace full of love.

The photos made me so indescribably *happy* that my heart overflowed with joy and love. I drew in a deep breath, clenched my teeth, and looked at Tyra. She was winding up a question but didn't get to finish because I'd bent over. Tears streamed down my face. I took deep gasps, trying to contain myself, but I couldn't dam up my joy.

The full emotional weight of the scene had hit me hard. Yes, I felt the bad things that had happened in the past: How my mom had divorced my dad and singlehandedly raised her three boys. But the tears came because of where she had led me, to this moment: me, a college-educated young man on the set of *ANTM*, on the precipice of winning and spring-boarding my career, an experience I was able to share with Mom, who loved us unconditionally and had sacrificed so much.

It had finally happened. I had cried in front of the camera, for the first time since the War Heroes fiasco.

The judges gushed over the photos. Of course, Mom stole the spotlight. Tyra loved her energy in the pictures, and Kelly called her a "genius." Tyra said that, while coaching me and Mom during the photo shoot, she and her mother noticed how Mom and I had a beautiful and natural relationship, a cool bond that they could feel. The judges gave us a score of 37 out of a possible 40 points, one tenth of a point behind first place finisher Mamé, and good enough for me to advance to the next stage of competition.

After judging finished, Anita walked up to me, a smile on her face. I pointed toward my eyes, bloodshot and raw.

Anita laughed and told me that in between shots during the judging, Tyra had asked if I had ever cried during interviews throughout *ANTM.*

"I told her that I tried like hell, but it was impossible!" Anita said.

But now, finally, Anita and *ANTM* got what they had so longed for: me locked in a moment of intense emotion, captured on camera.

With a sheepish grin, I repeated what I'd said to her right after she broke down during our interview.

"I told you. I cry tears of joy."

THE LAST DAYS OF THE competition were upon us. We did final photo shoots in a high school pool and at a run-down motel. Next, we delivered a nerve-wracking presentation in front of the judges. Then it was on to our finale, a fashion runway event with the entire *ANTM* cycle 22 cast reunited.

My castmates and I were given designer costumes for the finale event. Mine featured rings of black foam spikes that stuck out from around both of my shoulders. The spikes sometimes got into the way when I signed, which was mildly annoying. But even more bothersome were the black boots they made me wear, which were *heavy.*

Each of my castmates and I were to perform three runway walks. I huddled up with Miss J to practice my walk. At first he thought I was going too slow.

"Can you hear or feel the music?" he asked. I nodded; I could hear it, faintly.

"Walk in rhythm with the beat," he said. He patted his hand against his leg, mimicking the beat. "See? Your footsteps should be falling at this pace."

I had thought my initial pace, a normal, rhythmic pace, was fine. But I followed Miss J's advice and tried my walk again, much quicker this time.

"Perfect!" he said.

A field producer waved; it was time for my walk. I strode confidently out onto the runway. The crowd was packed, but the faces were all a blur to me; I kept my eyes on the runway, pacing myself to the speed that Miss J instructed. My boots felt like lead weights. I strained to pick my foot up each time but was then propelled forward by the boot's weight, increasing my momentum with every step.

When I exited the runway, Yu was waiting for me. I immediately saw that his hands were outstretched, palm down, waving vertically: the international gesture for *slow down.*

*Damn,* I thought. I'd taken Miss J's advice and sent it into overdrive. *Had I just ruined my shot at winning?* I had no time to despair—it was my turn on the runway again. I paced myself more slowly on my second and third walks and returned both times to positive feedback from Yu backstage.

I had rebounded, but I wondered if my first runway walk was bad enough to drop me to second place. All night at the *ANTM* mansion, I tossed and turned, thinking of that first walk. I cursed the heavy boots. If only I could have that first one back, I was sure I'd nail it. I didn't know if one subpar runway walk could topple three months of hard work, but there was a chance, and it killed me to think of it. I barely slept that night.

The next day, I stood beside Mamé in front of Tyra for the final judging.

Mom sat with Mamé's mother backstage, where they watched a TV showing the judging live. But the broadcast wasn't captioned, and the producers didn't provide an interpreter. Mom sat through the entire judging having zero clue what anyone was saying, except when I signed. The final judging ran through Mamé's and my performance from the first day to the last. On the big wall display were photos from competitions we'd won. Tyra and the other judges reflected on how much we had grown since day one. They outlined our strengths and highlighted noteworthy performances, then discussed our weaknesses and pointed out photo shoots where we'd come up short.

The judges debated our final runway walks. Miss J asked me if I could hear the music.

NO, I fibbed, hoping the judges wouldn't allocate so much weight to the runway walks in their final determinations of the winner of the entire competition. I needn't have worried; it didn't matter to Miss J.

"I loved it!" they declared.

"Yeah," Tyra agreed. "I loved that power coming forward."

Relief washed over me. At least that first runway walk wouldn't be a hindrance in the final judging—if I lost it would be because Mamé outperformed me throughout the competition, not because I'd messed up a single runway walk during the finale.

This entire time, my mom was watching, not understanding at all what was going on. She and Mamé's mom had been told to come running if their child was announced the winner.

In the judging room, the moment finally came. Tyra pointed toward the wall display.

My name appeared right next to the title *America's Next Top Model*.

I felt a surge of emotion and my chest constricted. A flood of tears filled my eyes, and I bent over to catch my breath and gather myself together.

Backstage, my mom was uncertain. Was that the winner announcement? she wondered. Then, awe and disbelief set in: Did they really just announce my son as the winner?

A handwave caught her attention, and she looked up to see the cameraman gesturing toward the hallway.

"*Go, go, go!*" my mom read on his lips. That moment, she knew for certain. She got up and ran down the hallway, all the way to the judging room.

Inside, confetti floated all around us. I hugged Tyra, then Mamé. Mom burst into the room, arms outstretched. I caught her and put my forehead to hers. We formed a little bubble inside our embrace and, exhilarated at my victory, I signed a brief message to her inside that little space we'd created just for ourselves.

In the scrum of hugs and high fives and cheek kisses, I spied Anita. I pointed toward my tear-filled eyes. "See? Again!"

She laughed and we hugged, and I was pulled away in the chaos.

Eventually, I wandered backstage, where I saw Mamé again, sitting with her mother. I was still in shock and dizzy and overwhelmed, but I wanted to congratulate Mamé. She'd been a fierce competitor, and the Top Model title could just as easily have been hers.

She said: "You're lucky! You're rich now."

My brain was still a hyperactive mess of synapses firing on overdrive, and I didn't understand what she meant at first. A beat later, I realized she was referring to the $100,000 prize that went to the winner. I had forgotten all about it. It wasn't that the money was unimportant—it *was* a nice part of the package. But I was thinking about the bigger picture. I had entered the *ANTM* competition to win the whole thing, but after winning, I had no plans to sit on my newfound pile of cash and count out dollar bills like a fat cat. *ANTM* was a springboard. Winning the competition could help launch my career and my platform. The *real* hustle had just begun.

More than that, the win wasn't all about me. I saw it as a victory for Deaf people everywhere. Winning *ANTM* opened opportunities to show myself embracing my Deaf identity and continue to fight for improved representation of our community in the media and on bigger stages with much larger audiences.

I had a hell of a lot more things to say about just how damn cool it is to be Deaf.

I felt all of this the moment my name appeared on the screen, declaring me America's Next Top Model, and moments after that, when, in that little bubble that Mom and I made as we hugged, I signed:

"We're going to change the world."

# 16.

# Fluid

One of the most personally earth-shattering things I have ever read in my life was a tweet written by a gay man I followed. He wrote: "The joke's on me. I had a childhood crush on this girl, but it turns out I'd really had the hots for her boyfriend the whole time. She was just my pathway to him."

I stared at that tweet a long time as my brain rearranged my childhood memories.

MY BEARD IS NEATLY TRIMMED and I'm wearing a biker hat, though I don't have a shirt on. The sun kisses my chest as I look off camera into the distance. I'm smiling subtly, a glint of mischief in my eyes. I don't recall exactly when this photo was taken. It's a nice shot and I wish I'd thought to use it as my profile photo on a dating app.

Unfortunately, someone else came up with the idea first.

The photo was posted to Facebook by a Deaf vlogger with a penchant for gossipy stories and a reputation for reporting, via ASL in self-recorded vlog entries, tabloid news about well-known Deaf community members. My newfound fame from *ANTM* had made me a target of his. In his post, he claimed that he had discovered me on a gay dating app. Someone had photoshopped the picture of me in the biker hat onto a screenshot of a user profile on the gay dating app the vlogger referred to, making it look as if I'd created it.

The story about me using the app was bullshit and the screenshot was a fake. But the vlogger's reputation and the veracity of his evidence were beside the point. My eyes floated to the bottom of the screen, where the number of likes, comments, and shares climbed steadily upward.

I took a deep breath and said to myself: *Remember Sweden?*

SWEDEN HAD BEEN THE FIRST stop of my summer 2013 Europe backpacking trip, the same trip during which I'd attended the Clin d'Oeil festival and met Alphonse. A Deaf Swede had invited me and a bunch of other local Deaf Swedes to his family home in the countryside. It was a gorgeous house in the middle of rolling grassy meadows that stretched for miles in all directions, and it had an in-ground swimming pool and a sauna out back. We'd brought a ton of booze and were partying it up in the sauna when I vaguely remembered that I'd once heard some time ago that Swedish people were very open-minded and that nudity was part of their culture, particularly when in saunas.

WHY WE-ALL CLOTHES-ON STILL? I asked my Swedish friends. WE IN SWEDEN. WANT-TO HONOR YOUR CULTURE, TAKE-OFF CLOTHES.

NO, THAT'S FINLAND THEIR CULTURE, NOT SWEDEN, one corrected me.

OH, I said. WELL, FINLAND, SWEDEN NEIGHBORS. GO-AHEAD HONOR FINLAND.

My Swedish friends protested and started making excuses. A guy next to me pointed to a girl sitting opposite him. ME KNOW HER SINCE KINDERGARTEN! CAN'T IMAGINE SEE HER NAKED.

COME-ON! NUDITY, NO-BIG-DEAL, I told them. BODIES, OURS, LIKE ART.

They didn't respond.

FUCK-IT, I said.

I took my swimming trunks off and sat back down, the sole naked guy sitting in the sauna. Ten seconds later, the guy next to me took his clothes off. Then the person next to him did, too. Soon, everyone in the sauna was naked, then all the others out in the pool ditched their clothes, too.

Buoyed by potent Swedish vodka and riding on a weirdish euphoria brought on by our nudity, we went nuts. We ran all around the yard, dove into the pool, ran back into the sauna. We must have gotten too rowdy, because the cops showed up, beaming bright flashlights into our faces and putting up their hands to avoid looking at our bare-naked bodies.

We gestured to them that we were Deaf and one cop took out a pen and a notepad. A girl stood in front of the cop and hopped, making her substantial breasts swing and bounce mere feet from the cop's face. Deadpan and unamused, the cop moved his notepad to block his view of the girl's chest. After telling us to pipe down, the cops left, the party died out, and we eventually put our clothes back on and went to sleep.

The next morning, the world had returned to its fully clothed equilibrium. It wasn't awkward, and we didn't look at each other any different. We'd had one brief bizarre and glorious night of unabashed nudity, and I thought that was the end of it. We'd move on, never to speak of the night. It was our little secret.

A couple weeks later I arrived in Reims for the Clin d'Oeil Festival. I was strolling around the festival with a group of my Deaf friends checking out booths, drinking cocktails from plastic cups, when a stranger approached me straight out of nowhere. He pointed at me and said:

THAT YOU!

I frowned and looked behind me to see if he was talking about someone else. He wasn't.

YOU AMERICAN START NUDE PARTY IN SWEDEN!

*The fuck.* I chuckled awkwardly and asked him how he knew. He said he heard about it from a friend on Facebook Messenger.

Reims was just the start of it. Later, at the Deaflympics, Deaf strangers walked up to me off the street.

AMERICAN NUDIST! They pointed and laughed.

Sicily, Italy, Czech Republic, Slovenia—anywhere I met new Deaf friends, the same thing happened, every time.

YOU AMERICAN BOY, GOT NAKED IN SWEDEN!

The news had seemingly spread to every corner of the European Deaf community. And all of the people I met who knew about it had found out through Facebook Messenger. The story of the nude party spread so rapidly because of a few key ingredients: it was a sensational story; it involved the small, tight-knit Deaf community; and it made use of a social media platform, Facebook.

Later, the Deaf vlogger's post shared these ingredients, with one big difference: during my European backpacking trip I was ordinary Nyle, and now I was Nyle the *ANTM* model. The vlogger's post came out when *ANTM* was midway through airing the cycle 22 episodes, and as each episode was released weekly, my celebrity seemed to increase exponentially.

In terms of information spread potential, the vlogger's claim of discovering me on a gay dating app was the Sweden nude party on *steroids*.

I was right. Within minutes after the post became public, I received texts from friends and acquaintances. Some came right out and asked me questions.

*Is this true, Nyle? Are you gay?*

I felt backed into a corner. I wasn't sure if I was ready for people to know yet, but at the same time, if I answered their questions with flat-out denials, I wouldn't be telling the truth. And even if I said no, would they believe me?

My close friends texted words of support. Fuck that guy, man. He's always so full of shit. I don't believe a word of it.

I appreciated that they had my back, but I had no idea how to reply to them. The gay dating app part of the story was bullshit—I had been on Grindr and other dating apps, but not the one the vlogger used in his fake image—but the gay part wasn't a total lie. The truth as I knew it then was that I wasn't straight. I didn't want to lie to my friends about my sexual identity. I left texts and other messages unanswered, and they started piling up on my phone.

I had to do something to stop the noise and give myself space to breathe. I wasn't anywhere near ready, but I saw only one solution: come out.

Before I could do so, I had two things to figure out first, and quickly. The first was: *How did I want to come out?*

I didn't believe in making a big public announcement, with fanfare and all that. Exploring sexuality is a journey, and people should be allowed to go on that journey at their own pace, without facing public pressure. Part of why I felt so strongly about coming out my way was the result of what I went through in college. A few times, rumors—all of them false—about me and guys swirled around campus. People would bring up those rumors to me directly, asking me, "Did you really kiss that guy?" with such disgusted looks that I felt compelled to immediately deny them and distance myself from an act that they had described with so much revulsion and disdain. It made me angry to think back to those moments, and I felt like I didn't owe anyone shit by coming out and bringing attention to the fact I wasn't straight after all.

I really didn't like the idea of coming out. Straight people never declare their sexuality. So why do LGBTQ people have to? The practice implies that the default sexual orientation is heterosexual, and anybody that isn't has to announce their sexual identity to the world. That is bullshit.

Unfortunately, the Deaf vlogger who'd outed me put me in a situation where I felt trapped, pressured by all my friends asking about my sexual identity, making me feel like I needed to say something quickly. But if I was going to come out, I was determined to do it on my own terms.

Another reason I didn't want to make a big announcement was

that I wasn't sure how to define my current sexual identity. That was my second question: *What do I come out as?* I knew from my brief encounters with men in the past that I liked men romantically. But I also thought I was still into women. I'd met a Deaf woman recently, and we were texting every day. In that direction, the sparks still flew. What did that mean? What did it make me? I had no idea. The only thing I knew was what I *was not*, and that was straight. But I didn't know what I *was*.

All these thoughts were rattling around my head, and I needed an outlet, someone to listen to me and help make sense of the jumbled mess in my mind. Fifteen minutes after the vlogger's post, I made a video call to Sarah, a friend I had known since childhood. I laid it all out—the vlogger's accusation, how I perceived my sexual identity, and my struggle in figuring out how to explain it. I told her about the numerous romantic relationships I'd had with women through high school and college. Some, like Hannah, I had loved deeply. Yet, I'd always been attracted to men, and more recently, I had begun to understand that I could be with them sexually, too. At the same time, though, I didn't think I was gay because of my attraction to women.

Sarah was an excellent listening eye. She heard me out and gave me space and time to sign out every thought that was rattling around my head. At one point, she made a comment in response to my description of my evolving, changing sexual identity.

"Everything has a fluidity to it," she signed.

There it was—the word "fluidity." It clicked with me, feeling just right. I googled the word and combined it with the term "sexual." Boom. I found what I was looking for: "sexually fluid," an actual term that some people used to describe their sexual orientation. As I read an article explaining the concept of being sexually fluid, my first thought was *THAT-THAT-THAT.*

Sexually fluid. That's me.

It basically meant that my sexual orientation could change at any time, depending on the situation and the people involved. My sexual orientation was fluid. This explained how I could have been with girls growing up, and how I was open to being with women and men now. My sexual attraction was flexible, evolving as I went. One article I read written by a sexually fluid person described how they went through phases, alternating attraction to one gender and then the other. They would be attracted to men only for a period of time—sometimes days, sometimes months—and then their attraction would switch to women only and continue for a time. That was exactly how I felt. I'd go through phases where I'd date men only, continuing my exploration of that part of my sexuality; and then I'd stop being with men and date only women. I'd understood bisexual people to be attracted to both men and women at the same time; this alternating attraction was why I thought the term "sexually fluid" described me better than "bisexual."

I was thrilled to find a way to explain what I was. So now I knew what to tell people, but I didn't know how to tell them. I knew I didn't want to make a big deal out of telling the world. So . . . I wanted to make it public, but not in a public way.

Then I saw a tweet from a random follower. He had tweeted me with a sweet and innocuous question: "Boys or girls? :)"

At least he'd asked nicely. There was zero judgment in his question, unlike the disdain-ridden questions I'd gotten in college. The smiley face was a sweet touch.

I replied to that tweet with a link to the article that explained sexually fluidity. That was it. Literally no other words were in the tweet. With that brief reply tweet, I officially outed myself to the entire world.

I closed Twitter and put my phone away for a moment to pause and breathe. Different emotions coursed through me. One of them was relief, the kind that made me literally breathe in deep and then out. *Ahhhhh.* There was no turning back, and that felt powerfully relieving.

The other dominant emotion was fear. What would people think? How would they take the news? Especially those closest to me, who had known me for my entire life. My family, my dearest friends. And it wasn't just the reactions of other people I was afraid of. The first twenty-six years of my life, I'd lived a lie. And now that I knew I wasn't straight, I felt like I was starting over, starting a new life. Who was I, really? This was all new to me, kind of strange and foreign. I needed to continue on my journey, and I hoped I would discover more of myself and become more confident in this new and evolving part of my identity.

With my emotions processed and my head clear, I picked up my phone and my eyes bulged. It had been just ten minutes since I posted it, but the tweet had gone viral already. There were so many retweets, likes, and responses. The vast majority were very supportive, and I was grateful. The news had caused a much larger fuss than I intended, but at least it was being met positively.

I reached out to my family quickly. It had been only a couple hours since the vlogger's Facebook post, but as fast as the news had spread, I was sure it'd gotten to my family already. First was my mom; I called her on FaceTime.

HI MOM, I signed, smiling. Seeing my mom helped calm my emotions. Out of everybody, I was the least worried about how my mom would react to the news. I was right.

"I'm happy for you, Nyle. I understand, and I support you fully."

We cried a little, happy and relieved tears. It felt really nice to talk with my mom about my sexual identity, to finally get it out in the open. There was only one issue. She'd learned about my coming out through a Facebook repost of my tweet.

"I wish you told me directly," she said. "I feel like I failed you. I didn't make you feel comfortable enough to be able to share with me."

I felt bad. Everything had happened so quickly, and I had felt pressured to come out immediately, I told her. I hadn't come out to her yet because I was *still* exploring and learning about myself. I reassured her that she'd never failed me. The opposite, actually. She helped give me the strength and confidence to explore my sexual identity. Wherever I ended up, I knew that she'd support me no matter what. As a parent, she got it: she had zero expectations or preferences for the gender of the person I was with.

"If I had just shown up, out of the blue, on your doorstep with a boyfriend, I know you wouldn't have missed a beat," I told her. "It would never have occurred to you to be mad. The fact that he was a guy wouldn't even have factored in at all. You would have hugged and kissed my boyfriend and welcomed him home for a home-cooked pasta dinner and wine and spent all evening getting to know him and telling him embarrassing stories from my childhood."

We laughed and wiped our tears away.

YES, YES, THAT-IS TRUE, she said.

Next, I texted my brothers. Nico was cool with it, no problem. Neal was, too, but at first he didn't fully understand what I was trying to say. He thought that I had been straight my whole life and it changed only after college when I started exploring my sexuality.

I called him on FaceTime to clear things up.

"I'm attracted to men, always have been."

"For real? Even while growing up?" Neal asked, dubious.

"Yes, I know for sure I wasn't 100 percent straight growing up."

He paused, thinking back to our childhood.

"But how come you never mentioned it? You had girlfriends and were with Hannah a long time. You never showed any attraction to men. How do you know for sure you weren't straight all this time?"

The questions Neal asked were valid, and he wasn't the only one who asked them. When I began exploring my sexuality and started dating men, I thought back to my childhood often. At first I couldn't clearly recall moments of attraction to men, and that clouded my thinking—I wasn't sure if those feelings had been there all this time.

And then I had read that tweet: "The joke's on me. I had a childhood crush on this girl, but it turns out I'd really had the hots for her boyfriend the whole time. She was just my pathway to him."

It hit me like a thunderbolt to the head. I couldn't clearly remember my attraction to men throughout my childhood because I'd brushed those thoughts aside, modified them to meet the expectations of society as I saw it. But after reading that tweet, I began seeing my memories in a new light—interpreting them differently, discovering their truth. And in my FaceTime call with Neal, I shared these truths with him.

"Do you remember the birthday Nico and I decorated our cakes as our favorite Power Rangers characters?" I asked Neal. "Nico's was the Red Ranger, and mine was the Pink Ranger?"

Neal chuckled and said he'd remembered.

"Mom and Dad thought the Pink Ranger was my favorite because I was crushing on Kimberly, the girl behind the Pink Ranger. For a long time, I went with what Mom and Dad were saying."

Neal nodded.

"I never told anyone that I also thought the Green Ranger, Tommy, was hot. Not because I thought it was wrong to have these feelings, but because I didn't consciously realize I was having feelings for Tommy. It never once occurred to me that I could be attracted to boys. It was like an invisible boundary existed in my mind that wouldn't allow it.

"It took me a long time, but very recently I finally realized why the Pink Ranger was my favorite. It was because the Pink Ranger was the Green Ranger's girlfriend. I remember the episode when Kimberly and Tommy had their first kiss—I was jealous. I wanted to be the Pink Ranger, so I could be with the man I was crushing on all along. If I was the Pink Ranger, then I could be loved by Tommy."

Neal was quiet for a full beat, letting my words sink in, before he said: "Oh, shit."

The Pink Ranger was just the first of many, I told Neal. Ariel in *The Little Mermaid* was another childhood favorite of mine; Prince Eric was the hottie I was truly after. Growing up, the female characters in TV shows or movies were often my favorite. I wanted to be them, because they got to be with the male characters I was crushing on. Subconsciously, I was projecting myself onto female characters, because they were my gateway to the guys I was attracted to.

"I was always sexually fluid while growing up," I told Neal. "Ever since I can remember, I've been attracted to men. I didn't fully realize it until recently, but it was always there."

"Damn," Neal said.

I thanked him for hearing me out. It was, and is, so important that my family know the truth. I was on the journey of a lifetime, and I wanted my mom and my brothers along with me.

Strangely enough, from far off, my dad was cheering me along too. Shortly after the Deaf vlogger made his post, my dad posted a video of his own to social media. To open his video, he said, MY SON NOT GAY. Though I had come out as sexually fluid, not gay, his comment was said in a way that looked down upon the entire LGBTQ spectrum. I cringed and thought, *Come on, Dad. Don't try to put me back in the closet.*

But then my dad kept talking. He implored the vlogger and other people to leave me alone, to give me time and space to figure myself out. My dad ended his vlog with: NYLE IDENTITY, WHATEVER HIMSELF DECIDE.

He was telling the world: "Nyle is whatever he wants to be."

It touched my heart. I hadn't spoken to him in the longest time and had never come out to him directly. Mom had told me that Dad once told her that he didn't tolerate gay people. Mom asked him what would happen if one of their boys were gay. NO! he'd responded.

That was once upon a time. The video showed me a different Dad. His message told me that he was changing and maturing, seeing and understanding life differently—for the better.

THE EVENTS OF THAT ENTIRE evening—the Deaf vlogger's post, the sexually fluid revelation, my coming-out tweet, and the conversations with my mom and Neal—passed while I was sitting alone in the basement of my uncle Charles and aunt Lisa's home in Staten Island. After *ANTM* filming ended I had crashed at their house; its proximity to Manhattan, the fashion and modeling capital of the United States, made it an ideal temporary home.

Minutes after I'd sent my coming-out tweet—and before I'd had the chance to talk with Mom and Neal—I felt footsteps coming from the basement stairs. My bedroom door opened, and my aunt and uncle came into my room. They never came down unprompted; I knew they'd come down because of my tweet.

My heart jackhammered against my chest. I was about to have my first face-to-face talk about my coming out with family members, and because it was with my aunt and uncle, I was extra nervous. They're both tall and imposing, with hard-cut Italian features. Culturally they were old-school Italians, with strong traditional conservative views. They'd been married a long time and had four kids—the very picture of the stereotypically perfect American heterosexual nuclear family. I loved them, but I didn't have a good feeling about how they'd react to their nephew being sexually fluid. Would they even understand the term?

YOUR TWEET, WE SAW. WHAT'S UP? my uncle said, getting right to the point.

The words struck the wall I'd built in my head like a stick of dynamite. The wall came down, stone by stone. Instantly I started sobbing, and my chest squeezed painfully, as if a two-ton boulder was pressing against it. I gasped, but it felt like no air was coming into my lungs. I started to sign, slowly, as I searched for the right words to say.

Softly, my aunt and uncle encouraged me to keep going.

The more I talked, the angrier I felt. The opportunity to come out when I was ready and felt fully empowered to do so had been stolen from me. My coming out, this conversation, everything I'd done that night, was forced on me. I still wasn't sure of my sexual identity and hadn't yet found the community of people who were like me, a community I felt I belonged to.

Amazingly, my aunt and uncle didn't judge me. They listened with an open mind, asked questions here and there, and genuinely tried to empathize with me. The conversation felt incredibly cathartic. I had underestimated my aunt and uncle badly—and I was never more happy to be wrong.

When I finally finished talking, my aunt and uncle were quiet for a bit. It was a lot, and they needed a moment to digest everything.

Earlier, my aunt had shown particular interest in my explanation of sexual fluidity, asking me a flurry of questions on the topic. Now, she had on a thoughtful frown, deeply absorbed in a moment of contemplation. I was quiet, too—exhausted and emotionally drained.

Suddenly, my aunt slapped my uncle on the shoulder.

"I think I might be sexually fluid."

My uncle and I stared at her.

"If not for you," my aunt continued, pointing at my uncle, "I'd probably be with a woman!"

My uncle frowned, then shrugged. I burst out laughing. All the anger, frustration, and other bad feelings came pouring out of me and were replaced with the love and compassion I felt from my aunt and uncle.

My family, man. I don't know where I'd be without 'em.

# 17.

# Boombox

It was Christmas morning, and Nico and I were seven years old. Nico knelt by the tree, ripping the wrapping away from his final present, a large rectangular box. His eyes lit up when he saw what it was: a boombox.

YES! He pumped his fist.

The boombox was pretty neat, Neal and I thought. We turned the volume knob to the max and smiled at how the boom boom vibrations on the floor felt on the soles of our feet.

But that wasn't enough for Nico. He picked the boombox up and placed it on his shoulder, the speaker on full blast inches away from his eardrum. Neal and I may have been Deaf, but our eardrums weren't numb. We winced, imagining the pounding that Nico's inner ears were taking.

Nico didn't pay us or the pain in his ears any mind. He just closed his eyes and kept rocking his head to the beat coming out of the boombox, the happiest boy in the world.

FACES ARE WINDOWS TO THE soul. Look at one closely enough, and you can sense what the person is thinking and feeling.

This is the ace up my sleeve when I interact with a hearing person.

I don't hear the pitch and emotion in their voices. Instead, I scan their eyes—are they looking directly at me, engaged? Or do they float elsewhere—or, worse, are they glazed with boredom? I watch their mouths—are they smiling at me, warm and genuinely interested in what I have to say? Or are they biting their lips, uneasy for some reason? All this information on a face gives me real-time feedback that I use to adjust my conversational approach on the fly.

My face-reading ability helped me successfully navigate countless conversations with hearing people throughout my life—until I stepped into the entertainment industry. The faces of the decision makers—the big shots—of the industry gave very little information away. During meetings it was difficult to read their faces and get a sense of whether they liked me, or how seriously they were considering offering me an opportunity I was pursuing.

Sitting in a room inside the ABC network's Los Angeles studio opposite an interpreter provided by the network, I saw that the executive producer of *Dancing with the Stars* was no different. She regarded me with a placid smile, even as she gave me a warm congratulations on my current success thus far on *ANTM*.

After I thanked her, one of her two assistants jokingly asked if I'd won. I hesitated, unsure how to respond. The final episode of cycle 22, revealing my victory, hadn't aired yet, and I was under a legal obligation to keep the outcome a secret. I was tempted to tell them, thinking it might improve my chances of being offered a spot on *DWTS*. After a beat, I thought better of it and instead teased them that they should watch and find out.

The executive producer smiled at this, showing mild amusement, but gave nothing else away. Her face was a *tough* read. I had zero clue how seriously she was considering me for the show.

After *ANTM* filming wrapped, I'd signed with a manager to help bring in and handle modeling work for me. But I wasn't securing a lot of gigs, at least not yet. I was itching for a bigger opportunity to come my way when my manager told me that ABC had asked me to fly to L.A. to meet with them and discuss the possibility of becoming a celebrity competitor on *DWTS*. I jumped on the next flight out. There were few opportunities bigger than *Dancing with the Stars*, which had an average audience of eighteen million viewers per week, much larger than *ANTM*'s.

One of the executive producer's assistants asked me about my family. I smiled and told them that I was the fourth generation in my family to be born Deaf and that my parents and brothers were all Deaf.

Finally, the executive producer's face showed signs of life. When she smiled, her eyes crinkled; it was genuine. I went on, talking about growing up in an all ASL household and how I'd gone to Deaf schools. She was hooked. The more I talked about my Deaf life, the more animated her face became.

When the questions dried up and the topic of my Deaf experience wound down, the executive producer's face resumed its earlier placidity. Then she looked me dead in the eyes and asked me: "Tell me, Nyle, would you make great TV?"

The question felt like a test. It didn't matter how much my earlier responses about myself had captivated her and her assistants. She was daring me to say out loud, with confidence, that my presence was worthy of her already successful show. Without a second thought, I said yes. It was a no-brainer. I imagined sharing stories about my Deaf experience and my Deaf community on *DWTS*'s massive platform. The show would give me the opportunity to help change perceptions of Deaf people for the better on a mind-blowing scale.

The executive producer smiled politely and told me that the studio was still considering its casting options for the upcoming season and that they might be in touch later if I were to be selected. I thanked her for her time and shook her hand. As I walked out of the room I scanned her face one last time. But I couldn't tell what kind of impression I'd made on her, good or bad, or if I had any shot at getting an offer to compete on the show.

It wasn't until I'd stepped out into the hallway that the thought occurred to me: *What if I did?* and I felt a twinge of fear. When I said

*Yes, I'd make great TV* to the executive producer, I was riding high on the idea of appearing on *DWTS*. But I hadn't yet thought it all the way through. Outside the office, taking a minute alone, I thought: *Shit, what would I be getting myself into?*

On *DWTS*, every week celebrity contestants and their professional dance partners performed choreographed dances live in front of an in-studio audience, a panel of judges, and a national TV audience. Each dance was given a score by the judges and the TV audience, which could vote by calling in or via the *DWTS* website. The show had a massive audience and its share of bells and whistles— gimmicky dance themes, for instance—but at its core it was a dance competition.

And I wasn't sure if I could dance at all.

Again, one more time: I wasn't sure I possessed the *skill that the show entirely revolved around.* Maybe I was going to make great TV by bombing so hilariously badly that people couldn't look away?

My qualms about my dancing ability weren't about being Deaf. I knew plenty of Deaf people who were incredibly talented dancers. No, at the heart of my unease was the fact that I had very little dancing experience, period. I wasn't even good for breaking out a nifty dance move or two at nightclubs. Was it even a reasonable expectation to learn to dance at a halfway passable level by the time the show began?

The more I thought about the idea of dancing in front of a national audience, the more terrified I became . . . until I thought of my twin brother, Nico.

NICO HAS ALWAYS BEEN FASCINATED by music. He craves it, obsesses over it. His ears work only slightly better than mine, meaning his residual hearing can detect sounds at around eighty to eighty-five decibels and louder (compared to ninety decibels for me). His being Deaf never bothered him—it just meant that he needed to find creative ways to be able to better listen to music. Like how, as a kid, he had played his boombox at max volume while carrying it on his shoulder. Or, when music started playing on the TV, Nico would scramble off the couch, crawl to the TV, turn up the volume, and lay down right there on the carpet, his ear hovering next to the set's speaker.

YOU DO-DO? COME-ON, STOP. YOUR EARS, HURT WILL, I chided him.

Nico ignored me. He wanted to learn what instruments created the different sounds he heard, what the lyrics said, how the beats were structured. He wanted to understand *everything* about music.

COME-ON, I told him. TRY-TRY HARD, STOP. YOU DEAF, SAME ME. Music was cool when you just felt the beats, but I thought Nico was taking it too far and that he was stupid to try so hard to listen to and understand music. Nico was *Deaf,* and Deaf people weren't made to enjoy music, I thought.

It's funny—I look back now and think: *Damn, internalized ableism took a firm hold on me when I was a kid.* I was pulling Nico down, thinking that he couldn't pursue his passion in music just because he was Deaf.

Thankfully, Nico continued to ignore me and kept doing his thing, no matter how often I put him down for it. Every time we got into the backseat of our family Dodge van, Nico pounded on the ceiling with his fist. The walls of the van *thud thudded* until Mom felt it and looked back.

TURN-ON RADIO! Nico said to Mom in the rearview mirror. The radio was always tuned to one specific station that Nico said played the best music: rap, hip-hop, and R&B. His favorite artists were Eminem, Jay-Z, and Sisqó.

A few minutes into the car ride, music blasting, Nico would tap my knee.

WHAT SONG IS-THIS?

Straining to hear the music and feel the beat, I racked my brain for anything that felt or sounded familiar. Nearly always, I shook my head and told Nico I didn't know. He sighed and told me the name of the song. Over time, I started to become impressed by Nico's uncanny ability to ID songs. How was he doing it?

It's different things, he explained to me. Sometimes it was the timing of the beats, how many *booms* and how often they came up in the song. Other times it was how loud the bass was. He could also recognize what instruments were being played, and even the voice of the singer.

Nico's study of music entered warp speed when YouTube started gaining popularity in the early 2000s. On the platform, he discovered music videos that showed lyrics in time with the song. PAH—ASL for "at last"—he had a tool that helped him learn the words to songs he loved.

In a way, YouTube was to Nico what television closed captioning, CC, was to my mom. She had grown up watching TV without CC, with no way of knowing, beyond lip-reading and visual cues, what people onscreen were saying. She had to invent dialogue and storylines. Later, in the 1980s, when closed captioning was introduced and became more widely available, Mom went back and watched shows from her childhood. *So that's what they were saying!* she thought as she read the captions. She was amazed at how different the actual dialogue and storylines were from those in her imagination.

Nico experienced a similar awakening while using YouTube. He'd had the other parts down pat—he could recognize musical instruments, beats, voices—and now he had the final piece of the puzzle: the lyrics. And it was a revelation to learn what all those songs were about, the messages they portrayed, the stories they told.

Sometimes he giggled as he read lyrics for the first time; he had no idea some of his favorite songs growing up had so many cuss words.

As he got older, Nico's passion for music grew. In college, he installed a 1,500-watt stereo system in the trunk of his car. He always turned it up to full blast when he drove, the windows rattling with every booming beat. When I joined him for trips back home to Frederick from Gallaudet University, I couldn't last more than five minutes listening to his sound system. It gave me a terrible headache, and I begged him to turn it off. Reluctantly, he would lower the volume, only because I was his little brother.

Today Nico is a professional DJ. He literally gets paid to play music at events. He has plenty of natural rhythm and dancing ability, which he uses to lead group dances at the events he deejays. Despite everything—his being Deaf, society's perception of Deaf people's ability to appreciate and understand music, the doubt fueled by internalized ableism he has had to endure from me, his own brother—he achieved his dream. His example proved to me that the unlikeliest feats were indeed within reach if you put your mind to it and ignored all naysayers. In a way, Nico and his relentless pursuit of his passion for music gave me the audacity to believe I could learn to perform complicated dance routines set to music on national television.

During my interview with the *DWTS* producer in L.A., she had asked if I could dance. Eager to make an impression, I said yes; to my great relief she didn't press further. It would be a few months before I heard from the producer again. In that long interlude, I had battled with my internal self-doubt, and thinking of Nico's example helped shift my perspective on dancing from petrified by the very thought to *maybe I can do this.*

Time passed, and I received very little communication from the *DWTS* producer. In December, the final episode of *ANTM* cycle 22 aired, announcing me as the winner. Then New Year's Eve came, and I received a text from the producer, wishing me a Happy New Year. She didn't say anything more, but I took it as a positive omen—at the very least she had me on her mind.

Finally, in February 2016, I heard back from the producer— offering me a spot on the show.

By then, I wasn't freaking out about learning how to dance. I knew I could do it, just like Nico had become a DJ.

*DWTS* SENT ME TO MEET my professional dance partner at a studio in Santa Monica. A photo shoot, complete with backdrop, lights, and a photographer, was arranged in the studio to set the stage for my introduction as a rising model who had just won *ANTM*. The plan was to have my partner walk in as I was modeling. I didn't know who my dance partner would be and vice versa—we'd both find out for the first time at the Santa Monica studio.

The blazing California sun turned the studio into an oven. Sweat ran down my body as I struck one pose, then another. Because it wasn't for a bona fide job for a client, my modeling was half-hearted. My mind was elsewhere, thinking about who my dancing partner would be. The minutes stretched on; it felt like the longest photo shoot I had ever done in my life. Finally, a producer waved me over.

"It looks like your partner is running late. Let's take five," he said, gesturing at a couch where we could sit down and relax while we waited. I sat down with Ramon, the same interpreter I'd worked with through *ANTM* filming. He continued to interpret for me for most of my time on *DWTS*.

As soon as I hit the couch, my mind started racing. Would my dance partner be easy to work with? How would she react to finding out that her celebrity partner wouldn't be able to hear music? Would my partner be patient enough to teach me—someone who'd never danced before in his life—how to dance?

Also, just as important, I really wanted to be paired with a top-level dance partner. Don't get me wrong, all of the professional dancers on *DWTS* are crazy talented—but certain pro dancers separated themselves from the field. The best of the best included Witney Carson, who'd won season 19 with actor Alfonso Ribeiro, and up-and-coming dancer Sharna Burgess, who'd placed second in the previous season and third the season before that. I was here to win, and I wanted a Witney or Sharna as my partner.

Ramon tapped me on the knee, knocking me out of my reverie.

"The producer just said your partner is on her way."

I took a deep breath and walked over to the backdrop and struck another pretend pose. I barely flexed my muscles as I posed; after every camera flash my eyes flicked to the door.

"Don't look right away when your partner arrives," the producer instructed me. "We'll tell you when it's time to look."

I turned my gaze back toward the camera lens and tried to keep it there, until Ramon waved for my attention.

"The producer just told me not to immediately come to your side when your partner arrives. He wants you to meet your partner alone and have your first conversation with her without an interpreter. After a couple minutes, I will step forward."

I chuckled to myself. This wasn't my first rodeo; I knew from my experience on *ANTM* that the *DWTS* producers were manipulating the situation to make for good TV. They were hoping to draw a dramatic response from my partner and capture it on camera. I was cool with it; I could handle myself for a few minutes communicating with a hearing person without an interpreter.

At last, the door opened and my partner emerged. While staring straight ahead at the camera lens, I strained to see my new partner out of the corner of my eye. There are studies showing that Deaf people have stronger peripheral vision than hearing folks, an improved ability to quickly catch and identify objects at the far edges of one's field of vision. Our bodies compensate for the loss of one sense by strengthening another. In the studio I stretched my Deaf superpower vision to its limit and made out the general physical features of my new partner: brown hair and a slender figure. She didn't look like Witney or Sharna. I racked my brain trying to think of other *DWTS* dancers but couldn't remember one that matched the features of my new partner. She descended the steps slowly and gracefully, and then stepped toward me, her figure coming into focus nearer the center of my vision.

Ramon waved. "Now," the producer said.

I dropped my fake-model pose and locked eyes with my dance partner.

"*Hello!*" she said. Right away I noticed her beautiful, warm smile. But it was unfamiliar. I waved back at her. She walked toward me, continuing to speak.

"*It's so nice, so nice to meet you.*"

I pointed to my ears and shook my head: "*I'm Deaf.*"

The gesture didn't stick with her; she kept talking at me, faster, the words coming too quickly for me to read on her lips. I put up my hands to stop her. Then I pointed at my chest and used an index finger to trace the letters of my name on my palm:

N-Y-L-E.

My new partner looked at the movement on my palm with a quizzical look. Then, in a snap, her face lit up with understanding.

"*Oh!*" she said. "*You're Deaf.*"

There was no mistaking her wide-eyed expression. She looked like the proverbial deer frozen in the middle of the road in the headlights of an oncoming car—a look I had seen and negotiated many times in my life. I imagined her brain being assaulted with questions: How do you teach a Deaf person to dance? What about music? How do you teach the concept of music to a Deaf person?

It would be up to me to help her answer these questions.

After she regained her composure, she mouthed, "*What do you do?*"

I traced letters on my palm again. *M-O-D-E-L.* She frowned and stared at my hands, trying to make out the letters I was tracing. At last, Ramon walked up, and I introduced myself again.

Then she asked, "Do you know who I am?"

I still couldn't place her. I had looked through the professional dancers that had competed in the most recent season on the *DWTS* website just the night before, but none of the faces matched the one before me.

I had no clue that one name was absent from the list of dancers on the website. Sidelined with an ankle injury, my partner hadn't been able to participate in last season's competition. Peta Murgatroyd was her name, she said. She had been a dancer nearly all her life. On season 14, paired with former NFL wide receiver Donald Driver, she had won the *DWTS* championship.

I did a mental fist pump. I was paired up with a champion!

As Peta talked, she kept her eyes on Ramon instead of me. Whenever you're in conversation with a Deaf person via an interpreter, it's best to look directly at the Deaf person. They are the one you are having a conversation with, not the interpreter. Looking away from the

Deaf person takes away the human connection two people have when conversing. Of course, Peta was new to Deaf culture and didn't know this yet. As she talked, Ramon tilted his head and gestured toward me, encouraging her to look at me instead. After a few minutes she got the hint and directed her eyes to me.

Eventually the cameras switched off. I was ready to stay and chat more and get to know Peta better. But she quickly gave me her phone number so we could text, said goodbye, and left, promising to be in touch to schedule our first rehearsal.

"That's weird," Ramon said.

"What do you mean?"

"You were supposed to have your first dance practice with Peta today, right after this."

My mind churned. Finding that her new dance partner was Deaf had come as a wicked curveball for Peta; that much was clear from the shock and confusion I saw in her eyes. I suspected that she cancelled practice to regroup and quickly create a whole new strategy to teach a Deaf person how to dance.

I was disappointed about practice being cancelled. Peta and I had only two weeks until the first dance competition. I had no dancing experience and absolutely no technical knowledge of dance movement. Because I faced such a steep learning curve, each practice session was incredibly valuable. But I told myself that the most important thing right now was to reassure Peta and build her confidence in me as her dance partner. In the car, I pulled out my phone and started tapping out a text to Peta. I told her I was thrilled that she was my dance partner and I believed we would dance great together.

The key to succeeding, I wrote, was to learn about each other. As a Deaf person, I came from a beautiful and unique heritage that included a multilayered culture, a visual language, and a wealth of stories. My plan was to give Peta a crash course on all things Deaf, and we would figure out how to weave Deaf elements into our dance performances. This was how some former *DWTS* competitors made their mark. A previous competitor, Noah Galloway, who was an amputee, had artfully told his story in his dance performances. Another power-ful example was Bindi Irwin, who gave a heartfelt dance tribute for her father Steve Irwin, the legendary Australian animal expert/TV show host, en route to her victory in the previous season.

You didn't win *DWTS* by just simply mastering the steps and movements of dance. To grab the Mirrorball Trophy, Peta and I needed to tell stories, inspire the judges, and capture viewers' hearts.

I ended the text message with a promise that I would work twice as hard as any other celebrity dancer on the show.

Peta texted back and thanked me for reaching out. She said she was excited to work with me and learn about Deaf culture.

"Our first dance lesson is tomorrow!" she wrote.

A SMALL CROWD HAD GATHERED outside the small private studio where our first practice was to take place. They waved for our attention and snapped pictures at us through the studio windows. Peta didn't mind them. She smiled for photographers briefly before turning toward me. Having learned her lesson quickly from the day before, she kept her eyes directed toward me instead of Ramon. Her smile was disarming, and her warmth melted away the nerves I felt before we started our first practice.

As we made small talk, Peta asked if I had any background or ex-perience in dance. I told her I had a Deaf twin brother who deejayed in his spare time and could dance pretty well.

This brightened Peta's spirits. "That's so cool!" she said.

"Unfortunately, I don't really have as much dance experience as my brother. Unless you count drunken dancing at night clubs. You know, mostly pelvic grinding."

I immediately regretted the joke when I saw Peta's face fall slightly. She mustered up a laugh, but I couldn't tell if it was a genu-ine laugh or one of nervousness. I quickly steered the conversation to safer ground.

Our small talk made me feel better about having Peta as a dance partner. But the question hung in the air between us: Would I be able to learn how to dance?

Without music, Peta eased me into my first lesson with a basic series of steps: Left, forward; right, backward. Peta and I stood side by side and I followed her lead, moving in sync with her rhythm. Left, forward; right, backward. We made it all the way through, no mistakes.

My confidence started to rise. Dancing wasn't so tough; I *could* do this. Encouraged, Peta moved me on to the second lesson she had planned: my first tango dance move.

Peta turned my body so that we again stood side by side. We stepped forward four beats, performed a 180-degree turn, and swept backward four more steps. Another test passed. Next, Peta wanted to perform the same tango move, but while facing each other. Our eyes locked and my hands in hers, my heart pounded. The competitor in me wanted to get this perfect so *bad*.

Peta led, moving backward, and I followed, moving forward. My feet quickly moved to fill the floor where hers just departed. Once I brought my feet down too early and clipped her shoes with mine. I grimaced, but we made it through the full motion.

We tried it again. This time I paced myself and there were no miscues. So far so good.

"Let's try again," Peta said. "A little faster this time."

The third try went without a hitch. Peta smiled at me; the doubt that was on her face earlier in the morning seemed to melt away.

Five weeks after that first practice—in the third week of the *DWTS* competition—Peta and I danced the tango. One moment, midway through the dance, Peta and I stood frozen in a hold. We were right by the stands and the entire studio was dimmed. Seconds ticked by, the anticipation building. Then, in an instant, a brilliant white light blazed on behind us and we exploded out of our hold. One, two, three, four steps forward, turn, one, two, three, four steps backward. Peta led and I followed, feet tapping the floor in rhythm, hips twitching and sashaying. It was the exact same move I had learned during my first morning of practice with Peta.

PERHAPS BECAUSE OF HER NATURE—SHE had a warm personality and showed that she cared about you as a person—Peta displayed a genuine curiosity about my Deaf identity. She asked questions gently without being too intrusive, and I was happy to answer them.

During one break, Peta asked me if I had an interpreter with me at all times and if Ramon had been my interpreter my entire life.

"Nope on both counts," I answered. I explained how I didn't have an interpreter with me day and night and that, like the vast majority of Deaf people, I spent 99 percent of my life without an interpreter. I told Peta that throughout my *DWTS* experience, including practices, interviews, and the actual competitions, Ramon would be my interpreter. But before Ramon, I had worked with many different interpreters—maybe hundreds—in many different situations, such as at school and doctor's appointments. And even now, I still worked with other interpreters in different settings, too.

Then it was my turn to ask a question.

"Do you speak with an accent?"

"Yeah," she said, giggling. "I was born in New Zealand and grew up in Australia. That's where my accent comes from. How'd you know?"

"I knew it!" I told her that I sensed something was different about the way she spoke when I read her lips. She enunciated certain words differently. Like when she said "No," her lips would exaggerate the *o*, rolling it longer than I was used to seeing. Sometimes I just couldn't read from her lips what she was saying, even when it was something simple and brief. It confounded me; I knew she had to have an accent.

She also told me that she'd started dancing very young and had travelled the world with fourteen other professional dancers, many of whom were also competing on *DWTS*. She'd known some of these dancers for a long time; they were like sisters and brothers to her. I had no idea, and it fascinated me that she was part of her own small little community in which everyone had known each other for so long, kind of like some Deaf friends I had with whom I went way back.

A phone call to Peta interrupted our conversation. It was a *DWTS* producer, informing her which dance we would perform during the first week of competition, which was less than two weeks away.

"Do you know the New York cha cha?" she asked me.

"No idea," I said. "I've never heard of it before." I was comfortable being transparently honest with Peta. After mastering the tango move in the morning, I felt I had proven to Peta that even though I was starting from zero when learning how to dance, I could learn very quickly. As long as I was honest, she would know where she needed to start when teaching me.

The New York cha cha is a dance with a lot of arm and hand whips and snaps. Like with the tango, Peta broke down the dance into sections and taught me each individual move first. Once I got the hang of the individual moves, we went through them all in sequence. After a few tries, I started to get the timing down right.

Dancing wasn't as easy as I'd initially thought after Peta taught me that very first basic move earlier in the morning. I struggled with some technical parts; for instance, Peta told me I needed to work on my hold. Instead of puffing my chest out and pulling my shoulders back, a perfect hold form, I kept slouching. But overall, I was making awesome progress. My leg movements and footwork were on point. My confidence was soaring.

Feeling myself a little bit, I turned to Peta. "Why don't we turn the music on?"

Peta giggled and shook her head. "No, no."

"Why not?" I asked. "What about the other contestants? Are they practicing with music?"

"Yes," she said. "But I'm not sure if you're ready."

I could understand Peta's hesitancy. At the start of the practice, she had no idea where to begin with me, a novice dancer who happened to be Deaf. Her strategy was to focus on the basics, breaking down each dance to its smallest bits, and walk me through each part slowly.

It didn't matter to Peta on that day how quickly I could perform each move—she wanted to make sure I built a good grasp of the technique and movement first. Once I'd mastered them, she would start putting multiple moves together. The last step in her dance training plan was to begin practicing in time to music, which would require me to nail all the technique and movements I'd learned at a much quicker pace. She didn't want to start that last step until later. It was a good strategy, and it worked—so well that I felt ready to dance to music after a half day of practice. Peta and I didn't have much time before our first competition. Every hour we spent practicing without music put us further behind the other competitors, who were already dancing to music.

"I want to practice and learn the way you would train any other dance partner," I told Peta. "You're doing an amazing job teaching me how to dance. I'm confident enough in my ability to learn and your ability to teach to start dancing with music on. We don't have much time left to practice. Let's start to push ourselves."

Peta agreed and switched on the stereo system. We assumed our start-of-dance pose and as the music began I followed Peta's lead. A minute later, I looked at Peta.

"How did we do?"

"Not bad," Peta smiled. "The dance itself was perfect. We were only slightly behind the music. We just need to quicken our pace a little bit."

We upped our pace over the next few tries, and Peta confirmed we were dancing in rhythm to the music. It was a good thing we started practicing with music on the first day, because it alerted us to a new issue early, giving us more time to solve it. Because I couldn't hear the music, I didn't know when to time different dance moves in our routine. For example, I didn't know when the music began and it was time to start the first steps of our cha cha dance. I'd start moving only when I saw Peta take the first steps, and that put me a split second behind her—which would cost us points in the judges' scoring during actual competition. We had to be in lockstep, from the first beat of the song to the very last.

After talking it over, Peta and I decided that the solution would be a cue from her. The cue should be subtle, built into the natural motions of the dance. We eventually brainstormed and used many different cues in our dances throughout the competition: rhythmic head nods, visible sweeps of the hand, hidden hand squeezes, carefully altered steps, discreet taps on the shoulder or back. For the opening to our cha cha dance, we decided on a soft upward turn of the head. Before the music began, we stood facing each other, our heads bowed, eyes downward. When she began lifting her head up, I would follow along, knowing the music had started and exactly when to take the first step of the dance.

We practiced this cue again and again and it worked without fail. It was effective, it felt natural, and it looked like an artistic movement, naturally blending in with our dance routine. It was perfect.

Piece by piece, Peta continued to introduce me to new elements of the cha cha—a hold, a move, a turn. We strung several elements together and practiced through them at once, again and again. Suddenly, in the middle of one of our dance progressions, Peta burst out laughing.

"What?" I asked.

She waved me off. "Nothing," she said. "Let's keep practicing."

We practiced our dance once more, and she laughed again. Throughout the rest of the practice, she would burst out laughing again and again.

"What? What's so funny?" I wanted to know, but she wouldn't tell me.

I had my suspicions, because I think I was feeling the same way. I couldn't believe how well this was going. Working with Peta was so easy. She wasn't just a talented dance teacher—she was a patient dance partner who asked me what I thought and worked with me to find solutions that felt right to both of us. I could see in her face that she was amazed that she could teach me to dance so easily.

After I got over my own amazement at my initial dance success, I thought about how attending Deaf schools growing up helped position me to learn to dance. Deaf schools are small, but the teachers, administrators, and parents have high expectations. It made you feel you wanted to join in many after school sports and other extracurriculars, which I did. Many of my fellow high school classmates played at least three sports and still had time to serve on the student body government and ace classes. My Deaf school experience helped me build a mentality that was open to trying new things, which helped me learn new skills quickly and instilled a competitive drive to kick ass in all of my endeavors. It prepared me perfectly for the pressure-packed challenge of learning how to dance in a matter of weeks and then perform in front of millions of people.

My natural athleticism also helped flatten out my learning curve. Back in fifth grade my skill at racing and tumbling had assisted me in winning over new hearing friends at the mainstream school; in high school I had excelled as the setter on the volleyball team; and now in *DWTS* practice I was quickly able to master the precise footwork and balletic turns of dance.

Overall, I couldn't have been happier with how the first day of practice went. Not just because I'd left a strong first impression after the abrupt cancellation of the first practice the day before, but also because it was an important step toward building trust between Peta and me. She had taken my lead on beginning to practice with music on, and it had worked out well. With increasing confidence, Peta could teach me more complex and advanced dance moves. We could progress through my dance lessons more quickly and Peta would be empowered with more freedom for creativity and complexity when choreographing our dances. All of these details would result in higher potential scores, and—just maybe—an eventual Mirrorball Trophy.

At the end of the day, *DWTS* interviewed Peta on camera. I went to the opposite side of the studio to sit down and soothe my aching feet. While I unlaced my shoes, Ramon nudged me.

"Because I can hear it," he said, "you should know what the interviewer and Peta are saying."

I smiled; for a brief moment I was back in the small auditorium with Tyra Banks and the CW executive, when Ramon interpreted their quiet conversation: HE SAID "I'M SOLD."

Ramon interpreted that the interviewer asked what Peta had thought of my first day. Peta said she was blown away. She was amazed with my ability to adapt and listen to her instructions. Though I didn't have any formal dance experience, I was learning very quickly.

It felt incredible to see her say these things.

A long time after we ended our run on *DWTS*, I asked Peta, "When did you sense that we had a real shot at winning the Mirrorball Trophy?"

Without skipping a beat, she said: "The first day of practice."

# 18.

# Silence, Deaf History, and the Last Dance

During Dancing with the Stars *practices, I wore special dance shoes. They hurt like a bitch. The edges of the shoes clamped the sides of my feet and cramped my toes. By design, the shoes kept my heels raised as I danced, forcing me to rely on little-used calf muscles to move around—leaving them sore as hell long after practice ended. My throbbing toes and calves screamed for relief as I stepped into a hot tub every night.*

*Wearing those shoes gave me a new appreciation for people who wear high heels. I can't imagine how their calves feel the day after a night of hard dancing on high heels at a club. Shout out to all you high heel wearers reading this.*

*However much I hated my dance shoes, I still wore them during practice every day—even the marathon practices that lasted six to seven hours. Noticing how I winced as I took my shoes off after one practice, Peta tapped me on the shoulder.*

*"You know you don't have to wear dancing shoes during practice? You can wear sneakers during practices, like I do, and save the dancing shoes for live competitions."*

*"No way," I told her. I wanted to simulate the experience of live dance competitions, and that included the shoes. I worried about other things, too, like not having the chance to break the shoes in and becoming comfortable moving around in them.*

*I kept wearing the shoes every day, until they became part of me. They kept punishing me with aching toes and calves after each practice, but I grew to love those shoes and the earned pain they inflicted on me.*

*I'll admit I was a little bit crazy. But you have to be if you want to win.*

THROUGH THE FIRST WEEK OF practice, one question lingered in Peta's mind: If the music was turned up loud enough, would I be able to dance to it without relying on cues?

The stereo system in our regular dance studio in Los Angeles wasn't loud enough for me to hear, so we couldn't try to answer Peta's question. But then, a week before the first live competition, I had modeling work in New York City, so we practiced at a dance studio owned by Peta's then-fiancé, Maks Chmerkovskiy, and his brother, Val. The studio had an obscenely loud stereo, one Nico would be proud of. It made the whole room shake; my teeth rattled with each *boom* and I could feel the beat deep in my bones. It was so loud that when Peta said something, Ramon couldn't hear.

"What?" Ramon shouted over the din. He bent his ear toward Peta and shook his head. Peta walked over to switch off the stereo, and the teeth-rattling beats abruptly stopped. Even in the sudden dead quiet I could still feel ghosts of vibrations shaking through my rib cage.

"Could you hear the music?" Peta asked.

"Oh, definitely," I said.

I rarely could hear music. It had to be turned all the way up for me to be able to catch slivers of the sound. The only place I can typically hear music is a nightclub, where the electronic music pulses so loud I could feel my eardrums bouncing like a trampoline with every beat.

Peta's face seemed to glow as she watched me take in the sheer acoustic force of the speakers. Finally, we'd get an answer to her question and find out how I'd do dancing while being able to hear the music.

At first, I was ambivalent about dancing to audible music. We had more than a week's worth of practice under our belt by then, and in all that time I hadn't heard a single beat of music. I relied entirely on the system of cues that Peta and I had created, and I felt more comfortable and confident by the day. Dancing had started to feel natural to me. When Peta and I were dancing, it felt like the entire world fell away. The fans and paparazzi that showed up outside the dance studios, the excitement and pressure of the *DWTS* competition, the self-doubt and uncertainty of being a Deaf dancer that constantly lingered in the back of my head, the endless whirlwind that my life had become since I first appeared on *ANTM*—all of that disappeared. On the dance floor, it was just Peta and me.

And now, it felt weird—disorienting, almost—to think about hearing the music while dancing after I'd practiced so often and successfully without having to factor it in. But I was willing to give it a shot because I trusted Peta.

Peta skipped over to the stereo to reset the music. We assumed our customary start position, facing each other with our heads bowed. I was supposed to keep an eye on Peta's head and wait for it to begin turning upward—my first cue.

I felt a faint twinge in my ears—was that the beginning of the song? My ears strained for the sound of the song's first beats. I thought I heard something, but Peta's head hadn't yet moved. Had I imagined hearing the beginning of the song?

Suddenly, I noticed Peta's eyes looking at mine—her head was already halfway through the upward turn. I had been so absorbed with trying to hear the beginning of the song that I was late to start the dance. I flicked my head and shuffled my feet into the dance's first steps, catching up to Peta's authoritative tempo.

Again, my focus drifted to my ears. I searched for the song's beats, trying to time them with the movements of my body. Sometimes I caught a beat correctly and timed a step in rhythm with Peta. It felt good when I did it right, like catching a wave while surfing. But then moments later I mistimed a turn, and I felt like I'd performed an embarrassing wipeout.

As I strained to listen and understand the music, my legs and feet and shoulders felt far away, apart from my mind. I missed steps, made turns late, and felt totally out of sync. It no longer felt like it was just me and Peta on the dance floor. Finally, the roaring music ceased, and the studio fell to a hush.

"My bad. I screwed up," I said. I hated failing; it gnawed at me.

"It's fine," Peta said. "It's only your first time trying to dance by following along with the music."

Even as audible as it was in the studio, the music made little sense to me. In each moment of the song, there were so many sounds—different instruments and voices, different pitches, different beats. I'd thought the dance cue beats would be easy to pick out, like single blips on a heart monitor. But the sound waves pummeling my ears in the studio were nothing like that. They were like multiple lines of jagged peaks: high and low, narrow and wide. I couldn't catch all of the peaks—some were at pitches I could hear well, others weren't, slipping past my ears. And I rarely could tell which peak was the beat that indicated the next progression of our dance.

Peta pressed play on the sound system and we took a second try at our dance routine. I figured out the beginning of the song and timed my head's upward turn with Peta's. We swept into the first steps firmly in rhythm. Peta turned and her eyes locked with mine. She had a smile the size of the Brooklyn Bridge. I smiled back and searched for the next beat—which never reached my ears. Late to the next step, I hurried to catch up with Peta. And then I thought I heard another beat and began the next step, only to find that Peta hadn't moved yet—I'd moved on the wrong peak.

I stopped and walked over to turn the music off.

"What's wrong?" Peta asked.

When it was just us, no music audible to me, Peta and I were *killing* it during practice. All of a sudden, with the music turned up so I could hear it, everything was thrown out of whack. No matter how loud the music was, my ears simply couldn't decipher the jagged peaks of the song. That was the problem. Why was I even trying? I was Deaf—I had been Deaf my entire twenty-six years of life and during that first week of excellent dance practice with Peta. On this day, with the music turned up so loud, I was trying not to be Deaf. The reason I was failing so miserably was that I wasn't being true to myself.

"In my life, I've never heard a single meaningful thing," I told Peta. "I never *wanted* to hear at all. I found ways to succeed without needing to hear. Like our first week, our practices had gone so well. My timing was spot on. The method we were using, with you dancing to the music and me following your cues, was working effectively. Why would we want to change that?"

In that moment it became crystal clear to me: I believed, deep down, that I could learn how to dance better than anybody else in the *DWTS* competition without needing to hear a single beat of the music.

"No music for me," I told Peta. "I want to focus on learning the moves, the timing, and keep working with and following you on the cues. That's all I need."

Peta nodded. I knew she had been excited to see how I could dance while hearing the music, and she was somewhat disappointed to see that the idea wasn't working out. But I could tell she understood. Like, *really* understood. She has this rare gift of empathy and compassion. She could put herself right in my shoes and understand, as close as possible for a hearing person, what I was feeling.

"You're right," she said.

She walked over to lower the volume on the stereo system, then pressed play. We stepped to the middle of the floor, facing each other. I stared downward in complete silence, eyeing Peta's head in the edge of my field of vision for the first cue. Without the anticipation of the music, I felt free.

A FUNNY THING ABOUT DANCING: it helped me put my math degree to good use. Because I couldn't rely on music to time dances for me, I had to do so by memorizing careful calculations. For every dance, I held many different numbers in my head—the number of steps and turns in each segment, the number of timed beats to remain in a hold or wait before beginning the next series of steps. All those numbers swam in my head somewhere in the background when I danced. After practicing a dance long enough, the timing became automatic to me—muscle memory, like shooting a basketball.

Once, however, my math brain's internalized dance timing became at odds with the music. On the days of live competitions, we'd have dress rehearsals—with cameras and cues, we'd go through the entire two-hour-long show. During our first dress rehearsal, something about Peta's and my dance was off. Peta kept telling me that I needed to speed up, but I couldn't understand how it was happening that I was behind. We'd rehearsed the same dance for two weeks straight; the precise timing of the dance was seared into my brain and muscles. There was no way I was dancing too slow.

A thought occurred to me.

"Peta, maybe the music is being played a little too quickly."

Peta didn't think so; the music sounded the same as all the times we'd practiced. I asked her to check just to make sure.

Coming back, Peta told me that I was right. The music was being played at a slightly faster pace than we'd been practicing to. For Peta, this minor difference in pace wasn't noticeable; it was something she could adjust to when dancing. But I couldn't. My Deaf math major brain had locked down the timing a certain way, and I needed the music to be played at the exact same pace every time. It was a huge relief to catch this problem during rehearsals, in time to fix it before the first live competition.

MOMENTS BEFORE OUR FIRST LIVE competition dance began, Peta tapped me on the shoulder.

"We have a small problem," she said. The music in the studio was being played quieter than she'd expected, and with the incidental noise from the crowd, she didn't think she would be able to hear the soft first beat that kicked off our first dance.

Then she shrugged and said, "Don't worry. We'll just wing it." She pulled me onto the dance floor.

This unexpected development terrified me. I already couldn't hear, and now Peta couldn't hear that first beat either? I had the timing of our dance set to the precise millisecond. What if we were late or early on the first move?

I had no time to think about what could go wrong, because the bright spotlight above the dance floor was already on me. I put on my best smile, showing my pearly whites and a face of cool confidence. Inside, though, my nervous system went into overdrive. The stage did that to me; I hated it with a passion. I didn't mind acting in front of a camera, where there were few eyes on me and do-overs were an option if I screwed up. Live on a stage, though, you couldn't hide any mistakes. And here, if I messed up, eighteen million people were watching.

My heart started pounding against my chest so hard I thought it would crash through. Fear gripped my body and my brain rained self-doubt all over me: *Ican'tdothisIcan'tdothisIcan'tdothis.*

But I had to.

When my hands wrapped around Peta's shoulder and waist, I started to feel a sense of calm. The audience, the judges, the background lights all faded away. It was just Peta and me again. She lifted up her head, the first cue, and we swept into our routine. Step and beat counts whizzed around my brain like spinning numbers on a casino slot machine; my body was on autopilot, giving way to muscle memory. In practice we had decided to add some extra sauce to the choreography—I ripped my button-down shirt open to show my abs and ran my hands through my hair, and our bodies grooved together in vertical waves near the end—and it was a hit. I felt good all the way through. When the dance was over, I raised my fist in the air and Peta pumped hers in exhilaration. In the audience my mom and brothers were cheering me on, and the other dance competitors high up in the balcony waved their hands—the Deaf equivalent of clapping applause.

The judges gave us a score of twenty-three out of a maximum of thirty, tied for the highest that week. Standing before the judges, Peta and I embraced in a celebratory hug.

AS I HAD TEXTED PETA the day we met, after she cancelled our first dance practice, the key to winning *DWTS* was to tell my story through our dances. Learning dances and executing them competently was indeed important; doing that work helped carry me in the first seven weeks. But by the final few weeks, the field had been reduced to the top dancers. Execution and skill could do only so much to separate us from the rest. To win, Peta and I needed to find an edge—something that set us apart from our competitors. That edge was my Deaf identity.

Throughout the first seven weeks, I could already see the impact that my presence as a Deaf dancer was having on viewers of the show—and not just those who were unfamiliar with the Deaf community, but also those who were close to it.

One example was a former speech teacher of mine from elementary school. She was of those teachers who had put me through endless repetitions of making single sounds in the hopes of helping me gain passable speech ability, before I decided once and for all to quit speech lessons prior to entering the third grade. Out of the blue, this speech teacher reached out to my mom to congratulate her on my run on *DWTS*. She said she owed me an apology for suggesting I wear hearing aids when I was her student, and that I had proven her wrong. To her, I had become a role model for Deaf people, showing that they *could* achieve their dreams.

The teacher's message surprised me and warmed my heart. It told me that just by being myself, a proud Deaf person, and performing well in my dances, I was helping change attitudes and perceptions toward people like me. Her message showed me I was doing something right and inspired me to try to make more of an impact by drawing on my Deaf identity and portraying it to the *DWTS* audience.

I sat down with Peta to figure out how we could blend in elements of my Deaf experience into our dances. Our discussion drifted toward the media attention I'd been receiving. Ever since my strong week one cha cha performance, some news outlets, bloggers, and media pundits had pegged me as a favorite to win the competition. Often they expressed amazement that a Deaf contestant could dance so well. One headline, from Time.com, read: "Nyle DiMarco is a Frontrunner on *Dancing with the Stars*—Even Though He Can't Hear the Music."

I loved the support the media was throwing behind me; it boosted my confidence to be singled out as a serious contender to win the Mirrorball Trophy. But I wondered, could they come close to understanding my experience as a Deaf man competing on the show? Did they have any idea what it felt like to be onstage, not hearing a single beat of the song, but still nailing my steps, moves, and turns?

That feeling—it's not something you can explain to someone. They won't get it, not until they experience it themselves. Realizing that was when the light bulb popped on for Peta and me: let's *show* the world what it's like to dance to no music. We started planning out how to mesh this new idea into the choreography of our paso doble dance for week 7.

The dance started with me standing behind a chain link fence, my hands gripping the metal wire, yearning for what lies beyond. Moments later, I stepped back, maneuvered into a turn, and pulverized the fence with a thundering kick, a literal metaphor that set the tone of the dance: I refused to allow any barriers to stand in my way. I stepped up to Peta and took her hand, and we swept into our dance.

A minute into our routine, Peta let go of me, leaving me surrounded by four male background dancers. The music started to fade away. We entered the climax of the routine: a full fifteen seconds of dancing to complete silence. I held my breath just before we started; this part had not gone well during practice.

When rehearsing the silent portion of the dance, I always nailed the count, hitting every beat on time from the moment the music faded until it came back. I was dancing like I always did, relying on my own head to time my count. The four background dancers, however, were used to having music to guide them. They needed that audible rhythm to keep them in sync. In total silence, they were lost. They kept screwing up the count, going too fast or too slow, throwing off our collective timing. Peta grew frustrated.

"Your timing is all off, guys," she scolded them.

"I'm sorry," one of the dancers responded. "We're not used to keeping the count without relying on the music."

Peta pointed at me. "He's been doing it all this time, and he keeps nailing this dance. You four are professional dancers. You need to figure it out, fast."

We ran through the silent dance routine again and again to no avail; they just couldn't get the timing right. It was startling to see how difficult my method was for professional dancers to master.

An idea came to me. I picked out one of the dancers, who had the best timing of the group, and showed him how to sign the numbers ONE, TWO, THREE, FOUR. This dancer would be performing in front, and I explained to the group how he could sign out the count discreetly, with his hand at his side. The other three just had to watch and follow along with his count, and our timing would be synced up. It helped; the four dancers' timing improved considerably in practice.

But the true test was the live performance. Would the signed count help us pull through? The music faded to complete silence, and I began the first step. Out of the corners of my eyes I saw all four dancers move in unison. We nailed the first progression, then the second. It was working: all five of us moved as one to a visual count.

In that silent quarter of a minute, I invited the audience of hearing viewers, in the studio and in living rooms all across America, into the world of a Deaf person. No music, just as I had told Peta the day we'd tried to dance with loud music. Only this time the experience was not mine alone, but also the entire audience's, whoever was watching along. No music—just dancing, making visual motion poetry to the numbers and counts memorized in my head, and signed out by the lead dancer, but invisible to our audience.

We earned a score of twenty-nine from the judges for our barrier-breaking, deafeningly (pun shamelessly intended) silent paso doble.

As good as that dance was, Peta and I saved our most powerful message for last.

THE PRODUCERS TOLD US THAT the Mirrorball award announcement would take place outdoors, just outside the *DWTS* studio where live competitions took place. They had constructed a large stage and arranged seats and five-row-high bleachers around it. We would perform our final dances inside the studio, then sprint to the outdoor stage for the Mirrorball winner announcement. This news took Peta by surprise; Mirrorball winners in past *DWTS* seasons had always been announced inside the studio.

I started getting texts from my friends that they had gotten tickets to attend the Mirrorball winner announcement. Among them were my friend Jonaz, who had helped me make my *ANTM* tryout video, and my ex-girlfriend, now good friend Hannah. Some of my other Deaf friends were even flying in from out of town to watch. I was confused at first. I knew *DWTS* made their tickets available early in the season and they had run out of tickets. But because they moved the winner announcement outside, more seats became available and so *DWTS* had started giving away tickets again. And, as evidenced by the dozens of texts I was getting from Deaf friends and acquaintances, the show was prioritizing members of the Deaf community in the ticket giveaways.

It was an incredibly meaningful gesture by *DWTS*, and I was thrilled that my friends in the Deaf community would be there with me for this special moment. Though the *DWTS* producers had never said as much, I suspected that the audience vote—buoyed by Deaf community members—had given my scores a boost week after week. The audience could vote online or by phone; plenty of Deaf voters used the online method, but many voted by phone, too. They used videophones and made their calls using Video Relay Service, which provides

ASL interpreters to facilitate phone conversations. It's basically Face-Time, but with a third party on the call—the interpreter—translating between spoken and signed languages. Every Monday night as episodes aired, Deaf voters flooded the Video Relay Service with calls to the *DWTS* line, helping propel me to the finals of the competition.

But the ticket giveaway to Deaf fans made me overthink a little bit. Was *DWTS* doing this because they viewed Peta and me as favorites to win the Mirrorball? Or—I gulped—was I going to stand there on that outdoor stage and take my defeat in front of hundreds of my Deaf friends?

I forced myself to push these thoughts aside. I had final dances to prepare for, and one in particular excited me—Peta's and my freestyle contemporary dance.

By the final weeks of the competition, Peta was well versed in Deaf history. I had told her the story of Clerc and Gallaudet and how they established the first Deaf school in Hartford, Connecticut, which helped to form ASL and created a model that was replicated by scores of new Deaf schools across the United States. Empowered by accessible education and being able to communicate freely in ASL, Deaf Americans flourished. I shared with her other powerful moments in Deaf history, like Dr. Stokoe's research and declaration that ASL is a language, and the Deaf President Now protest at Gallaudet.

I also told Peta about the darkest moments in Deaf history and the blatant oppression, injustice, and discrimination that Deaf people have endured. How, for centuries, sign languages were looked down upon, and the idea that they were legitimate languages was scoffed at. How prominent and powerful people like Alexander Graham Bell advocated for the removal of sign language from the education of Deaf people and how they used eugenics on Deaf people to ban us from marrying and procreating. I recounted the Milan Conference for Peta, telling her that 163 hearing men and only a single Deaf man mandated oral education for Deaf children all over the world, and in the process banned the use of sign language in Deaf schools. How the far-reaching and devastating effects of that conference stretched across generations and continents, eventually touching my Deaf grandparents, my parents, and my brothers and me.

Peta and I decided to make the Milan Conference the basis of the story that we would tell in our freestyle contemporary dance for the final week of the *DWTS* competition. Peta helped me find a song that felt just right: Disturbed's version of the Simon & Garfunkel song "The Sound of Silence."

The song lyrics told a story that, to my eyes, paralleled the oppression that the Deaf community had faced throughout history. The song's protagonist, a metaphorical representative of the Deaf community, is isolated from his fellow people, who are hearing. He tries to communicate a message to them, one that I interpret as the Deaf community's plea to live our lives the way we know best—with sign language. The reasons why are so obviously, *blatantly* clear to us. As a visual communication method, it's naturally accessible to us. And as Dr. Stokoe's research proved, our signs were not a rudimentary system of gestures but rather a bona fide language; thus, when we used it, we were helping build the parts of our brain that recognized the patterns of language. Sign language is something uniquely *ours*, a beautiful creation made with Deaf minds, hands, and bodies. When we use it, we feel truly content, truly ourselves.

Deaf people can't fathom how any hearing person outside of our community could disagree with our line of thinking, especially when they have not walked in our shoes or come anywhere near close to understanding what it was like to live as a Deaf person. But they did anyway. Countless times, throughout the centuries, we have tried to hammer home the point that sign language allows us the best chance at a successful and fulfilling life.

In the song's story, the protagonist's voice, a lone spark of hope, is drowned out by the continuous chatter of other people. These people, outsiders to our community, keep talking among themselves. They decide what is best for Deaf people *without* the input of Deaf people and impose their solutions on us.

The protagonist's, and our, message fades away, unheeded.

All that remains is the sound of silence.

This silence, to me, is not the audible silence created by Deaf people using sign language, but the oppressive silence that occurs when a tremendous injustice is being inflicted upon a community, and no one outside of the oppressed community stands up to fight it. The song spoke to me, and I knew that it would also speak to people watching our dance.

There was just one problem. When we asked Disturbed for permission to use the song for our *DWTS* finale dance, they said no.

Their response caught me off guard. We *had* to dance to that version of "The Sound of Silence." I hadn't even entertained the possibility of dancing to any other song. After thinking it over, I thought if Disturbed understood how much the song meant to me and how I envisioned it helping tell the story of my community, I could change their mind. I wrote a letter to the band, describing the oppression that Deaf people faced throughout history, including the Milan Conference. Disturbed's version of "The Sound of Silence," I wrote, was powerful and moving and would help me tell the story of my often-overlooked community's history in my finale dance. The goal of the dance was to help the world better understand what Deaf people went through—and are still experiencing—and to enlighten minds and hearts, and build allies to help better Deaf lives.

The song's first lyric is "Hello darkness, my old friend." At the end of my letter I pleaded to Disturbed to help the Deaf community escape the darkness and break free from the centuries of systematic oppression we faced.

It felt like a year and a day passed before I received a response. When it did finally come, I let out a huge sigh of relief—Disturbed had graciously agreed to let us use their cover of the song. I was, and am, grateful to Disturbed for helping me tell the story of my community.

With permission secured for the song, the final piece had fallen in place for our dance. All there was left to do was go out and perform it.

PETA AND I STOOD AT the center of the dance floor. I sensed that the audience was quiet and tense in anticipation of our performance. There was little movement in the stands, which I could see out of the corner of my eyes even with the lights dimmed. Somewhere to one side, in the section of the stands reserved for friends of family of competing dancers, I knew my mom and brothers were watching, ready to cheer me on no matter how I performed. Behind Peta and me, a prop grand piano was aflame. A fitting backdrop, as my dancing would always go on, with or without music.

Just before the song started, Peta climbed behind me and wrapped both of her hands around my head, one leg over my shoulder, and the other around my waist. She held me tight and heaved the burden of her physical weight upon my shoulders, forcing me to carry her.

Our dance was an allegory, and Peta and I took on opposing roles. I played myself, a Deaf man, and represented my Deaf community. Peta, in a more conceptually abstract role, embodied the systematic oppression that the hearing world imposed on Deaf people.

The moment the dance began, I pulled Peta from me, fighting off the hearing world's oppression. Almost immediately, she rebounded and embraced me chest to chest, mimicking how the hearing world is stubborn and suffocating in its pursuit of control over Deaf people. I broke apart from her again and, as we circled each other, I followed her lead in putting a finger to my mouth, an initial accession to the world's silent response to the Deaf community's oppression.

I caught Peta as she fell backward, then traced my fingers across her throat. Each tap of my fingers was a word that gets caught in my throat whenever I try to use my voice to speak. I thought back to the time the *ANTM* casting director Rachelle asked me to use my voice in our interview. I remembered how uncomfortable the request had made me feel, and how it made me think that no matter how fluent I was in my natural language, ASL, it would never be enough. The hearing world has always placed a higher value on the ability to communicate using our mouths and has kept coercing Deaf people toward this method of communicating. As I tapped each finger on

Peta's throat, I was declaring to her—and to the hearing world—that this method does not work for me.

I lowered Peta to the floor. My message had been sent and I was ready to walk free. Not so fast; Peta caught my ankle and tripped me up. We gripped each other's heads and grappled as we picked ourselves up from the floor. I was trying to stand up for myself, but the hearing world was pulling me back in its oppressive grip.

In tandem we covered our mouths with our elbows, continuing to reinforce the silent oppression of the Deaf community. Peta stepped away, and I covered my mouth with both elbows, completely immersed in my struggle to meet the hearing world's misguided expectations: to speak flawlessly using my mouth, to flourish in school despite the ineffective oral education that has been imposed on Deaf children for generations.

Peta then sprinted back into my arms, and we swept away into the next segment of our dance. I swung my arm around, a desperate attempt to freely use my hands and express myself in sign language, only for Peta to block my arm mid-swing.

In that moment, Peta was the teachers who sat my grandma down in the corner in a dunce cap when she signed in school; the school superintendent who took away my mom's Speech Student of the Week pin; my dad's father and brothers, who refused to learn ASL to communicate with him; my elementary school teacher, Miss Dawes, who had less ASL fluency than I did when I was a kindergartener, and who told me I wasn't ready to learn if I wasn't wearing hearing aids. With her forehand blocking mine above our heads, Peta was all of the hearing people who oppressed me and my Deaf family based on our hearing ability, the 163 hearing men who voted for oral education and to ban sign language for Deaf children at the Milan Conference, and millions more from thousands of years of hearing society forcing Deaf people to stop using sign language.

We broke apart again. As I stubbornly kept moving my hands and body, she reluctantly followed along, finally conceding to the true spirit and nature of my Deaf being: using sign language.

I picked Peta up for a final embrace. Instead of wrapping her arms around my head as she did at the start of the dance, she bent her waist and moved her torso away from me—giving me the space and freedom I'd fought for throughout the dance.

I put her down, and we each placed one hand over the other's mouth. And then we moved our hands away, our bodies leaning away from each other until our hands caught the other's. We stood there, our bodies leaning in opposite directions, but held together by our hands. There is no separating the Deaf community from the hearing world. We have to coexist, and the way to do so is to give Deaf people the freedom to live and communicate the way we want to, which includes using sign language.

The moment the dance ended, the audience broke its own silence. Hands clapped and waved and fists pumped. I turned to Peta and kissed her on the forehead. We had finally done it. The story had been told better than I could ever have imagined.

I EMERGED ONTO THE MIRRORBALL announcement stage to find hands moving everywhere. All over the outdoor bleachers for the audience were Deaf people chattering away and cheering for me with their hands. It was a surreal sight.

A few feet away to my left was my fellow finalist, the mixed martial arts fighter Paige VanZant. She had performed incredibly well this season, too. It wouldn't have surprised me if *DWTS* awarded the trophy to her; she deserved it.

But I wanted to win so bad. Peta and I had worked hard throughout the competition. We poured everything we had into that last dance. If we walked away without winning, I would still take pride in what we had accomplished together. But our goal was the Mirrorball Trophy.

Standing onstage before my fellow Deaf community members, I felt like we were on the cusp of a historical moment—not just for me, but for my entire community.

The pause right before the winner was announced felt like an eternity. I waited and waited—and then I felt Peta explode beside me. A beat later I saw the interpreter sign my and Peta's names. I wrapped Peta in my arms.

Emotion came pouring out of me. The moment marked an overwhelming culmination of an incredible year-plus journey. *ANTM* filming had begun in March of the previous year. From then on so much had happened; my life had felt like an insane blur. For both *DWTS* and *ANTM*, I had endured countless filmed scenes and interviews, intense moments of competing, and nerve-wracking moments of judging. I'd flown all over the country and overseas for gigs, interviews, and meetings. I'd met so many new people, fans who loved me and the message I was spreading as a proud Deaf man. And along the way, somehow, I had made time for major personal growth, coming out as sexually fluid. And now it was May, fourteen months later, and I had, in the span of five months, won two major reality show competitions.

Fans from the bleachers began climbing onto the stage—momentarily frightening the *DWTS* hosts and security officers—and crowded around us. Someone heaved me up on their shoulders. Perched high up above the stage, I could see the Deaf hands in the crowd waving in the frenzy, free and jubilant. I saw that some people—Hannah and other Deaf friends from my childhood and Gallaudet days—had tears of joy running down their faces, mirroring my own at the moment. It felt like a moment to rejoice for my entire Deaf community. The Deaf people in the stands that day, and in the Deaf community all across the United States and the world, had all taken part in my journey. They'd backed me up from day one. They voted like crazy for me in *DWTS*'s fan vote. When I most needed it, they poured in love and support and urged me to keep going. The Mirrorball win was theirs just as much as it was mine.

I raised my hands, joining my Deaf brothers and sisters in our celebration.

# 19.

# Embracing Me

As a young boy I learned of a Deaf man who was a legendary track sprinter. He dominated in international Deaf events for more than a decade, collecting enough medals to fill up his closet. As I grew older I would hear news of his athletic feats from my teachers and coaches at school.

After he hung up his track cleats, he stayed close to the sport and became a coach. He ran the high school track program at a Deaf school and coached the USA Deaf Track & Field team. An accomplished athlete and coach, he gained the deep respect and admiration of his peers in the international Deaf track and field community.

He was handsome and charismatic, and had a sculpted, muscular figure and a swagger. Women flocked to him, drawn to his impressive physique and magnetic personality. He eventually settled on one lovely woman; they married and had two children. The former star Deaf athlete aged well into the role of the macho patriarch of a picture-perfect family. The man loved his wife and children, and from the outside the family looked to be very happy.

Then one day, unexpectedly, the Deaf man died by suicide. The international Deaf community was shocked and devastated. Nobody *had seen it coming, and nobody could quite understand why it happened.*

WHEN I CAME OUT AS sexually fluid, media outlets picked up my story and amplified the heck out of it. *The Advocate*, a well-known LGBTQ magazine, included me in an article featuring celebrities who had come out so far that year, 2015. At the top of the article was a row of headshots of recently out celebrities, and next to my photo was Miley Cyrus's. I was astonished and flattered and, quite frankly, terrified that such a public spotlight was being shined on my coming out.

Recall that I wanted to come out in a quiet and understated way rather than stand onstage and scream my news to the world. Whatever my intentions, I was onstage anyway.

I needn't have worried, because the media recognition led to an outpouring of support from the LGBTQ community. Many advocacy organizations reached out to invite me to events supporting LGBTQ causes, including the Trevor Project, an organization that provides crisis intervention and suicide prevention services to young LGBTQ people. The Human Rights Campaign, a national organization championing equality and human rights for LGBTQ people, asked me to give a keynote speech at their annual event, the HRC National Dinner—one of the highest honors of my life.

IT WAS EASY FOR ME to be proud and comfortable in my Deaf identity. The key was the sense of belonging to a community. Between my family, our friends, and the Deaf schools I attended growing up, I felt comfortable with and accepted by others like me. We shared a pride in our culture and language that made me feel I was right where I was supposed to be.

In the Deaf community, though, I came across few gay men who had similar interests to mine. To date, I met only one Deaf gay person whom I considered to be masculine-presenting and athletic—the star basketball player at Gallaudet.

After I came out, I started making more of an effort to look for gay people I could relate to, to see if I could find a community where I felt I belonged. This was much harder than I thought it would be. Today, the sophisticated algorithm on Instagram scans my profile and activities and expertly recommends dozens of gay men who are the same age and share the same interests as me. But back in 2015 and earlier, I had to find and meet them the old-fashioned way, by attending parties and get-togethers. The LGBTQ events and galas I was invited to helped in this department, and I met a ton of cool gay people at them.

There was just one problem: my new gay acquaintances were hearing and didn't know ASL. Every interaction I had with them, I had to pull up the Notes app on my phone or use a pen and paper. Our written conversations were slow and superficial. I wanted so badly to talk with these new friends whom I was getting to know in a language I truly felt comfortable with—but I couldn't.

Many of the LGBTQ people I was spending time with had never before met a Deaf person and were ignorant of my culture, lived experience, and language. The burden fell on me to explain all of that to them. My first dates with hearing gay men were excruciating. The minute I sat down with them, a hail of questions would begin raining down on me.

Wow, your parents are Deaf?

Oh, your brothers, grandparents, aunts, and uncles, basically everyone in your family are Deaf, too? You're the fourth generation to be born Deaf in your family?! Amazing!

Oh—how do you sign [insert swear word]?

Hey, just curious, why don't you get cochlear implants?

Boom—before I knew it, the dinner date was ending before I had the chance to talk about ordinary stuff that interested me, like the best bike routes to hit, cool new trails to hike, and the movies and TV shows I'd seen recently. We'd leave the table still at square one in all aspects of getting to know each other, except one—my Deaf life had been laid bare for my date to thirstily drink in, quenching their curiosity.

I'd leave those dates thinking *I'm not your goddamn science project,* chuckling to myself in wonder at how badly they went. When a date feels like an interrogation, it's a major turn off.

As I started to build my career in the entertainment industry, I found myself interacting more and more with hearing people in general. It's a position I'd not found myself in before, having grown up in a Deaf family and attending Deaf schools. In this new stage of my life, I felt the intense exhaustion brought on by communication barriers and cultural disconnect issues like never before. I became uncomfortable around hearing people in general. It was tough for me to just be myself around them. I developed social anxiety and started limiting my interactions with hearing people, and as a result, went out less often with hearing gay friends.

My sexual identity journey stalled.

AROUND THIS TIME, I OFTEN traveled to different colleges and events around the country to give presentations. After one event, I was sitting in a green room backstage when an older Deaf man barged in uninvited. I was about to politely ask him to leave when I noticed how peculiar he behaved. Something was off about him; he seemed nervous and anxious. I wanted to make sure he was okay, so I relaxed and started making small talk.

I tapped him as being a gay man instantly. It was obvious in the way he talked and looked at me. My gaydar was blaring, just as it had when I picked out Alphonse in the Clin d'Oeil Festival crowd all those years ago. Now I noticed this man had a ring on his left-hand ring finger. Then he mentioned that his wife was waiting for him outside.

*Ahh,* I thought. I nodded along.

Then he finally signed the question he was there to ask: "I heard that you're not straight?"

"Yes," I told him. "I'm sexually fluid, which means I can be attracted to both men and women."

"That's impossible. Are you serious?"

Anger flared inside my belly. This man had some nerve, first barging into my backstage room, and now openly challenging my sexual identity.

THAT MY PROBLEM, I told him. I'd faced reactions like his—immediate doubt, comments like "Are you serious?"—countless times since coming out, which pushed me a step backward in my journey of self-discovery. I knew people reacted like this partly because they couldn't believe that anyone could be attracted to more than one gender, but also because I didn't fit the harmful and dangerous stereotypical picture that they'd created in their heads of a queer man. We were expected to look and act a certain way. The truth is that queer men can present as feminine and masculine and everything in between, and we're all beautiful just the way we are.

ME GROW UP, PEOPLE ALWAYS ASSUME, ME STRAIGHT, I told him. NOT TRUE.

I looked closer at him and saw no hint of judgment or pity. Instead I first sensed confusion, then envy. He stared back at me intensely, perhaps longing for a life he'd never got to live. Maybe he'd always been closeted and never showed his true colors or embraced his true self. I felt bad for him. I wondered how different his life could have been if he'd come out a long time ago, and how many Deaf LGBTQ kids he could have helped and inspired along the way.

The man nodded at me, confusion and envy still clouding his face. I smiled back at him. I wanted him to know that I was okay—I was proud of and happy with who I was. And he could be, too. After a moment, he changed the topic, congratulating me on my success. We talked for a few minutes more, and then he left.

I don't hold anything against him. Everyone's journey is unique, and how society viewed and treated LGBTQ people was way different when he was young. But my conversation with him was a wake-up call. It told me that I had to fight through the frustrations I was feeling with my hearing gay friends. I had spent my entire childhood and young adult life ignoring a significant part of myself, my sexuality. Repressing my true self once ate away at me like a cancerous growth, but I was able to push back when I started dating men and came out as sexually fluid. If I slowed down now, though, my former shame and need to hide who I was would come back with a vengeance. The only way to heal was to push forward, keep learning, and stretch my boundaries, no matter how uncomfortable I was at first.

I started to make progress with my hearing gay friends. With patience, I taught them how to sign, and about the Deaf culture and community. They began to be more sensitive and aware of how important communication access was. They made a conscious effort to include me in group conversations. When they started doing so, I felt welcome, like I belonged.

Soon I started to create very real connections with hearing gay friends through shared moments that carried so much weight, such as when we talked about the time we first realized we weren't straight. This experience is a key touchstone for an LGBTQ person and one that varies in detail but is in essence the same for all of us. I shared my Pink Power Ranger story with my friends, and they told me theirs. One friend's moment came as he watched the movie *Bring It On* and thought the male cheerleader character, Les (played by Huntley Ritter), was smoking hot. That moment resonated with me. YES! I responded to that friend. I totally remembered thinking that the cheerleader was *hot* when I first saw the movie—and realizing that I couldn't talk about how I felt with anyone else. The memory came alive now, in a different light, a source of joy and relation as I talked about the experience freely with my friend. It was validation from a fellow person who'd gone through what I had. The shared understanding helped me think that I belonged.

SEXUALLY FLUID, THE IDENTITY I first labeled myself with, had once fit me like a glove. The more I immersed myself into the gay community, though, the less attraction I felt toward women. Long before I came out, back when I had a wall built up around my thoughts and feelings toward men in my head, I could be attracted to women and experience physical and emotional passion with them. My relationship with Hannah was a prime example of that. But after those walls came down and I allowed myself to freely have feelings toward guys, I realized that the emotional and physical connection I could have with men was just as strong as what I'd shared with women. The more I dated men, the stronger these feelings became. Inversely, my feelings for women grew weaker and weaker.

That is, with one exception: Deaf women. Where most hearing gay men I dated fell short—they asked too many questions about my Deaf life, failed to make an effort to learn ASL, and habitually left me out of group conversations with hearing friends—certain Deaf women made me feel powerfully myself as a Deaf man and could connect with me intimately on levels that would always be out of reach of hearing people. I found that I was especially attracted to Deaf women who grew up attending Deaf schools, were born to Deaf families, and who used sign language with the grace and beauty of a from-birth signer. It's difficult to explain why I felt—and feel—this way toward culturally Deaf women. There was something about them that aroused my emotions: the way they carried themselves with confidence, their ease with their native sign language, their sureness in knowing who they were as Deaf people. I was drawn to how they shared my understanding and love of Deaf humor and delighted in trading jokes about our own community and culture. A naturally sign-language fluent Deaf woman playfully and cleverly mocking the tendencies and habits of Deaf people—there were few things in this world I found more sexy than that.

The powerful chemistry I felt toward such women is beyond the realm of explanation, I think. Because it's driven by cultural forces known and experienced only by Deaf people in our world, I know it's impossible for a hearing person to 100 percent understand why I felt this way. It was confusing to me, too, because it felt like it conflicted with and pushed against the overwhelming tide that was my burgeoning attraction toward men. But I couldn't deny what I was feeling. As I continued to date more and more men, from time to time, I would meet a whip-smart, wisecracking, confident Deaf woman who tugged at my heart.

Still, even with the exception of an occasional Deaf woman that attracted me, I could feel the compass needle of my romantic attraction orient itself primarily toward men. As the needle swung in that direction, I began wondering if sexually fluid was no longer the true way to describe me.

I SAW A PARALLEL BETWEEN my struggle in understanding my sexual identity and that of a Deaf person who had been raised from childhood in the hearing world, without learning ASL or meeting other Deaf people—like my college friend Barry. His experience entering the Deaf world at Gallaudet University, learning ASL, and finding his community of Deaf peers, was an awakening. Like many other Deaf people who'd been raised in the hearing community, he was tired of scraping by with spoken communication and trying to pass as hearing. Within the Deaf community, he could truly be himself.

Similarly, I was tired of passing—as straight, and later, as sexually fluid.

This transition was difficult for me to come to terms with. It was a process that involved undoing countless social inputs I'd received through my childhood and young adult life—such as my dad teasing me about the Pink Ranger being my girlfriend. I grappled with the idea that if I wasn't with a woman, I couldn't fulfill the Deaf community's expectations of me. The schools I grew up attending, Texas School for the Deaf and Maryland School for the Deaf, had ultracompetitive environments that were a double-edged sword: they pushed students to do their best, but also reinforced rigid and harmful social frameworks of so-called acceptable behavior, interests, and sexual identity. Conditioned by these schools' environments, I wanted to grow up to meet their picture of the ideal—heterosexual—family: me, a Deaf man, with a Deaf wife, with Deaf children we'd raise to be ASL fluent and culturally proud of their Deaf identities as well as excellent students and successful athletes. It was such a narrow, specific ideal, but one I'd bought into completely. When I was with Hannah, we'd lie around in bed talking late into the night about the Deaf family we'd build together. We had the plan all laid out: we'd have our first kid by the time she turned twenty-seven, and I twenty-six.

But there came a point when I started to ask myself: Who do I want to wake up to in the morning? With whom can I experience soul-mate levels of connection? As far as my sexual identity, with whom did I feel most truly myself? The further I delved into my sexuality, the more my answer to all of those questions leaned toward "men."

And so my perception of my sexual identity shifted—from sexually fluid to queer.

IN THE FALL OF 2017, the winding path of my sexual identity journey looped all the way back to Europe, the continent where, four years earlier, I had my first kiss with Alphonse. This time I was in Europe not as a backpacking tourist, but as a working man with photo shoots and modeling gigs on my itinerary. One night, on a break from work, I went out to dinner with a group of Deaf Europeans. Midway through the meal, I learned that the Deaf man sitting across from me was gay. We talked, and he asked me if I knew the famous American Deaf track sprinter who had grown to become a legend in the track and field community. I told him yes, I knew of him, and was genuinely saddened when I'd heard of his suicide.

I saw grief touch the man's face. He asked me if I'd known the sprinter was not straight. I said I hadn't.

The man said that he'd met the Deaf sprinter at an international Deaf track and field meet back in the early 1990s. The man had attended as a fan and was immediately attracted to the sprinter. He didn't think his feelings would be reciprocated, as all evidence pointed to the sprinter being straight. But when they met at a bar later that evening, the sprinter discreetly came on to him. They spent the night together at the hotel, the first night in what would become a decades-long secret romance. They would meet up every year or two at different international track and field events, the man attending as a fan and the sprinter first as a participating athlete and later a coach. At night they would sneak off together, cherishing the few moments they had together.

The man respected the sprinter's preference to stay discreet. But he longed to be free and open with him, the man he loved. One time, during an international competition, he asked the sprinter if he would give up his life in America and move to Europe to be with him for good. The sprinter told him he couldn't. He had a family back in America, and he couldn't let anyone else know about his sexual identity.

"We parted," the man signed, "and I wondered how long it would be before I saw him again. I never did. Soon after that, he took his own life."

Learning that story was my snapping point. It angered me so much how one man could hide his true identity for so long, and how it could drive him to suicide. It pained me to know that the pressure the sprinter felt to keep up the perception of heterosexuality had prevented him from showing the world his true self.

I had only one life left to live, and I couldn't waste any more time. I made a promise to myself then and there that I would be true to myself. I couldn't let anything stop me—not even the communication struggles I'd had when trying to connect with hearing gay friends that I'd met at galas and events. I was getting better at creating connections with hearing gay people, and I had to keep at it.

By being true to myself, I was developing an image of myself as a masculine-presenting Deaf queer role model. That was the first step toward creating a community of people like me. Deaf LGBTQ people, young or old, might see themselves represented in me, and feel inspired and secure enough to come out. Together, we could build a community.

Before I put myself out there, though, I had to start at home. My first step was to be honest about my sexual identity with everyone I loved and cared about—all of my family and closest friends.

At the time I had come out to my entire family about my sexual identity—except my grandparents. Even after I publicly announced that I was sexually fluid, my grandparents remained unaware. They weren't that active on social media, so they didn't catch wind of the news when it first came out. I was kind of waiting until the time was right to tell them, but my conversation about the Deaf sprinter made me realize I couldn't wait any longer.

As soon as I returned to the States, I went straight to my mom's house and walked down the stairs to the basement, where my grandparents lived. They had been watching TV, but when I sat across from them I had their full attention. They smiled at me, but I think they could tell that something was up because of my unexpected visit, and by the way I looked at them.

I was scared to tell my grandparents, probably more than I was when I told any other family members. I was mostly afraid of how my grandma would react. She is a buttoned-up, reserved lady, with a penchant for tradition and views strongly trending conservative. In contrast, my grandpa was more emotionally open and had a big heart. Him, I wasn't worried about.

YOU KNOW TODAY GENERATION, DIFFERENT? I asked my grandparents. YOUNG PEOPLE NOW MORE PROGRESSIVE, OPEN-MIND?

They nodded in agreement.

WE NOW MORE ACCEPT-ACCEPT PEOPLE DIFFERENT RACES, ETHNICITIES. DIFFERENT IDENTITIES. LIKE SEXUALITY.

YES, YES, they murmured.

WELL, ME ATTRACTED-TO MEN.

I braced myself for my grandma's reaction. To my astonishment, she didn't seem bothered.

OH, THAT'S FINE. YOUR LIFE, she said. Internally I rejoiced. Grandma, the toughest hurdle in the basement, had been cleared. She had reacted so favorably that I had no doubt my grandpa would have any issues with it. I turned to him.

Grandpa was shaking his head, a stern frown on his face. When he does that, it's extremely intimidating. He has strong Italian features, and his typical outfit includes a gold chain necklace and wristwatch and a white tank top undershirt. The man looks like a mob boss in his off hours.

His reaction stung. My journey had been relatively easy thus far. My coming-out conversations with my mom, brothers, aunt and uncles, and friends had all gone very well. They had embraced my sexual identity without a second thought, each of them helping ease the burden I'd felt before sharing with them. Everybody I had talked to treated me well.

Grandpa was the first to express disapproval, and from his reaction I got a small taste of the bad coming-out experiences that others had gone through. I knew I'd been lucky so far.

I tried to explain to him how being queer was who I was. My queer identity was there when I was born and was still with me now. It'd be with me for the rest of my life.

Grandpa shook his head again. He didn't understand, or he didn't want to. We talked a little while more, and he made a comment about the stereotype of queer men being feminine. Grandpa was reinforcing this harmful stereotype, and I wanted to bust it right then and there.

I took out my phone and pulled up a photo of a guy I used to date. He was six foot four, used to play Division 1 football, had a handsomely sculpted physique, and, as a bonus, was a tanned, dark-haired Italian hunk. He stood an inch taller than me in the picture.

HIM, ME BEFORE DATE. I showed Grandpa the photo.

He stared at it. I could see the cogs turning in his head as he remade his mental image of what a queer male looked like. Finally he moved his hands.

HIM HANDSOME.

YES. BIG AND STRONG, TOO. BEFORE HIM PLAY FOOTBALL, PURDUE UNIVERSITY.

Grandpa raised one of his bushy eyebrows. HIM NOT FEMININE.

Not all queer men are feminine, I told him. Some are, yes. There are many queer men, living life differently. Not all of us are the same. We can be both masculine and attracted to other men.

Grandpa nodded then turned to Grandma with a mischievous grin.

ME DIVORCE YOU AND MARRY HIM, he said, pointing toward my phone.

STOP, Grandma said, slapping him on the shoulder. Grandpa turned toward me, his grin growing wider and his gold chain glinting in the basement light, and winked.

RECENTLY, I WAS EXCHANGING TEXTS with Millie, the first friend I told about my kiss with Alphonse. She said, "People grow and change over time. Why can't our sexual identities change with us?"

Her words struck me. They helped me realize I shouldn't view my sexuality as being frozen in time. It evolves and grows along with me as I become older.

One of the most important things I learned about the LGBTQ world is that it is a massive, inclusive umbrella of sexual identities. So many people exist at different points along the spectrum between straight and gay. One's sexual identity is a complex, layered, and interlinked web of factors, and exploring and making sense of this web is a lifelong process.

Every day, I'm continuing to make strides: learning more about my sexual and emotional attractions, staying true to myself, embracing me. In the eyes of many of my friends in the LGBTQ community, I'm still a baby, so young and new. I know I still have a lot to learn. Staying in tune with my sexual identity is an ongoing journey—I think it'll be never-ending.

For the moment, though, I know that I am truly happy.

# 20.

# Home Movies

The first movies, silent films, were naturally accessible for Deaf people. Displaying the text of the characters' dialogue onscreen wasn't an afterthought but a necessary feature because there was no audio component to those films. Their voices useless, actors leaned on nonverbal ways to present action and emotion—facial expressions, gestures, body language. All of these were visual communication skills that sign language-fluent Deaf people were familiar with.

It isn't a stretch to imagine that Deaf people could have had an influence on the stars of the silent film era—even the biggest one of all, Charlie Chaplin.

Off-screen, Chaplin enjoyed collecting art, and one of his favorite painters was a Deaf man named Granville Redmond. The two men became friends, and Chaplin valued Redmond's art so much he set up a studio for Redmond at his lot in Los Angeles. Later, Redmond would go on to appear in a few of Chaplin's movies.

Many traits of Chaplin's unique gifts for nonverbal visual story-telling ran parallel to those of sign language speakers. His eyebrow movements and hand gestures in particular brought to mind an ASL speaker. In some movies, Chaplin even went so far as to actually use ASL signs.

*It makes one wonder: How much of the silent film master's legend-*
*ary acting talent can be attributed to his Deaf friend? No one knows*
*for sure. Very little historical documentation exists on their relation-*
*ship. But I suspect that Redmond had far greater influence on Chaplin*
*than he has been given credit for. Redmond's contribution to Holly-*
*wood, one could say, has been hearing-washed away.*

*Eventually, silent films gave way to talkies, and just like that,*
*communication access to movies fell out of Deaf people's reach. Ever*
*since, we've worked tirelessly to regain it. We've made progress, but we*
*have a way to go. Even now, we're still working, fighting to claim our*
*rightful space in Hollywood.*

LOOK AT-THIS, NYLE, DAD SAID, handing me a piece of paper marked
with a pencil.

My jaw dropped. Staring back at me from the page was Spider-
Man, mid-swing between skyscrapers, one hand holding a web rope,
the other shooting out another web rope. The drawing was so realistic
that Spider-Man looked like he was about to jump off the page and
into my living room.

Dad chuckled and told me to keep it, and if I wanted, he'd draw
more pictures for me.

I thanked him and ran off to hang up the drawing in my bedroom.
I was excited about the drawing, but I was relieved too. When Dad
was drawing, that meant he was in a good mood. Creative work did
that for him. It was his outlet, and the impressed reactions he got
from others boosted his self-esteem. His artistic ability helped him
make up the intellectual and emotional ground he'd lost to his peers
due to language deprivation and a poor education. He would never be
as book smart as many of the educated Deaf peers he met at college
and thereafter, but his creative mind was a force. It gave him what
he saw as a potential path toward success and equal footing with his
Deaf peers.

My dad was at his very best creative self when he was on the stage
or acting in front of a camera. His bread and butter was physical

comedy. His acting style evoked shades of his heroes, the legendary comedic actors Charlie Chaplin, the Three Stooges, Robin Williams, and Jim Carrey. He had the uncanny ability to transform into different characters—an animatronic figure with stiff hinges for joints and a robotic manner of signing, a vaudevillian cane-wielding narrator with a Charlie Chaplin–inspired costume (complete with black tux, fake toothbrush mustache, and bowler hat) who communicated in an unusual mix of gesture and ASL, a white-faced mime who led his straight-faced foil (my uncle Robert, Mom's brother) on absurdly funny adventures. In one solo stage skit, he took on the roles of five separate characters, each a musician playing an imaginary instrument; he'd breathlessly tap a fake piano one moment and puff his cheeks out, cross-eyed, into a pretend flute the next. He'd turn a sly eye mid-act to the audience, drinking in their laughter. Nothing gratified him more than making other people laugh.

Dad's dream—one that would redeem himself in his own eyes and the eyes of his Deaf peers—was to become a famous professional actor. His day job was at the post office, but nights and weekends he hustled in pursuit of his dream. All day, every day, he thought of characters to play, skits to perform. He polished his craft at home, filming and editing skits using a handheld camera we owned. Over time, he put together a complete solo show, uniting all his characters and skits.

Dad was invited to perform his show at Lexington School for the Deaf when Neal, Nico, and I were students there. It was a success, and word spread to other Deaf schools in the Northeast, and he was asked to come and perform for their students.

*It's all coming together*, Dad thought. His solo show was making waves, and one day it would help him springboard to Hollywood.

"I'm getting close," he told my mom. "One day, I'm going to make it big."

NYLE! ME YOUR BIGGEST FAN! YOU MIND US TAKE-PICTURE?
The arm wrapped around my shoulder and the phone camera clicked before I had a chance to smile. The stranger flashed me the

I LOVE YOU sign as they walked away. Immediately, my arm was grabbed by another stranger. I turned to see a man holding a giant iPad tablet; he was on FaceTime with somebody I'd also never met.

THIS-IS MY SON, AT HOME, the man said. MIND SAY HI?

His son stared back at me on the iPad, slack jawed, eyes dazed and starstruck. I had time for one quick wave before a hand hooked my shoulder, slid down my arm, and stuffed a piece of paper in my hand. I unfolded it to find a phone number and looked up to see a young lady wink and sign, CALL ME.

Tap-tap. Another stranger's hand, on my shoulder. I looked. She was an older lady, about sixty-five.

YOU EVEN HOTTER IN PERSON THAN ON SCREEN, she said, a flirty look in her eyes. I froze, unsettled at the sight of an older woman making an overt, no-holds-barred run for my affection. I fought my hesitation, forced a smile, and posed for a picture. But she didn't pull out her phone. Instead she looked me up and down, and one corner of her lips curled up into a frisky, lustful half-smile.

HEARD YOU HAVE MATH DEGREE, she said. THINK YOU CAN GO BACK CLASSROOM, TEACH?

Her hands and face taunted me as she mocked the career I'd pictured for myself. She laughed when she finished signing—one part flirting, and one part scoffing at the sheer absurdity of picturing me standing in front of a classroom of Deaf students, a piece of chalk in hand, and behind me, a blackboard with differential equations scrawled all over it.

She blew a kiss while walking away, and I looked past her at the crowd of people encircling me. There was supposed to be an organized queue, but all semblance of crowd control had been lost long ago. All around me was chaos: hands waving for my attention and signing my name, saying LOOK, NYLE!, phones filming and flashing, faces popping up out of nowhere just inches from my eyes.

I looked away from the crowd, and there, in the distance, a familiar shape caught my eye: the Tower Clock. Amid the chaos surrounding me, that iconic feature was the only thing that reminded me that I was at Gallaudet. At the time, I was still a contestant on *Dancing with the Stars*, and I'd taken a brief break from my daily dance practice with Peta to fly out for an appearance at the university.

Only three years had passed since I had graduated with my math degree at Gallaudet. Since then, my return visits were sporadic; I spent more and more time in New York and Los Angeles in pursuit of my career. But I looked forward to every chance I had to return to campus, because it was unlike any other place in the world. On the Kendall Green campus, I was surrounded by Deaf and ASL-fluent people—my community, people who understood my culture and lived experience, people who could truly relate and empathize with my deepest frustrations and sincerest joys as a proud Deaf man. Communication access occurred naturally, automatically—I could eavesdrop on a conversation at the next table over or drop into a quick and easy conversation with any person I passed in the hallway. On campus, people didn't see me as that Deaf person but as me—Nyle DiMarco.

When you drive through the front entrance of the school, there's a small dip at the curb that your front tires lean into before bumping up the driveway onto campus. Before this visit I was so excited to feel once again that sharp dip and bump, because it meant I was *home*. It might seem a silly thing to one who has never felt it, but the real ones know. Gallaudet alumni stretching back decades have felt the same sensation at that dip and bump—your heart flutters a little, and a deep, welcoming warmth washes over your chest. That small bump told you that you had entered a mecca of Deaf culture, and that your community awaited within to welcome you in your language.

Post dip and bump, though, this visit was turning out quite differently than I had pictured it. Nyle from three years ago, the anonymous and ordinary undergraduate student who had roamed this same campus, could never have predicted the chaos I found before me.

When I first got onto *ANTM*, I was hoping to make a mark, have a little success that I could build on. But I could never, even in my wildest dreams, have predicted that I would not only win *ANTM*, but also start to compete on an even more famous reality show immediately afterward. Everything had happened so quickly; I'd had so little time to process the details. I hadn't yet fully realized the impact I was having on people who had been watching me on *ANTM* and *DWTS*, at least not until I found a mob of frenzied fans, every one of them screaming for a piece of me, in my home, the Gallaudet campus.

Another unsettling thing was that all of those people were treating me like somebody they knew intimately. Partly that was a direct result of my being on reality shows. I wasn't playing a character; I had appeared as myself. And those shows cut cast members open, peeled back the layers, and showed the world who they were. People who watched those shows grew to learn so much about me that I seemed like a lifelong friend.

When planning the visit, Gallaudet officials had insisted on having security officers by my side. I blanched at the idea at first; Gallaudet was my *home*. I didn't want to walk around separated from my community, my *friends*, by uniformed officers. But now I saw why they had insisted. Even then, the security officers weren't enough; in the middle of the event they decided an additional security measure was needed and ushered me to a tent.

When it was time to end the meet and greet, a Gallaudet official came up to me inside the tent and laid out the game plan.

"There's a golf cart ten yards away," he told me.

Needing a golf cart to get off the Gallaudet campus was another thing that would have made undergraduate student Nyle knock the back of my head and say, "Get off the weed, dude." But on this day in my strange new life, it was a very real and necessary thing.

The Gallaudet official continued: "One security officer will go out first, you and I will follow, and the second security officer will flank us. We'll move quickly and get out of here."

I emerged from the tent to face the mob again. Faces, phones, hands everywhere. Strangers grabbing me all over, waving, signing for my attention. Enveloping me, suffocating me. The security officers helped clear the way, and we eventually made it through to the golf cart and drove away, leaving the crowd behind.

As the cart rolled up to the campus's front entrance, I sat in silence, digesting what I'd just undergone. One moment stood out at me: the older lady who had mocked me about becoming a math teacher. After what I'd experienced today, I knew that there was an undeniable truth to what she had said.

At the time, my modeling career was slow to take off. I wasn't getting enough gigs to count on them as a dependable source of income. And, with the end of my *DWTS* run in sight, I began to feel pressure. Where could I go from here?

I'd once thought that becoming a math teacher could be my fallback plan. But after the event at Gallaudet, I couldn't see that happening. I could only imagine students asking me endless questions about *ANTM* and *DWTS* and trying to flirt with me. Becoming a math teacher and living the ordinary life that I'd once pictured for myself within the Deaf community now felt like an impossibility.

So where could I go from here?

ONE AFTERNOON WHEN WE WERE kids, Neal, Nico, and I were lying on the floor poring over our Pokémon cards spread all over the carpet when Dad tapped on our shoulders. We turned around and saw that he was holding his video camera on his shoulder, a big excited grin on his face.

MAKE MOVIE, WANT?

My brothers and I looked at each other and shrugged. Why not?

Dad said the movie would be about his favorite superhero character, Spider-Man. He pointed to the places where he wanted us to stand and fed us our lines. We followed his direction, scene by scene, until we wrapped up the story line he'd thought up. It surprised me how fun it was. When Dad acted out the lines the way he wanted us to recite them, it made us giggle. He winked at us, knowing how funny he was being. When we nailed a scene, Dad hollered and pumped his fists, and we cheered along with him. It was a foreign feeling: We were having fun *with* Dad, not in spite of him. For once he wasn't absent or being violent. He was present.

After we made that first movie, every once in a while Dad would ask if we wanted to make another one. Each time he asked, we jumped at the chance, knowing how fun it would be. But eventually, he wanted to make movies more and more often. Then he asked almost every day. We quickly got bored with it.

Once we said no, but he wouldn't accept our answer.

COME-ON! FUN, WILL.

Afraid of what he would do if we kept saying no, we went along with him, but making movies now wasn't as fun as the first times we did it. It felt like a chore.

One time Nico and I had a friend from school coming over. We had the whole day planned: trading Pokémon cards, going out for a ride through the forest by our home on our BMX bikes, jumping on our trampoline in the backyard. It was going to be *lit*.

But when our friend arrived, Dad walked toward us.

HEY KIDS! MOVIE, WANT MAKE? He grinned.

NO. WE PLAN GO RIDE-BIKE.

YOUR FRIEND ENJOY ACT MOVIE, WILL. He turned to our friend and told us that he'd thought up a story that needed one more actor in addition to his three boys, and it was a perfect coincidence that our friend was here.

Our friend smiled and said, OKAY, SURE.

Dad flashed a thumbs-up sign. GREAT! FUN, WILL!

I gritted my teeth and went along, but this time it wasn't fun at all. I watched Dad as he gleefully directed and filmed. He was present, again, but now I understood why: the situation was on his terms, doing something that *he* loved. He didn't seem to care whether *we* had fun. The home movies weren't for us boys; they were for him—a way for him to hone his own craft, and at the same time train us on its finer points. He was projecting his dream of becoming an actor onto us.

From that day forward, I made it a point to avoid moviemaking. I watched Dad from afar, ready to bolt if he went near the closet where he kept the video camera. By the time the camera was out of the closet, I was often already halfway down the block on my bike.

After a while, Dad stopped trying to force us into making movies with him. But the bad taste still remained. His home movies sucked every iota of fun out of acting. For a long time, even after my mom divorced my dad and we moved away, I instinctively avoided acting. I didn't try out for school plays from middle school through college.

It wasn't until after college that I gave acting a shot again. Eventually I landed a guest role on *Switched at Birth*. Once I'd had to choose *ANTM* over *Switched at Birth*, but later, when episodes of cycle 22 were airing, I was fortunate enough to receive a second offer to appear on the show. The experience reminded me how I enjoyed performing in front of the camera; there was a joy to acting that I'd missed for so long.

And so as I rode on the golf cart, still feeling ghosts of the hands that had grabbed at my chest, my math teacher fallback plan disappearing into the realm of the impractical, I thought: *Just maybe, acting could be my way forward.*

HOLLYWOOD. THAT WAS WHERE I needed to go. The more I thought about it, the more it made sense. Media representation was an issue I talked about often during my time on *ANTM* and *DWTS*: Deaf people rarely showed up on our screens. It was even rarer for Deaf people to appear as characters in productions that eschewed the typical woe-is-me Deaf storyline; I seldom saw Deaf actors taking on roles of ordinary characters who just happened to be Deaf and were going out and doing and experiencing everyday stuff. Deaf people had indeed made strides in Hollywood—the most notable example was Marlee Matlin, who won an Academy Award for Best Actress for her work in *Children of a Lesser God*, and there were numerous other Deaf actors succeeding in the industry. But it wasn't enough. There was a ton of room for more Deaf representation on TV shows and in movies.

In a way, working to break through in Hollywood and helping create representation for people like me was similar to the pivotal turn in my sexual identity journey. The same fight was going on in Hollywood, and I wanted to jump in.

When I started, I wasn't sure what to expect. I had some advantages, certainly. My appearances on the two reality show competitions had helped me build a significant platform. My social media accounts had large followings. My core messages—embracing your identity and taking pride in what makes you different—resonated hugely with my growing audience. What I stood for helped reinforce my brand, which was becoming more and more well-known. The people I met and the relationships I created along the way, with celebrities, executive producers, agents, and the like, added to my growing network. These were all important tools available to me in my pursuit of Hollywood.

In 2017, not long after my *DWTS* win, I met with my manager and agent to formulate a strategy. We decided to cast as wide a net as possible.

"Let's not limit my auditions to just Deaf roles," I told them. "I want to try auditioning for hearing roles."

And why not? There were already few enough Deaf roles out there, and I didn't want to wait for them to come my way. I knew that my auditioning for a hearing role would probably shock some casting directors or producers. It might make them uncomfortable, but was necessary. A role was written for a hearing character because creators and writers likely hadn't even imagined the possibility of having a Deaf character in their story. Just by showing up, I might stretch the boundaries of their imagination a little bit, push them outside the box, make them consider adding different dimensions to the role. In the end I might not get the job, but at the very least I'd plant an idea in their heads to consider including Deaf characters in that or a future production.

A second decision I made was not to request interpreters for in-person auditions. This was a tough call. It meant I was sacrificing access, which is not something I recommend for any Deaf person going into a job interview. There are protections, like the Americans with Disabilities Act, that give us the right to communication access accommodations in these situations. But I'm also a realist. Producers, scared off by the need to provide an interpreter—and the associated cost—might write me off before even giving me a chance to show what I could bring to their production. So I went without. I was able to get by in auditions without an interpreter because auditions were brief and got straight to the point, reciting the scene for the audition. The only tough part was when a production assistant fed me lines—I had to keep a close eye on the assistant's lips to understand what they were saying and figure out when it was time to recite my lines in ASL. It wasn't easy, but I never had any major difficulties. And anyway, for most auditions, I taped myself signing out lines and sent the video in—an option I often volunteered to casting directors, since it would save me the difficulty of auditioning in person without an interpreter.

Despite my strategy, my auditions mostly fizzled out. I did snag a few acting jobs, but all of them were for guest roles, so I was a temporary visitor on the TV show for an episode or two, and that was it. I kept hunting for more substantial and longer-lived roles. Once I came close with a Deaf role in a legal comedy, a well-written multidimensional character who had been accused of a crime and was being defended by the show's protagonist. My audition went well, and the casting team showed serious interest in me. When I got a call from them a while later, my heart was beating silly; I really wanted the role.

But instead of telling me they were giving me the part, they told me they were removing the character from the show. They had cold feet, fearing that the way the character was written would create backlash from the Deaf community.

This really poor excuse made me FIRE-IN-THE-BELLY angry. Don't use potential backlash from an underrepresented community to justify removing a character representative of that community. There's a right way to create a minority character, and doing so takes commitment and work: Engage the community and ask community members to help you create and flesh out the character. Make a meaningful attempt instead of wimping out and blaming the community for caring how they're represented. This show was actually already doing something right by seriously considering me, a Deaf actor, for the Deaf role. I could have been asked to consult on developing the character and his story. But it didn't matter now; it was too late. The role had vanished into thin air, shot dead by cowardice before it ever came alive.

As my auditions ran into dead end after dead end, one constant recurrence started to bug the hell out of me. I hungered for feedback from the casting directors who evaluated my auditions, but I never received anything substantial. They nearly always said that my audition was fantastic, which was frustrating because 99 percent of the time, none of the people who judged my audition could understand the language that I was communicating in. My auditions were in ASL; my evaluators weren't fluent in it. Of course they had no constructive feedback—they didn't understand anything I was saying. The "your acting was great" feedback they kept providing felt empty. But it was all they could give me.

I decided to take another tack and work through my network. I remembered someone I'd met during a *DWTS* red-carpet event who said he knew a big-shot Hollywood producer. I reached out and asked him if he would introduce me to the producer. He happily obliged, setting up a brunch meeting at a 1950s diner in Beverly Hills.

"Oh, Larry King's going to be joining us, too." he added. Neat, I thought. It'd be a fun honor getting to meet King, a living legend.

At the diner, as I walked up to the table, the producer stood and looked me up and down. He spread his arms wide, and as he started talking, I pulled out my phone and turned on the speech-to-text translation feature.

"Oh my," he said. "You have the look of a big-time Hollywood movie star."

My cheeks burned. After I'd been rejected for so many roles, the comment gave me hope and lent legitimacy to my acting aspirations. When you get told no again and again, you start to doubt yourself and think, *Am I crazy for believing I can do this?* Receiving that compliment from a bona fide producer told me, heck no, I'm not crazy. I *can* do this.

I took my seat next to Larry King. He craned his neck, frowned at me, and asked (my phone translating): "How did you get here?"

I gave him a frown of my own. *I drove here*, I typed on my phone.

His eyebrows sprang up his forehead. *"You can drive?"*

I blinked. Did the legendary Larry King really just ask me that? Stifling my incredulity at the insulting insinuation behind his question, I jabbed my thumb toward the parking lot and told him my car was parked over there. He squinted out the window to verify my offering of evidence. I ignored him and turned my attention back to the producer for the rest of the meeting.

The producer asked me about my rise to fame, my experiences on *ANTM* and *DWTS*, my acting background, and the roles I'd auditioned for. In turn I picked his brain and asked him what directors and producers looked for in auditions. As our brunch ended, we agreed to meet again later with his partner, with whom he ran a production company that turned out massive blockbuster movies. With the genuine interest the producer was showing toward working with me, I had the feeling our discussions could result in a big part, potentially a leading role, in a film.

I went to the next meeting with the producer and his partner with a mental portfolio packed with project ideas. In a flurry, I pitched them all to the pair, but, strangely, nothing seemed to stick. I started to think that they might have been trying to get to know me better and were waiting for the right idea to strike. I was wrong.

When I'd finished talking, the producer asked: "Nyle, what do you think of doing a reality show on you and your family?"

The idea caught me off guard. All the ideas I'd touched on in our first meeting were for movies or scripted TV shows. This pair's production company was known for blockbusters, not reality shows. I'd walked into the meeting thinking feature film, and they'd flipped my expectations upside down.

"I'm not sure I like the idea. I've already done two reality shows, and think I might be done with that. I don't want to be typecast as a reality TV guy. I know I'm capable of doing much more, including movies and TV shows."

They said they were intrigued by the idea of allowing the viewer an inside look at a Deaf family. I didn't disagree, but I really didn't want to go in this direction. I wanted to act, to do movies and TV. The producer and his partner didn't seem interested. They didn't say so outright, but I sensed they thought it would be difficult to write Deaf characters. I kept trying to nudge the discussion toward my suggestions, dropping hints on how we could incorporate Deaf experiences into scripts. But they firmly held on to their reality show idea. We'd reached a stalemate. I shook their hands and left.

Not long after, I met with a casting director. As soon as he saw me, he said that I had a glow about me. I took his words in stride, remembering how the producer's "You have the look of a big-time Hollywood movie star" comment had ended up working out for me. I told him about myself and what I wanted to do in film and TV. We threw around ideas, and he shared information about the different production teams he was supporting. For each show he was working on, I gave him suggestions on how a Deaf character or storyline could be integrated. He seemed to consider them all with an open mind, an encouraging sign.

Just before I left, he told me not to worry.

"The stars are going to align for you," he said.

I fought to keep my face from collapsing with exasperation. It might have been an okay mantra to live by in this industry as an able-bodied person, but that destiny stuff doesn't work for people with disabilities. I knew I had to work ten times harder than the next person to succeed in Hollywood. If I didn't, nothing was going to happen.

What irked me even more was that the casting director's company had worked with some big-time TV shows. He knew how the industry operated and was fully aware of the *power* that people like him had over the fates of aspiring actors. If our conversations resulted in acting opportunities for me, it would be because he pulled strings, not because destiny played a role.

I didn't have a great feeling after meeting with that casting director, and it turned out I was right: in the follow-up, he had nothing for me. All the production teams he'd relayed our ideas to liked the concept of adding a Deaf character but couldn't quite figure out how to make it happen.

"We're not sure how to write you into any of our projects," he said.

I shook his hand, restraining myself from crushing it into powdered rubble, and walked away.

After all that, I was back to square one. Still trying, futilely and endlessly maddeningly, to break into Hollywood.

*God,* I thought to myself. *Am I turning into my father?*

BY WORD OF HAND, THE Northeastern U.S. Deaf community learned about the solo show that Dad created and performed at Lexington School for the Deaf. Deaf schools around the region invited him to perform in front of their students. These Deaf school students loved him and his zany, physically expressive acting style. Dad thirstily absorbed their laughter and compliments; they slowly filled up the void in him where his self-esteem should have been.

The New York Deaf Theatre caught wind of Dad's solo show and invited him to perform a skit with them. He was ecstatic. Momentum was snowballing, getting him closer and closer to his dream. One of the theater organization's founders, a legendary comedic actor, was enthralled with Dad's skills. Even though the cofounder was gay, she joked that she was in love with Dad.

His path forward was like a ladder, he told my mom. He just had to continue to climb to the next rung above. He'd started with his solo shows, now he was working with the New York Deaf Theatre, and perhaps the next rung would be the National Theatre of the Deaf, NTD, the prestigious theater organization. And then springboarding from NTD to the biggest stages of the world wouldn't be unheard of. It had happened before; one of NTD's alumni was Phyllis Frelich, who went on to star in the Broadway production of *Children of a Lesser God* and win a Tony Award for Best Actress. Another was Linda Bove, who was a mainstay on *Sesame Street* for more than three decades. If Dad could just get into NTD, he would be one rung away from a life of fame and success.

Dad gave a fabulous performance in his skit with the New York Deaf Theatre. The cofounder gave him rave reviews. Dad was hyped; he was so close to achieving his dream. The call from NTD would come any minute, he figured.

He waited for the call. And waited. And waited.

It never came.

He was crushed. His self-esteem, once buoyed by his burgeoning acting aspirations, fizzled along with his dreams of becoming a famous actor. He sank back to his old ways, returning to using drink and drugs to nurse his damaged soul.

DAD'S BIGGEST MISTAKE WAS THAT he waited for the call to come. He sat back and hoped the stars, as the casting director said to me, would align for him.

I couldn't repeat his mistake. If I waited for Deaf roles to be written and then hoped to get selected for them, I would do a ton of waiting, and, after all the waiting was done, I would leave Hollywood behind the same as I'd found it—with sparse, insufficient Deaf representation.

I wasn't giving up on my goal of making it in Hollywood, but it was time for me to rethink my approach. Waiting for Deaf roles to be written wasn't going to cut it. I would need to help create them instead. I wouldn't be the first to try this approach—Marlee Matlin had several executive producer credits under her belt, and two Deaf writer/actors, Shoshannah Stern and Joshua Feldman, had created *This Close*, a TV series on the Sundance TV channel that featured themselves and many other Deaf actors, including myself in a guest-starring role. These Deaf actor/producers were breaking new ground. I wanted to help them blaze this new path for Deaf representation in Hollywood.

I called my manager and agent together for another meeting.

"I'm done auditioning and hoping roles will come my way," I told them. "Let's start creating Deaf roles, for myself and other Deaf people out there."

And so my journey began on the other side of the camera, as a producer. Producers are the people who make all the magic happen. Stories get created at their hands. It was the ideal path forward for me—as a producer, I would have the opportunity to tell stories I wanted to tell while also creating on-camera roles for myself and other Deaf actors.

There was one problem: I'd never been a producer. I had very little idea of the work involved and no clue where to start. At first it was slow going. The casting director wasn't quite right when he said the stars would align for me. But the stars were indeed there, and I moved them until they were in the perfect position.

My first opportunity was the *Children of a Lesser God* production on Broadway. The play, made famous by the Oscar-winning movie starring Marlee Matlin, had been a 1980s Broadway mainstay long before the film adaptation came along. And now it was returning to Broadway with an all-new cast that featured talented up-and-coming Deaf actress Lauren Ridloff. The show's producers called me and asked for public relations and marketing support, to help drum up buzz on the show. They offered to pay me for consulting services. Keep the money, I told them. I would do what they asked me to, but only if they made me a coproducer. I told them that this production had Deaf folks onstage, which was awesome, but it would be even better if they had Deaf people backstage on the production team, too.

To my amazement, they accepted. Just like that, I got my first producer credit, which helped get me into a network's room for my first production pitch meeting. The production was a sitcom featuring a Deaf family, which I'd worked with a CODA (child of Deaf adult/ adults) writer to create. The idea, my very first pitch, wasn't quite polished enough. The decision makers in the room were hesitant about selling a show featuring a family that communicated primarily in ASL. The pitch was declined and the idea was eventually shelved.

But: I'd gotten a pitch meeting under my belt, an accomplishment in and of itself. Not everything was going to fall into place immediately; it was going to be a long journey, slow and steady, one step at a time. I just had to keep hustling—and I had to keep faith. Somewhere on the horizon was my breakthrough, I believed. I had to keep moving toward it. That was all I could control—how hard I worked, and my mindset. The rest would take care of itself.

My breakthrough eventually did come, although in a rather roundabout manner. I received word through a friend at Gallaudet that a production company was interested in doing a reality show on its students. Intrigued, I reached out and was quickly connected with Eric, an executive producer working on the idea. For Eric, connecting with me was providential; when he first started working on the project, his talent agency had suggested that he get in touch with me. And now all of a sudden I was trying to get in touch with him. He couldn't pick up the phone fast enough.

Eric told me the cast for the reality show had already been chosen, and he shared photographs of each cast member. Fortunately, most of them were familiar to me. It hadn't been that long since I'd graduated from Gallaudet, and I followed a few current students on social media. I'd seen and gotten to know—albeit superficially—some of the cast members through my friends' Instagram videos and stories that featured them.

"I love the diversity of your cast," I told Eric. "There's so much variation in the lived Deaf experiences of your cast members. Some of them come from Deaf families, had signed all their lives, and had attended only Deaf schools growing up. Others were born into hearing families and had attended mainstream school growing up. There's a wide range of ASL fluency among your cast, from natively fluent to new signers."

I pointed to one cast member, Daequan. "You can tell he started learning to sign recently."

Eric's eyebrows popped up. "Really?"

I nodded. "He's learning quickly, but his fluency is not the same as that of someone who signed from birth. He might get there one day, but right now you can tell he's new. And that also tells me something about his background—that he was probably mainstreamed."

"Huh," Eric said. "I didn't realize all that."

"There's so many layers to explore with your cast, so many storylines you could spin."

Eric nodded, processing the information.

"How well do you know the Deaf community?" I asked him. "How much do you know about ASL, Deaf culture, and the lived experiences of Deaf people?"

He admitted he was just starting to learn—and wanted to learn a whole lot more.

I decided to tell him the story of Barry, my friend from Gallaudet who'd never learned ASL until he enrolled there. About how hard he'd worked for four years to become better at ASL, only to find that Deaf Kindergarteners had more ASL fluency.

Eric was captivated. He began to see the layers I was talking about, the potential stories that could be told about the different dimensions of the Deaf experience.

"There's so many different ways for a Deaf life to unfold," I told Eric. "We're not a monolith, all of us one and the same. But to find these stories, dig deep enough, link the threads, and tell them compellingly, you need Deaf people on your team. We know ourselves, our community, our experiences. You'll get so much more authenticity that way."

Eric agreed, a thousand percent. Then he did something I never expected. He opened the door and extended me an invitation.

"Do you want to be a coexecutive producer on this project?"

It's one thing for someone to ask for advice from a member of an underrepresented community for a project. It's another thing entirely to ask them to stand alongside you and help you make the thing. I was thrilled and honored to get that offer from him.

With me onboard, the production team prepped and made a pitch to Netflix. To their credit, Netflix was also thrilled that I was on the team. They pushed hard for representation of minorities, both in front of and behind the camera, on the productions they backed. Netflix liked our reality show idea, but they wanted to see more before they committed to it. If we put together a sizzle reel (a short, promotional teaser), they told us, they'd come back to the table and give us a serious look.

Encouraged, we went back to Gallaudet, rounded up the cast, shot different scenes and interviews, and threaded together a seven-minute reel. We called Netflix to tell them we were ready, and they invited us for another meeting.

Eric and the production team asked me to lead the pitch. I was honored to do it. It felt right—a Deaf person getting the opportunity to stand in front and tell a story from his community.

I remember the moment I first stood before the Netflix development panel, just before I dove into my pitch. I had been nervous as hell going into the meeting, but right then I felt a strange calm. I was pitching a show, but I was essentially telling *my* story. The Deaf story. The story of myself, my mom and dad, my grandparents, my brothers, and so many of my Deaf friends.

I started out by telling the Netflix panel about myself. How I was born into a Deaf family, the fourth generation in my family to be born Deaf. How ASL was my first language growing up. How I'd attended Deaf schools all my life and had been surrounded by Deaf peers and role models growing up. How I'd attended Gallaudet, the world's only liberal arts college for the Deaf.

Every one of these facts, unremarkable and ordinary to me, elicited amazement from the panel.

I segued into the pitch of the reality show and introduced our cast. I talked about how different their experiences, backgrounds, language, education were from each other's and from me.

"This is a reality show about young college students. They're going to date around, hook up, get drunk, fight with each other and their families, battle personal demons, and, through everything, try to figure out their place in life. All stuff that young college students go through. These students just happen to be Deaf."

The sizzle reel played, and then it was time for questions.

I love questions and answers during meetings when I'm pitching a Deaf-centered story. The questions, often about the Deaf experience, were easy to answer. I drew from my own life and stories shared by my Deaf peers and spoke from my heart. And every time, the listeners are hooked.

I have no doubt that my steadfast pride in my Deaf identity is the reason. I love being Deaf so much; I love everything about the uniqueness of my and other Deaf people's existences. I'm fascinated by it, and I want to share everything about it with other people. I've found that this enthusiasm can be contagious. When I talk about the Deaf experience with passion, others are infected by my enthusiasm. They want to know more.

This phenomenon isn't unique to me or the Deaf community. I believe that it happens anytime an individual embraces who they are. They become confident, self-assured, and *passionate* about their identity and everything that sets them apart from other people. Just then, the different qualities the person and community have—a missing sense, a distinct language, a proud culture, a steadfast re-silience in the face of oppression stretching back for millennia— become glowing marvels. From them, you can spin stories: Stories that teach and inspire. Stories that include people from all walks of life, people who may become role models for children, who may have been searching all their lives for someone else out there who is just like them.

When differences are embraced, stories become magical.

Before the pitch ended, I made one final pledge to the Netflix panel. With this show, putting Deaf people in front of the camera was just half of our goal. To tell these stories featuring Deaf people, we aimed to hire Deaf people behind the camera. Producers, camerapeo-ple, directors, editors—Deaf talent in all these roles. To me, this was the cherry on top of our pitch. If we won this deal with Netflix, it would be a monumental step forward for Deaf people toward better media representation, toward claiming our earned space in Hollywood.

The pitch ended, and I scanned the people on the Netflix panel. Their faces, like those of the *Dancing with the Stars* executive producer and every other Hollywood industry big shot I'd encountered so far, were unreadable. I smiled to myself and wondered, *If I ever reach that echelon of success, would I be able to hide my emotions as well as they did?*

After a moment I decided, nah, I could never do that. My Deaf-ass ASL-trained face would give everything away.

And there'd be nothing wrong with that. It was long past time to do things differently in Hollywood.

A WEEK LATER, I WAS at the gym, lifting weights—always on the grind, never relaxing. Pausing between reps, I saw that I'd just gotten an email from Netflix. They were greenlighting the show, which would come to be titled *Deaf U.*

Right then and there, in the middle of the crowded weight room, I let out a holler.

# Resources

*Furthering Your Deaf Education*

This brief list of selected resources will guide you as you delve deeper into your Deaf education. Some of these resources were a huge help to me in writing certain historical and cultural portions of this book. If a part in *Deaf Utopia* touched you and you'd like to learn more, look for that topic in bold here; the associated resource will take you on a learning path into the topic.

*Controlling Our Destiny: A Board Member's View of Deaf President Now* by Philip Bravin (Gallaudet University Press, 2020)

*Deaf President Now! The 1988 Revolution at Gallaudet University* by John Christiansen and Sharon Barnartt (Gallaudet University Press, 1995)

*Deaf Mosaic*, episode 402 (Gallaudet University, 1988)

> If you want to learn more about the **Deaf President Now protest**, start with these resources. Bravin, a Deaf man, was a member of the Gallaudet University Board of Trustees at the time of the protest, and in his book he offers an insider's perspective of the events of the protest. *Deaf President Now!* is the comprehensive and authoritative written account of the protest. *Deaf Mosaic*, episode 402 is a documentary episode dedicated to the protest, complete with interviews with protest leaders and participants and footage shot during key moments of the protest.

*When the Mind Hears: A History of the Deaf* by Harlan Lane (Random House, 1984)

Lane offers a meticulously researched and eloquently written history of **Deaf education** in Europe and the United States. The broad sweep of Lane's pen brushes over the tales of Abbé de l'Épée and Abbé Sicard and the famed Institut Royal des Sourds-Muets in Paris; the oralist movement in Europe; Thomas Gallaudet, Alice Cogswell, Laurent Clerc, and the founding of the American School for the Deaf; and the Milan Conference.

*Audism Unveiled* (DawnSignPress, 2008)

This documentary, published by Deaf-owned company DawnSignPress, paints a powerful and deeply intimate picture of the damage that **audism** inflicts on Deaf people.

*Signing Black in America* (The Talking Black in America Project, 2020)

*The Hidden Treasure of Black ASL: Its History and Structure* by Carolyn McCaskill, Ceil Lucas, Robert Bayley, and Joseph Hill (Gallaudet University Press, 2011)

*Signing Black in America* features Black Deaf people sharing their stories and experiences, and is an excellent place to start learning about **Black ASL**. If you want to dive a little deeper, check out *The Hidden Treasure of Black ASL*. Many of its authors were featured in the *Signing Black in America* documentary.

*The Invention of Miracles: Language, Power, and Alexander Graham Bell's Quest to End Deafness* by Katie Booth (Simon & Schuster, 2021)

I touched briefly on **Alexander Graham Bell** and his relationship to the Deaf community in a few places in my book. Booth's book is a great resource to learn more about that less often chronicled side to Bell.

*Made to Hear: Cochlear Implants and Raising Deaf Children* by
   Laura Mauldin (University of Minnesota Press, 2016)

*Hearing Happiness: Deafness Cures in History* by Jaipreet Virdi
   (University of Chicago Press, 2020)

   In my book, particularly the first chapter, I allude to **how the
   medical field views deafness primarily as a problem to be
   fixed**. The two books I've listed here give further insight into
   that perspective. *Made to Hear* is written by a sociologist who
   examines, from that professional lens, the process by which
   cochlear implants are provided to deaf children, and the greater
   medical and scientific establishments that support the practice.
   *Hearing Happiness* is a richly researched history of the cures
   that doctors, scientists, and businesspeople—many of whom
   I'd call quacks—have created to treat hearing loss, and the
   marketing language that has accompanied these often zany, and
   occasionally deadly, inventions.

ON THE TOPICS OF DEAF culture and history and the Deaf experience, there are lots of great books (fiction and nonfiction) and
documentaries—too many to list them all here. But the following suggestions are a good place to start.

*Chattering* by Louise Stern (Granta Books, 2011)

*Deaf Again* by Mark Drolsbaugh (Handwave Publications, 2008)

*Deaf Culture: Exploring Deaf Communities in the United States* by
   Irene W. Leigh, Jean F. Andrews, Raychelle L. Harris and Topher
   Gonzalez Avila (Plural Publishing, 2016)

*Deaf Gain: Raising the Stakes for Human Diversity* by H-Dirksen L.
   Bauman and Joseph J. Murray, editors (University of Minnesota
   Press, 2014)

*Deaf Heritage: A Narrative History of Deaf America* by Jack Gannon (National Association of the Deaf, 1981)

*Deaf in America: Voices from a Culture* by Carol Padden and Tom Humphries (Harvard University Press, 1990)

*Everyone Here Spoke Sign Language: Hereditary Deafness on Martha's Vineyard* by Nora Ellen Groce (Harvard University Press, 1985)

*Inside Deaf Culture* by Carol Padden and Tom Humphries (Harvard University Press, 2006)

*Introduction to American Deaf Culture* by Thomas K. Holcomb (Oxford University Press, 2012)

*Through Deaf Eyes,* a film by Lawrence Hott and Diane Garey (WETA Washington, D.C., and Florentine Films/Hott Productions, Inc. in association with Gallaudet University, 2017)

*True Biz* by Sara Nović (Penguin Random House, forthcoming 2022)

*Understanding Deaf Culture: In Search of Deafhood* by Paddy Ladd (Multilingual Matters, 2003)

IF YOU'RE INSPIRED TO LEARN ASL, you may want to start with The ASL App, which was created by Deaf people, and, at the time of this writing, contains more than two thousand signs and phrases. Another great option is to seek out a class. Many local libraries and community colleges offer ASL courses at varying fluency levels. Try to find one led by a Deaf instructor. The last and best method of learning is by immersion in the Deaf community. Make new Deaf friends, attend Deaf events, show up at a gathering of a Deaf club, spectate at a sporting event at a Deaf school.

TWO BONUS BOOK RECOMMENDATIONS!

*Gay Like Me* by Richie Jackson (HarperCollins, 2020)

This love letter from Jackson, a gay father, to his gay son, details Jackson's experiences with the LGBTQ movement and the HIV/AIDS epidemic. Jackson fears that the modern gay generation lacks the same pride and grit as the generation he grew up in, and risks undoing decades of the LGBTQ movement's progress. This book not only resonated with me as a gay man, but I also drew parallels between the father's descriptions of modern LGBTQ people's attitudes and those of young Deaf people today. The lesson I take from *Gay Like Me* is that all young people of underrepresented groups have to recognize the work of the people who came before them and strive to make things better for the next generation.

*The Ethical Slut* by Dossie Easton and Janet W. Hardy (Celestial Arts, 2009)

What I love about this book is that while it illuminates different types of relationships, it emphasizes that the foundation of a successful, healthy relationship (including friendships) is communication. I personally think everybody should read this book.

# Acknowledgments

So many people played a part, big and small, in the stories in this book. I cannot thank each and every one of you here, but please know that I am grateful for your contribution. What follows is a small selection of valued contributors, and my appreciation for them.

To my manager, Sami Housman, I have a million thank-yous: For that cold email after seeing me on *ANTM*. For believing in my true potential. For remembering a bit of ASL from your Deaf high school friends. For sticking with me and helping change minds in the entertainment industry on disability and Deaf inclusion—a massive undertaking that alone requires hours and hours of educating and advocating, often without pay. Not many would be up for the challenge and even fewer would have the forward-thinking mindset required to succeed. And scarcer still are the very best humans, who have the (unlimited) imagination needed to stretch what's possible. And only one meets all of the above criteria—and possesses your unmatched passion. I'm glad you're in this fight with me.

To Robert Siebert—Bobby—we've come a long way from when we were roommates our freshman year at Gallaudet, new friends who barely knew each other but formed a fast bond over boozy nights with cheap beer and fruit-flavored vodka. Later, when I was thrust into the limelight, you became an important sounding board, helping me set up the Nyle DiMarco Foundation and determine its mission: supporting Deaf kids' early-language acquisition. Four years ago, we first talked about writing this book. Things have changed so much in that time—you became a father, not once but twice—yet you stuck by me and your commitment to this book never wavered. Translating ASL to English is no easy task, and you must have piled hours upon hours of interview footage into your hard drive—heck, at one point I probably took up more hard drive space than your partner, Danielle, and your boys, Tobias and Brody, combined! I don't know how you found the time in your busy life to work on this book (it's almost like you have an eighth day of the week), but I'm glad you did—I couldn't have done it without you.

And to Ramon Norrod, for weathering the storm with me on *ANTM* and then *DWTS* back-to-back. When I most needed it, you sacrificed a ton of your personal time—time with your husband, especially—to ensure that I had a top-notch communication experience. And then you became a thoughtful guide, helping ease me into the LGBTQ world with sheer patience, care, and kindness.

To Grayson Van Pelt, a fantastic communication partner and an amazing soul—you brought vivid color to my meetings and laughter to my work life, and became a valued LGBTQ mentor to me.

To Tyra Banks, who discovered me, gave me my first shot, and amplified my voice. And then, after you crowned me America's Next Top Model and the cameras switched off, you remained by my side, nudging me, advising me, cheering me on. You're still here, in my corner, and I'm grateful for your steadfast support.

To Cassie Jones, my editor. You believed in this project, even back when it was little more than an inspired idea and a few dozen pages of raw material. And then you helped turn that idea into this book. Thank you for driving this project forward with your endless optimism and thoughtful and precise feedback, for your patient and informative explanations of the inner workings of the book publishing process, and, above all, for your willingness to dive into the Deaf world. The things you did—taking ASL lessons and googling up Deaf topics like International Sign—led to thought-provoking questions and informed insight that made the book immeasurably better. I appreciate you, very much. And to Jill Zimmerman, thank you for giving the book a close read and spotting issues that whooshed past our eyes and would have gone unnoticed if not for your valuable contributions.

To Phyllis Steele, my first—and only—girl sleepover guest in middle school. I'm grateful for our decades of friendship. Thank you for being you and for always being up to discuss new and different perspectives.

To the brilliant Deaf artists Christine Sun Kim and Ravi Vasavan, thank you for generously allowing me to use and paraphrase your definition of <0/, or Deaf Power.

And last, but not least, to my family: my mom, Donna; my brothers, Neal and Nico; Grandpa Charles, Grandma Janice, Uncle Charles and Aunt Lisa, and Uncle Robert. You made me the person I am today. Thank you for putting up with my random and sometimes bizarre antics. For unconditionally embracing me for who I am. For giving me the space and freedom I need to wander off on my own . . . and always coming to bring me back home.